CASE IN POINT[10]

Complete Case Interview Preparation

Special Section on Government and Nonprofit Cases

MARC P. COSENTINO

CASE IN POINT 10th edition
Complete Case Interview Preparation

P.O. Box 60137 Santa Barbara CA 93160

ISBN: 978-0-9863707-4-8

Library of Congress Cataloging-in-Publication Data:
Case in Point: Complete Case Interview Preparation / Marc P. Cosentino – 10th ed.
Library of Congress Card Number 2001117521
Printed in the United States of America
First Printing 1999 – Second Edition 2001 – Third Edition 2004 – Fourth Edition 2005 – Fifth Edition 2007 – Sixth Edition 2009 – Seventh Edition 2011 – Eighth Edition 2013 – Ninth Edition 2016 – Tenth Edition 2018

MBA Analytica

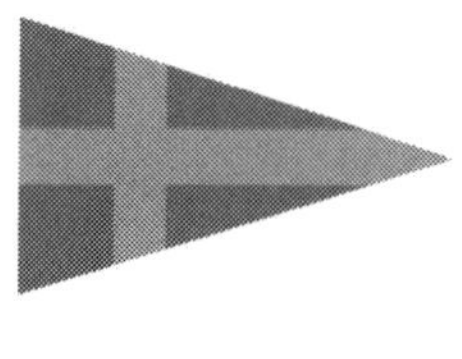

Published by Burgee Press, Santa Barbara, California

AMAZON REVIEWS — CASE IN POINT

★★★★★ Secret to success – consulting case interviews. In graduate school I browsed many books on consulting case interview preparation. This was the only book I read. The clear, consistent way of thinking through how to manage case interviews made sense. Rather than focusing on formulas, frameworks (e.g., Porter's Five Forces), or just examples, Cosentino classifies cases into sensible categories and coaches the student through how to think about answering. Additionally, he gives valuable tips on how to get comfortable in the interview. The true proof, however, was that I interviewed with the two top strategy consulting firms and received offers from both. I would highly recommend this book to anyone considering interviewing with top strategy consulting firms.

★★★★★ Outstanding prep for case interviews. Case in Point is in my view the best book of its type on the market. The top firms vary their cases from interviewer to interviewer; Cosentino's book provides a good system for tackling any case that you're presented. This book got me extremely well-prepared for my interviews. I just received a summer associate offer from what's arguably the top consulting firm, despite my non-business background.

★★★★★ As a self-proclaimed "casehead" I can tell you the man has it covered. I've read everything else out there and there are no original thinkers left. I owe Cosentino everything.

★★★★★ Great book for consulting preparation. Cosentino's compilation of cases is a superb way to prepare for management consulting case interviews. Not only does he provide a wide variety of cases (from market-sizing to acquisition opportunity to dipping profits) he also offers several helpful frameworks for approaching consulting cases in general. I would highly recommend this book to anyone planning to do consulting interviews – and they're tough!

★★★★★ Having a job interview? Use this book: it's a must. I used this book as a tool to prepare for interviews, and it really helped me. In this tough period, I followed the Ivy Case Method proposed, and it didn't fail. The book presents in a very readable way what to expect in an interview and how to create your best strategy. I'm usually very skeptical about these kinds of books, but I must say that Cosentino is able to attract the reader and through anecdotes and concrete examples, keep the reader's interest till the last page. Definitely a must.

★★★★★ Got me a consulting job! I was VERY nervous about getting a good job after school. I compared several interview guides and found some to be incomplete and others to be too long and confusing. Cosentino's Case in Point was easier to understand and covered the key techniques/frameworks behind case interviews. I practiced the sample cases and I eventually got a job in strategy consulting.

★★★★★ Case Interview Bible. If you are like me, then you had never seen (nor heard of) a case interview before business school. By practicing the methods taught in Marc's book, you will be able to tear through case questions with thoroughness and efficiency. Considering that many companies are switching to case style interviews, it would be a mistake not to hone your skills in this area. I recommend this book to anyone in business school as well as to any job seekers looking to nail an interview.

Dedication

To my parents.

Acknowledgments

A big shout-out to Professor Brendan Boler of the McIntire School of Commerce at UVA and all his students. Special thanks to Mukund Jain who contributed cases.

The Government/Nonprofit section would not have been possible without help from Evan Piekara, Katie Lonergan, and Deshika Wickramasinghe, all Georgetown MBAs who now work at BDO. Thanks to all for contributed thoughts and material.

Also by Marc P. Cosentino

Case in Point: Case Competition. Creating Winning Strategy Presentations for Case Competitions and Job Offers
Case in Point: Graph Analysis for Consulting and Case Interviews
The Harvard College Guide to Consulting Case Questions
The Harvard College Guide to Consulting
The Harvard College Guide to Investment Banking

Note to the reader

FROM MARC COSENTINO: In *Case in Point 10* I have streamlined the material; the book was getting too long. I reduced the number of sample cases and focused on cases that are relevant, challenging, and sophisticated – with plenty of graphs and lessons built in. I like to think that I craft a case, not just write a case. I've added material upfront that reflects the changes taking place in case interviews across the globe, and I've added three new cases and developed a special section on government and nonprofit cases.

The mind is wondrous.
It starts working the second you're born
and doesn't stop until you get a case question.

1 : Introduction

Our client is Netflix. The company hired us to develop a game plan for how and when it should shutter its DVD-by-mail membership services. Where do we begin?

Consulting firms are in the business of renting out brains. Consultants are paid to synthesize massive quantities of foreign data, toss out the irrelevant information, structure an approach to a given client issue, and hypothesize logically and creatively for people of power and influence (such as bigwigs at Netflix). That's why consulting firms put so much weight on the case question – because it allows them to judge how logically and persuasively a potential consultant (i.e., you) can present a case. In essence, a case interview is a role-playing exercise. **Keep in mind that in most cases there is no one right answer. Dialogue is always more important than consensus. You should put yourself in your client's shoes, and produce outcomes rather than projects**.

In order to nail a case interview, you need to know both how to prepare and how to perform. This book will help you do both. It walks you through the overall consulting interview, teaches you how to conduct your research, tells you what the consulting firms are looking for in a candidate, explores the various types of case questions and then introduces you to the Ivy Case System™.

As a career officer at Harvard University for over eighteen years, I helped more than ten thousand of the nation's top students prepare for case interviews. During this time, students tirelessly memorized individual frameworks and then struggled to decide which one(s) to apply. All the while, the case questions given by consulting firms, as well as by a growing number of companies in various industries, had become increasingly complex. The standard frameworks of the past, while still valuable, weren't enough to solve these sophisticated cases. I developed The Ivy Case System™ in order to simplify things. This system will allow you to make an impressive start (without a long and awkward pause) and ensure that you approach the answer in an organized and logical way. The difference between a framework and a system is that a framework is a tool, and a system is a process with all the tools built in. The Ivy Case System™ is the most sensible and comprehensive case interview strategy you can learn.

Keep in mind that case questions help educate you during your job search by acting as a self-imposed screening device. Is this the type of work you want to be doing? Is this the type of environment in which you can learn and flourish? You need to ask yourself, "Do I enjoy problem solving? Do I enjoy these types of questions and issues?" Case questions can and should be fun.

The best way to prepare is to hunker down and (a) read this book and don't skip any pages; (b) attend all case question workshops sponsored by consulting firms or your career services office; (c) practice with your econ professor, roommates, friends, and anyone you know who worked or is currently working in consulting. Sounds like you had better start reading ...

2 : The Interview

Relax, it's worse than you think. If you figure the odds of being chosen for an interview, having all the interviewers like you, and making it through seven to ten cases, you'll be spending next semester's tuition on lottery tickets. But you know what? You faced much tougher odds when you applied to a top school. Not only were you accepted, you even thrived. So forget about the odds and concentrate on you. If there was ever a time for tunnel vision, this is it. Besides, the recruiters don't know about the time you ... well, they don't know and we're sure not going to tell them. So head into your interview with a clean slate.

> **FIRST-ROUND INTERVIEW**
> Usually two 45-minute back-to-back interviews. The first person spends 25 minutes talking to you about you (why consulting?), asking for examples of leadership, persuasion, failure, and team experience. Next, a small case, likely a small-business problem. She then ends with your questions for the company. The second person spends 10 minutes breaking the ice and then gives you a full case, taking up 25 to 30 minutes and often including charts for analysis. The last few minutes are taken up with your questions.

This chapter will walk you through a first-round interview and show you how to prepare properly for each step. Some firms set up two back-to-back 45-minute interviews for the first round. In these interviews, one interviewer spends more time questioning you about yourself and gives you a short case question, while the other interviewer spends less time on you and more time on the case.

+ Introduction

You get called, offer your clammy hand, and then lie and say, "It's great to be here." Nothing to it; you did it the last time you had a blind date. (Let's hope this goes a little better.)

Cliché time: You never get a second chance to make a first impression. Eye contact, a pleasant smile, and a firm handshake are paramount.

+ Questions About You

The first part of the interview is all about "getting to know you." McKinsey calls it a PEI, or a Personal Experience Interview. They will ask you to come up with several examples of times when you influenced or persuaded a group, about your relationship-building style, and about goals that you set for yourself and were successful in meeting. Interviewers will ask you several questions drawn from your résumé (and anything on your résumé is fair game). They may even ask, "Your life is a newspaper article. What's the headline?"

What they are looking for:

- confident, easy demeanor; strong communication skills (Are you a nervous wreck?)
- leadership ability and initiative (Forget about the time you organized that keg party.)
- ability to be a team player (Do you play well with others?)
- drive, aspirations, energy, morals, and ethics (Do you have any?)

In this part of the interview you should be responding, not thinking. In the case questions you're going to do enough thinking to last you a week. You need to research yourself beforehand. Look at the list of the most commonly asked questions in a consulting interview. You may not be asked any of these questions, but if you take the time to write out the answers or, better yet, bullet-point the answers, you will be forced to think about things you haven't thought about in years (or ever).

Don't be surprised if the interviewer asks, "Tell me about a time you persuaded a group to do something they didn't want to do." You offer your answer and you then hear, "Great, give me another example." It is common for interviewers to ask for two or three examples for the same question. When thinking through your answers, go three stories deep. Remember to bullet-point your answers instead of writing passages. People try to memorize passages, but unless you're Gwyneth Paltrow, there is no way you're going to deliver your answer and make it seem real.

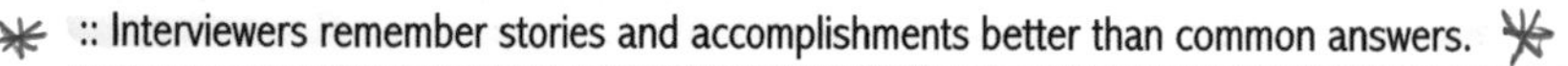

:: Interviewers remember stories and accomplishments better than common answers.

For once in your life you want to get labeled. If you tell the interviewers your captivating tale about windsurfing across the English Channel, at the end of the day when the interviewers see your name on the list, they'll remember you as "the windsurfer." Everything you spoke about will come back to them. If they see your name and think, "Which one was he?" your candidacy is over.

COMMONLY ASKED CONSULTING INTERVIEW QUESTIONS

If you take time to answer these questions before the interview, you will be more articulate and focused when it comes time to perform. When you're ready, have a friend videotape your responses. Critique your posture, facial expressions, and the confidence level in your voice. Do you say "yes" instead of "yeah"? Did it take you 20 seconds to explain something you could have explained in 10 seconds?

- Tell me about yourself.
- What are you doing here?
- Why consulting?
- Why did you pick your school?
- What do you think consultants do?
- What do you know about this job and our firm?
- Why would you choose our firm over our competitors?
- How are your quantitative skills?
- What percentage is 7 of 63?
- Tell me of a time you showed leadership skills.
- Tell me about a time you were a team player.
- Give me an example of a time you influenced or persuaded a group.
- Tell me about a recent crisis you handled.
- Have you ever failed at anything?
- Tell me about a time you took the initiative to start something.
- What type of work do you like to do best?
- With which other firms are you interviewing?
- Which other industries are you looking into?
- What accomplishments have given you the greatest satisfaction?
- What experiences/skills do you think are particularly transferable to our organization?
- Why should I hire you?

How do I answer?

Three of the most problematic interview questions are:

- Have you ever failed at anything?
- With which other firms are you interviewing?
- With which other industries are you interviewing?

How do you answer these truthfully?

Q1: Have you ever failed at anything?

Say yes! Everybody has failed at something. People fail all the time. That's how you learn.

Do's: Do talk about a failure and what you learned from that failure. Better yet, talk about how you failed, what you learned from that mistake, then how you turned it into a success. A perfect example comes from Michael Jordan. He failed to make his high school basketball team his freshman year, yet persevered and became a basketball legend. Have a story to tell; make it memorable.

Don'ts: Don't talk about a personal failure. Stay away from anything that is going to make the interviewer feel uncomfortable, e.g., "I never got to straighten things out with my dad before he passed away" or "My girlfriend dumped me" or "I couldn't outrun that police car when I was seventeen." Interviewers don't want to hear it. The other thing they don't want to hear about is an academic failure. If you did fail a course, they would know about it and ask you why it happened.

> A DOZEN REASONS TO ENTER CONSULTING
>
> Just in case you're not sure, below are 13 (a baker's dozen) of the most popular reasons students go into consulting:
>
> 1. You'll work with and learn from very intelligent and articulate people.
> 2. You'll develop a vast array of marketable skills in a prestigious environment.
> 3. The learning curve never ends.
> 4. You'll receive exposure to the corporate elite: the way they think, act and analyze their problems.
> 5. You'll be exposed to many industries.
> 6. You'll work as part of a team.
> 7. You'll solve problems.
> 8. You'll make organizations more efficient.
> 9. You'll work on multiple projects.
> 10. You'll travel.
> 11. You'll improve your chances of being accepted into a top business school.
> 12. It will always look great on your résumé.
> 13. The money's good.

With which other firms are you interviewing?

It's okay to tell them that you're interviewing with other consulting firms. Competition's tough; you'd be foolish to put all your energy into just one firm. However, you must be able to tell them why they are your first choice and what makes them better in your mind than the other firms.

With which other industries are you interviewing?

Consulting goes hand-in-hand with three other industries. While interviewing for a consulting position, it's okay to mention that you are looking at investment banking, private equity, and/or strategic planning. These positions need the same qualities in a candidate and require similar job skills. In fact, McKinsey's and BCG's biggest competitor is Goldman Sachs – not each other.

+ Why Consulting?

You know the interviewer is going to ask you why you want to be a consultant: not only should your answer be immediate, but you must also look the interviewer right in the eye. If you look away, it indicates that you are thinking about the question, and that's enough to end the interview right then and there. You should have given this answer a great deal of thought long before you walked in to the interview. While I don't want you to memorize your answer, I do want you to memorize bullet points. This makes your answer focused, linear, and of an appropriate length. Avoid talking aimlessly. Having several good reasons that you want to be a consultant isn't enough. It's not always what you say but how you say it and, most important, what they hear. Your voice should carry sincerity and enthusiasm.

They may ask you about your quantitative skills. This could be followed by a small math question such as, "What's 100 divided by 7?" or "Nine is what percentage of 72?" The questions aren't hard, but they might take you by surprise. It may be time to break out the flash cards.

During the first part of the interview, you're being judged. The interviewer is asking herself whether or not she'd like to work and travel with you. Are you interesting? Engaging? Do you have a sense of humor and like to have fun? This is better known as the "airport test." The name comes from the question, "How would I feel if I were snowed in with this candidate for nine hours at the Buffalo airport? Would we have a lot to talk about, or would I have to pretend I was in a coma so I wouldn't have to talk?"

The interviewer is also measuring your maturity, poise, and communication skills, while thinking, "Would I feel comfortable bringing this candidate in front of a client?" An important part of the "maturity test" is to determine whether you think before you speak. I had a student who, when asked what percentage 3 of 17 is, blurted out "Eighty percent." (I don't know how he got into college, either.) For him that interview was over. He might as well have gotten up and walked out because nothing was going to save him. Not because he got the wrong answer, but because it was clear that he didn't think before he spoke. If he does something like that in an interview, what is he going to do in front of a client? I couldn't trust him, and if I can't trust him, I am not going to hire him.

The second part of the interview is the case question. These questions carry a tremendous amount of weight. You can pass the airport test and be as poised and articulate as John F. Kennedy, but if you fumble the case, that's it.

PRE-INTERVIEW QUESTIONS

1. What type of consulting does the firm do?
2. In what industries does the firm specialize?
3. How big is the firm? How many domestic and international offices does the firm have? How many professionals are in the firm?
4. What kinds of training programs does the firm offer?
5. What type of work does an associate consultant do?
6. How much client contact does a consultant have the first year?
7. Does the firm have a mentor program?
8. How often do first-years sleep in their own beds? What's their travel schedule like?
9. How many hours make up a typical work day?
10. How is a case team picked?
11. How often are consultants reviewed?
12. How many consultants does the firm expect to hire this year?
13. How does that compare to last year?
14. Where do consultants go when they leave the firm?
15. Is it possible to transfer to other offices, even international offices?

Alternatively, if you hit a home run on the case but have the social skills of Napoleon Dynamite, then you have bigger problems than getting a job. We'll cover the case questions in depth in Chapter Three.

+ Your Questions

The last part of the interview requires a good deal of research about both the industry and the company. In addition, if you can find out who will be interviewing you, you should be googling them to see what articles they have written or issues they are involved with. You can bet that they will be googling you. In your research, you should be looking for answers to the pre-interview questions. Questions for which you can't locate answers become excellent questions for you to pose to your interviewer. However, before you ask your first question, if there is anything critical that you didn't get a chance to bring up in the interview, now is the time. Simply say, "Before I ask my first question, I just want to make sure you understand ... " Get it out before you leave the room. If you don't, you're going to kick yourself all the way home, and even worse, you'll never know whether that statement could have turned the tide in your favor.

The best ways to collect these answers:

□ **Attend career fairs and speak to the firm representatives.** Pull out your list of questions and ask three or four. Make sure that you try to turn this meeting into a conversation. At the end, thank the reps for their time, ask them for their business cards, and inquire whether it would be all right if you called or emailed them with further questions. At this point, no one is going to judge you on your level of company knowledge. They are there to provide information and hype the firm.

□ **Scour the company's website.** This will let you know how the firm sees itself and the image that it's trying to project.

□ **Talk to alumni and classmates** who used to work for the companies that you're interviewing with. Often, career services offices will be able to match you up with alumni who are working in a specific industry. Interviewing past employees can be very enlightening. They will tell you more about their old firm in half an hour than you'll learn by spending two hours on the internet. Plus, they'll tell you things that you'll never find on the internet. They can be completely objective; they don't have to try to sell the firm.

□ **Attend company information meetings.** Get your name and face in front of firm representatives so that they can associate your face with your résumé. While these people don't have the power to hire you, they do have the power to get you on the interview list. Top-tier firms often get 400 résumés for 100 first-round interview slots. Snag that interview slot by networking and schmoozing with firm representatives every chance you get. One of the best-kept secrets of company presentations is the value of arriving early. If a company presentation is scheduled to start at 6 p.m., show up at 5:40. Most students won't arrive until 6 p.m. or a little after, but the firm's representatives show up at around 5:30 to make sure that the room is set up correctly and the cheese table is laid out nicely. If you show up early, not only will it impress the consultants, but it will allow you to get at least five minutes of quality face time with one of them. They are more likely to remember you if you visit for five minutes at the beginning of the night than if you hang around until the end hoping for 90 seconds of their time. They are also more likely to have their business cards with them. Remember to ask for those business cards and send a follow-up email.

□ **Search** *The Wall Street Journal*, CNBC.com, Bloomberg.com, and other online sources for articles and information on the firm. This allows you to be current on any firm's news.

□ **Visit sites such as Glassdoor.com to get ex-employee and peer insights on the firm**. Take your written list of questions with specific facts or figures you've dug up when you walk in to the interview. This shows that you have done your homework and have given this interview a great deal of thought. Besides, if you freeze up, it's all right there in front of you.

+ Why Should I Hire You?

This is your opportunity to shine and to market yourself. But before you launch into a laundry list of skills and attributes, you may want to simply state that they should hire you because you want to be a consultant. Then, reiterate all the reasons that you brought up earlier when they asked you, "Why consulting?"

Consulting firms look for "low-risk" hires. You're a low-risk hire if you've worked in consulting, liked it and want to return, or have done your homework. You know about the travel, the type of work, working on projects, and working as part of a team. Consulting firms' biggest fear is that they will spend a lot of time and money recruiting, hiring, and training you, only to have you bail out after six months because consulting isn't what you expected. If they aren't convinced that this is what you want to do, then it doesn't matter how talented you are; it's not worth it for them to extend you an offer.

Students receive job offers in consulting for four reasons:

1. They are able to convince the interviewer that they are committed to consulting and know what they're getting into (e.g., type of work, lifestyle, travel).
2. They can demonstrate success-oriented behavior.
3. They exhibit good analytical skills when answering case questions. (That's where we come in.)
4. They are able to articulate their thoughts, create a positive presence, and defend themselves without being defensive.

Now you understand the structure of the interview for the first round, and the subsequent rounds are not all that different. The second round is often held at a nearby hotel and usually consists of two interviews, both 60 minutes in length, each with a heavy focus on case questions. The third round is typically held in the firm's offices where there are five interviews, 60 minutes each, again with a heavy emphasis on case questions. During all the rounds you can expect to analyze many charts. In addition, some firms give written cases requiring you not only to analyze the information but also to design charts to back up your recommendations.

There are other kinds of first-round interviews. Some firms conduct phone interviews while others conduct group case interviews.

+ First-Round Telephone Interviews

Sometimes your first-round interview will be conducted over the phone. Sometimes this is a screening interview; you may get a case question as well. Things to remember: if possible, go to a quiet and private place. Turn off the TV and lock the door so no one barges in and interrupts you.

Most important: you are your voice. That's all the other person on the phone has to go on. Your voice should be upbeat and enthusiastic; speak clearly and with confidence but not arrogance.

Finally, lose the calculator. I know it is tempting to have it right there, but if you get the answer too quickly, or the interviewer can hear buttons clicking, you're sunk.

+ First-Round Telephone and Skype Interviews

In addition to all that, for a Skype interview you will need to dress up as you would for a regular interview. I've heard stories about the interviewee dressed nicely above the waist, but wearing pajama bottoms, shorts, or sweat pants. Normally this wouldn't be a problem, unless you have to get up and retrieve something. Also, be aware of your background. What can the person on the other side of the computer see of your environment? If you have an inappropriate poster hanging on your wall, you might want to remove it or angle the camera away from the poster. I Skype with students from around the world, and I'm always interested in the background – what their apartment or dorm room looks like. It gives me additional information on their personalities and organizational skills.

+ First-Round Group Case Interviews

McKinsey and other firms sometimes hold group interviews for non-MBA graduate students as part of their first-round interviews. During a group interview, consultants look more at the group dynamics than at how the group answers the question. Does this candidate have the ability to build relationships, empathy, and teamwork? On one hand, you are a competitor of the other people in the group, but on the other hand, for this moment in time you are teammates. People who are aggressive and try to dominate the conversation don't get called back. Remember, consultants work in teams, and if you're not willing to be a team player, then you're out.

In my business school classes, the professor rarely called on anyone who had his hand raised while someone else was speaking. This indicated that the hand-raising student wasn't listening to his classmate and had his own agenda. Like a business school case class, you are expected to build on what others have said, and move the discussion forward, not take it off on a tangent or in your own direction, or move the discussion back because you had a point you wanted to make.

+ Stress Interviews

Well, they're back. Stress interviews. They usually come in one of two forms. The first type is the two-on-one (you're the one). The interviewers ask you question after question without giving you much of a chance to answer. They'll make unfavorable comments to each other about your answers, dismissing your answers as amateurish or ridiculous. They may even turn rude and snappish.

Why do interviewers do this? They put you through this to see how you react. Can you defend yourself and your answers without becoming defensive? Can you maintain your cool and your professionalism? Can you handle it if someone snaps at you, or will you crumble and cry?

The second type is the silent treatment. The interviewer doesn't smile; he usually sits in silence waiting to see if you start talking. If you ask the interviewer a question, he'll usually shoot back a one-word answer. He might question many of your statements, making you explain even the simplest of answers.

Why do they do this? They'll tell you that silence leads to stupid statements, where the interviewee will blurt out irrelevant conversation just to fill the space, and it's important to know how you would react in a situation like this with a client.

Sometimes during a case you'll be asked to make a decision. You will be asked to choose between A and B. If you choose A, the interviewer will look you right in the eye and say, "Let me tell you why you are wrong." If you had chosen B, he would have looked you right in the eye and said, "Let me tell you why you are wrong." It doesn't matter which one you choose, he is going to tell you why you are wrong. Again, he does this to see how you react. Do you turn red? Does your jaw tighten or do your eyebrows shoot up? Clients are going to challenge your findings and ideas all the time. The interviewer wants to make sure you can handle criticism when he gets in your face.

While he is telling you why you are wrong, if you don't find his answer very persuasive, then simply say, "That was an interesting argument, but I didn't find it compelling. I'm sticking with answer A." That's what he wants you to do: Stick with your answer if you think you are right. Defend your answer without being defensive.

If in his argument he brings up something that you didn't think about, and now that you're thinking about it, it changes everything, admit that you were wrong. Simply say, "That was a very persuasive argument, and to be honest, I didn't think about the inventory issue. I think you're right; I think B is the right answer." There is no shame in changing your answer if you were wrong. It shows that you are still objective and open to reason. Remember, one of the main reasons corporations hire consulting firms is a firm's objectivity. If you can remain objective about your answer, then you are one step closer to being a consultant. What the interviewer doesn't want you to do is change your answer just because he said you were wrong.

Rules for stress interviews:

- Don't take it personally.
- Try not to get flustered.
- Roll with the punches.
- Watch what you say; make sure it is relevant to the interview.
- Remain confident.

+ Confidence

To add to the fun, while all this is going on, you need to sound confident even if you don't feel confident. If your confidence level is too low, they're going to question everything you say. There is an old saying about Yalie professors: they're often wrong, but never uncertain. You need to carry that same mindset into your interview. Even if you are uncertain, you need to remain confident.

+ Advice for International Students

Over my 18 years at Harvard, I've advised thousands of international students pursuing careers in consulting. Most of these students initially wanted to work in the U.S. before returning to their home countries. While many were successful, like their American classmates, most were not. Consulting jobs are very competitive and highly sought after. I offer three additional pieces of advice for international students.

1. Be honest about your communication skills. Much of the interview process is driven by communication skills. Are you truly fluent in English? Do you have an accent? How pronounced is it? A couple of years ago, I worked with a brilliant Chinese student. He did very well in the mock case interviews I gave him; however, his language skills, particularly his presentation skills, were poor. While his understanding of English was excellent, his verbal and written skills left much to be desired. Against my advice, he applied to the Boston offices of all the top firms. While he received a number of first-round interviews, he didn't get a single second-round interview. He found himself competing against American Harvard students, and he didn't stand a chance.

2. Think long-term and play to your strengths. I met several times with a Russian student. Her English was excellent, she could articulate her thoughts, and she had a good command of "business English." While she had an Eastern European accent, she was easy to understand. Her grades, work experience, and extracurricular activities were just okay, but nothing great, so she faced some pretty stiff competition from her American classmates. She wanted to work in New York. Her problem was in landing that first-round interview. We talked about thinking long-term. If she applied to the Moscow offices of these firms, she would have a significantly better chance of being hired than if she focused just on New York. She knew the language, the culture, and the economics of the region, and she had a degree from a prestigious American university. She could work in Moscow for two years, then transfer back to the U.S., which is exactly what she did.

3. Come back to campus in case-fighting form. Summer internships are tough to get, so don't be discouraged if you don't land one. I have a pocketful of stories about students who didn't land a summer internship but did find a full-time consulting job upon graduation. There are many more full-time opportunities than summer positions, but they are still very competitive. Don't waste your summer; use it to become a better candidate come autumn. The first step is to secure a summer job where you will be developing some of the same skills you would if you worked in a consulting firm. The second step is to practice your cases over the summer. I had a brilliant student from the Caribbean who had no business experience but plenty of great leadership experience. He received four first-round summer internship interviews. He made it to the second round with two firms but did not receive an offer. He spent the summer working for a large international financial agency in Washington, DC, where he wanted to settle. He spent the summer contacting alumni who worked in the DC offices of the two major consulting firms and invited them out for lunch, coffee, or a beer. He learned about their firms, and he made great connections within those offices. Every time he sipped a coffee or drank a beer with them, he asked them to give him a case question. This went on all summer long. When he returned to campus in September, he was in case-fighting form and had many supporters within each firm. He ended up with full-time offers from both McKinsey and BCG.

To summarize:

- Strengthen your communication skills.
- Think long-term and play to your strengths.
- Come back to campus in fighting form.

+ Advice for Industry Hires

If you are applying as an industry hire, there are a few things you need to know. While most of the hires made by the big consulting firms are university hires, the number of industry hires has been increasing, although it is still around an 80/20 breakdown of university over industry. Having years of experience in a particular industry isn't always a good thing. For example, if you have ten years' experience in the healthcare industry, some firms might be reluctant to hire you for your industry experience because you come with certain prejudices or beliefs about an industry. The firms are worried that if you see a problem with a client, you are going to solve it the same way you solved it when you worked in healthcare. They like people who can look at a problem objectively, with no preconceived notions. They will, however, draw on your industry knowledge when building industry files. So don't be surprised if you are assigned to new industries at first.

The interview process is somewhat the same. If you are applying to McKinsey, you'll probably be asked to take the written exercise that most non-MBAs have to take. The first round might consist of three one-hour interviews, which will have both a personal experience component as well as a case. I'd be surprised if the cases you get touch on your old industry. They want to test your thought structure, not your industry knowledge.

They will expect you to be more confident than a university candidate, more professional in your demeanor. Another thing to remember is that you will enter the firm at the same level as a newly minted MBA (unless you bring a host of clients with you). You may be reporting to someone years younger than you are. Keep in mind that these firms are meritocracies and you can move up as quickly as your talents allow. In fact, you want to enter at that level; it will give you time to get your sea legs and establish yourself. And now, at last, it's time for ...

3 : Case Questions

A case question is a fun, intriguing and active interviewing tool used to evaluate the multi-dimensional aspects of a candidate.

+ What Firms Look For

Consultants spend a great deal of their time on the road or at the client's site. They work in small teams and are sometimes put in charge of groups of the client's employees. Often, consultants work under great pressure in turbulent environments while dealing with seemingly unmanageable problems. It takes a certain type of personality to remain cool under pressure, to influence the client without being condescending, and to be both articulate and analytical at the same time. The business of consulting really is the renting of brains, packaged and delivered with an engaging and confident personality. As you work through the case, the interviewer is asking: Is this candidate ...

- relaxed, confident and mature?
- a good listener?
- a good communicator?
- engaging, enthusiastic and intellectually curious?
- exhibiting strong social and presentation skills?
- asking insightful and probing questions?
- able to determine what's truly relevant?
- organizing the information effectively and developing a logical framework for analysis?
- stating assumptions clearly?
- comfortable discussing the multifunctional aspects of the case?
- trying to quantify his response at every opportunity?
- displaying both business sense and common sense?
- thinking creatively?
- rolling with the punches?
- defending himself without being defensive?

+ Case Preparation

Case questions can be made simple through preparation and practice. I never like to equate an interview with a test, but they are similar in that the more you prepare, the better you'll do. Maybe you've experienced the feeling of being so prepared for an exam that you can't wait for the professor to hand it out so you can rip right through it. Case questions are the same. Firms look to see whether you have that "rip right through it" look in your eyes. It's called confidence.

Some of my students, even after they got the job, would come into my office and ask me to give them a case. They loved doing cases. To them it was no different from working a crossword puzzle. They loved the intellectual challenge, and they learned something every time they did one.

One of the best ways to learn how to answer a case is to write your own case. You are basically re-engineering the process. You need to think of a structure, plus the answers to all the questions that an interviewer would ask.

+ Interview Evaluation Forms

Every firm has its own individual evaluation form; however, what they look for is the same. Some are broken down into analytics (structure, quant acumen, and good use of data), communication (eye contact, articulation, listening, asking probing questions, and note layout), and personal (enthusiasm, self-confidence, teamwork, original thought and intellectual curiosity).

To use one example, the Bain & Company interview evaluation form is broken down into three areas; value addition, client/team, reality check, plus a final summary rating. You are rated 1 to 5 in several categories under these areas, with 5 being the highest score.

(Value Addition)

Under value addition you have five categories; structured problem-solving, business judgment, quant skills, creativity and drive to results (80/20), plus a final overall value addition score.

(Client/Team)

Here also are five categories plus a summary score. The five areas are drive/achievement, team skills, communication, professionalism, and leadership.

(Reality Check)

Under this heading, the interviewer is asked to answer three questions. Is this person interested in Bain? Would you have this person on your team? The Airport Test – and, would you pass on or give an offer to this person?

(Summary)

Finally you get an overall interview rating.

In the first two sections there are spaces for the interviewer to write comments under two headings, strengths and weaknesses, and topics to test in next round.

I don't care who's giving the case, whether it's Amazon, Pepsi, BCG or McKinsey, they all look for the same four things: structure of thought, confidence level, communication skills, and going beyond the expected answer – creativity.

+ Types of Case Questions

Case questions generally fall into one of three major categories: back-of-the-envelope questions (which are often called market-sizing questions), factor questions, and business case questions. It's quite common to find a market-sizing question enclosed within a larger business case question. Whether fun or frustrating, all case questions are valuable learning experiences.

MARKET-SIZING QUESTIONS
Base your answer on logic and assumptions.

Structure
Listen to the question, then label the case: population based, household, or preposterous?
Ask clarifying questions only if you don't understand the question or terminology.
Lay out your structure first and the steps you'll need to answer the question, then go back through it with the numbers.
Assumptions
Don't worry if your assumptions are off; the interviewer is more interested in your thought process than whether your assumptions are correct.
If your assumptions are way off, they will tell you; otherwise they'll let it go.
Base your assumptions on some sort of logic, otherwise the interviewer might press you on how you drew that conclusion.
You can group several assumptions into one number; e.g., the 20% takes into account X, Y and Z.
Math
Estimate or round off numbers to make calculation easier.
Write all numbers down.
Answer – sanity check
Review the final answer to see if that number makes sense. If not, say so, and pick a number that makes more sense.

(Market-sizing Questions)

Market-sizing questions surface all the time and can be found during any round of interviewing. Sometimes it's a stand-alone question, but most often it's embedded in a larger case. When I hear a market-sizing question I like to label it. Is it a population-based question, a household question, or a preposterous question? Regardless of the type of market-sizing question, your answer should be based on logic and assumptions.

There will be instances when your assumptions are wrong. Sometimes the interviewer will correct you; other times she will let it go. **The interviewer is more interested in your logic and thought process than whether your assumptions are spot-on.** If you are still concerned, you can always say, "I'm not that familiar with this market, so if my assumptions are off, please correct me." Ninety percent of the time, the interviewer will tell you not to worry about it. However, everything you say has the potential to be questioned – be ready to defend your assumptions, as they should be based on some type of logic. If you just pull them out of the air, you're risking the interviewer aggressively challenging your assumptions and your credibility.

During a market-sizing case you don't get a chance to ask questions. You can ask questions only if you don't understand something. If they rattle off a string of initials, industry jargon or slang, and you're not sure what they mean, ask. You don't lose points for asking clarifying questions. These questions are tough enough to answer even when you do understand all the information.

When I go into a market-sizing question, I've already memorized several key facts and numbers. I don't want to be caught flatfooted, and I don't want to pull numbers out of the air that are going to be difficult to work with. I want numbers that are going to be easy, numbers that I'm familiar with, so I can do calculations with confidence.

Here are some key numbers that you should memorize:

- U.S. population is 320 million
- Life expectancy of an American is 80 years
- Even distribution between the ages: so there is the same number of 2-year-olds as 72-year-olds. We know that this is not true, but in a case like this, it's fine to assume, thus 4 million people per age group.
- 80 million per generation
- 100 million U.S. households

Regardless of where you're interviewing, you should know these key facts for your country or region. Also, don't use your friends as a sample population. Chances are you're at an elite university and your friends are unlikely to represent the general population. And remember to use easy numbers, numbers you can divide and multiply without much problem.

As they give you the question, write everything down. Determine and label the question. Next, ask questions only if you don't understand the questions or terminology. Finally, lay out your structure, then go back through it and fill in the numbers. That way you get a second bite at the apple as you work through the problem again. Base your assumptions on some sort of logic. And take advantage of grouping assumptions together. You can say something like, "The 20 percent takes into account X, Y, and Z."

Population-based questions

Population-based questions are often broken down by generation (0-20, 21-40, 41-60 and 61-80) or 80 million people per generation. To calculate a subset of each generation, use 4 million people per year, thus the number of people in their twenties would be 40 million (4 million people x 10 years). Sometimes you might want to break it down by men and women (50/50 split).

□ How many new smartphones were sold in the U.S. last year?

- Make assumptions and break the population down by generation.
- Determine the number of cellphones in each generation.
- Calculate the number or percentage of smartphones out of each generation's number of cellphones.
- You may want to draw a chart to show how well organized you are and how logically you think. It also makes it easier for the interviewer to follow your thought process.
- Review the final answer to see if that number makes sense. If it does not make sense, tell the interviewer that you think that number seems high and pick a new number that seems more reasonable. You don't have to go back through the process again, they know your process. It was just that one of your assumptions was off.

Assumptions: 320 million Americans, life expectancy of 80 years, even distribution among the ages. I'm going to divide it into generations, 0–20, 21–40, 41–60 and 61–80. That means 80 million people per generation.

Kids 0-12 or 52 million American children don't own cellphones. Out of the remaining 28 million kids I'll assume that 20 million have a cellphone. Out of that 20 million I'll assume that 10 million have a smart phone. These are older kids and they're technology driven.

Reason through your numbers for each generation and fill in the chart as you go along.

	Population	No. Cellphones	No. Smartphones
0 – 20	80m	20m	10m
21 – 40	80m	60m	50m
41 – 60	80m	60m	50m
61 - 80	80m	60m	40m
		200m	150m

We came up with 150 million smartphones in the U.S. However, the question called for the number of smartphones sold in the U.S. last year. The average cellphone contract is two years, but with the rising cost of cellphones and less impressive feature upgrades, I'll assume that people are holding on to their phones longer. I'm also going to assume that more people are buying refurbished phones. Taking all that into account, that means that 75 million are eligible. I'll assume 80 percent will upgrade to a new model. That means 60 million (75 X .80) will upgrade. I'll also assume that 20 percent of the 25 million (200m – 150m / 2) regular cellphone users eligible for an upgrade will switch to a smartphone, which equals 5 million. Thus 65 million smartphones were sold last year.

Now you may not agree with all my assumptions, but as long as you can follow my logic, I'm fine.

(Household questions)

There are times when you will want to break down the 100 million U.S. households by income level. According to a graph published in *The Wall Street Journal* in the summer of 2016, approximately 30 percent of U.S. households are high-income, 50 percent are middle-income, and 20 percent are low-income.

□ How many televisions are there in the U.S.?

- Draw/design a chart and fill it in as you go along (see below).
- Break households down by income levels.
- Assign the number of households per income level.
- Make assumptions about the number of TVs at each income level.
- Total them up.
- Add to that total an estimated number of non-household-owned TVs.

I'm going to break the U.S. market size down by household incomes: high, middle and low. I'll assume there are 30 million high-income households making up 30 percent of the total U.S. households and that they have on average three TVs per household. That makes 90 million TVs.

Middle-income households make up 50 million homes or 50 percent and they average two TVs. That leaves the low-income households at 20 million. I'm going to estimate 1 TV per household, or 20 million.

Income	Households	# of TVs	Total TVs
High	30m	3	90m
Middle	50m	2	100m
Low	20m	1	20m

That gives us a total of 210 million TVs. Review the answer to see if it makes sense. If it does not, adjust the answer, but not the process. Because it seemed to make sense, I'll add another 20 million non-household TVs to the count. That 20 million takes into account TVs found in schools, airports, hotels, hospitals, nursing homes, restaurants, and sports bars. That gives me a total of 230 million TVs in the U.S. Where did I get the 20 million non-household TVs? I pulled it out of the air, but I justified it by naming the venues that make up that number. You may want to add that the number of TVs might have been higher, but today many people watch "TV" on their computers or tablets or even phones.

□ How many garden hoses were sold in the U.S. last year?

- Determine the U.S. population and break it down by household.
- Estimate the number of households in the suburbs and in rural areas.
- Calculate the number of those households that have a yard and are in need of a garden hose.
- Add in businesses that use garden hoses to get a total.
- Estimate the life of a garden hose.

Assumptions: 320 million Americans, 3.2 people per household, thus 100 million households.

I'm going to estimate that 50 percent of the households are either suburban or rural. That makes 50 million households. I'll assume that 20 percent of those homes are apartments or condos. That narrows us down to 40 million households that most likely use a garden hose. Garden hoses are relatively inexpensive, so people are likely to have two hoses, a hose in the front yard and a hose in the back yard. That makes 80 million hoses. To that number, I'd like to add another 10 million hoses, which can be found in nurseries, zoos, and other outdoor facilities. Most of those businesses have at least two hoses.

We are now up to 90 million garden hoses. Hoses aren't replaced every year. I'd say that they are replaced every three years unless they run into the business end of a dog's tooth. So we take 90 million hoses, divide that number by 3 and come up with 30 million garden hoses sold each year.

(Worldwide market-sizing)

Whenever you get a worldwide market-sizing case, don't start with 8 billion people. Instead, pick one country, make assumptions, and then extrapolate out.

□ What is the worldwide market size for bulletproof auto glass?

- Make a list of possible customers or users (militaries, Fortune 500 companies, governments, the mob, drug lords, celebrities, and armored trucks).
- State that you are going to figure out the size of the U.S. market and extrapolate.
- Make assumptions, e.g. 2 percent of all U.S. cars have bulletproof auto glass (or bpag). The U.S. makes up 10 percent of the world market.
- Determine the U.S. market size by:
  - Breaking the U.S. households down by income levels
  - Estimating the number of cars in each income group
  - Adding non-household cars to the count

Income	Households	# of Cars	Total Cars
High	30m	3	90m
Middle	50m	2	100m
Low	20m	.5	10m

That gives us a total of 200 million cars. To that total, I'm going to add 40 million commercial vehicles. Where did I get the 40 million? I pulled it out of the air. It's not the number that is important, it's what makes it up. In this case, the 40 million includes government cars, armored cars, military vehicles, taxicabs, limos, university-owned cars, delivery vans, 18-wheelers, and rental cars. We now have a grand total of 240 million cars on the road. If 2 percent of U.S. cars have bpag that means there are 4.8 million cars. If 4.8 million is 10 percent of the worldwide market, then the total worldwide market is 48 million cars.

(Preposterous cases)

Preposterous market-sizing questions are usually stand-alone questions. These are asked not only to test your math skills, but also to see how you handle the absurd. The best advice is to roll with the punches, do the best you can, but have fun with it. They love people who love solving problems, so keep a sense of humor and attack it logically. These are questions like how many jelly doughnuts fit into the leaning Tower of Pisa? Or how many slices of pizza does it take to reach the moon? Or how much does a 747 weigh? I would be shocked if you received a preposterous question from a consulting firm. These are often given by companies that don't have a lot of practice or skills in giving case questions. It's a little scary to think, after how many years of school, that your job comes down to a question like this.

(Factor questions)

Factor questions usually start with "What factors influence ..." or "What key issues would you consider when ..." Factor questions are gaining popularity, particularly with non-consulting firms, companies such as Johnson & Johnson, Coach, Taco Bell, and Amazon, who use cases when interviewing for finance, marketing, or supply chain analysts.

Factor questions are used when time is short and interviewers can't devote significant time to walking you through an entire case, but want to see you think in broad strokes. They may also pop up in place of stand-alone market-sizing questions during first-round interviews. Factor questions last ten to fifteen minutes, where a full case could last up to forty minutes. Even though they are more conversational, the firms are still looking for the four key things: structure of thought, confidence level, communication skills, and creativity.

Some questions might require a recommendation. If so, state your recommendation, and then mention the risks and next steps.

Examples might be...

Johnson and Johnson: What factors would you consider when developing a new drug?

Taco Bell: Marketing is suggesting that we add french fries to the menu. What are some of the key issues to consider?

Amazon: We are thinking of putting a new distribution center somewhere in the Midwest. Where would you put it and why?

FACTOR QUESTIONS

- The best way to approach these questions is to think in broad terms and try not to get too detailed.
- Ask a few clarifying questions upfront, maybe make an assumption or two.
- Think the problem through and lay out your structure. If you just wrote down whatever popped into your head, make sure you prioritize this before you answer.
- Figure out a key metric in which to measure success.
- The interviewer may ask you questions, and may question what you ask.
- Go beyond the expected answer. Be creative.
- When making your recommendation, mention risks and next steps.

+ Written Group Case and Tests

Over the last couple of years more and more firms have turned to written cases; particularly in the second and third rounds. Monitor was the first to pioneer the written case. Since then firms have added a few new twists to the process. The interview can go something like this:

Scenario 1: You arrive for the interview and are handed a written case (usually about five pages: three pages of text and two of charts). You are given 20 to 30 minutes to read and take notes. When your time is up, a consultant comes into the room and you are expected to "present" the case, much as you would in a business school class. More often than not a discussion ensues. Chances are you will be touching on the same points you would if given a verbal case.

Scenario 2: The interviewer hands you a written case (usually three pages). You are given 30 minutes to read it, take notes, and draw up three PowerPoint slides to go along with the case, one of which needs to be a chart. You have no calculator, no computer, which means no PowerPoint or Chart Wizard, just three plain sheets of paper. The consultant comes back in and you present the cases as you would to a client.

Scenario 3: You are sitting in a conference room. A consultant comes in and gives you an 80-page document and tells you to read it and be prepared to discuss it in 30 minutes. In a case like this, what you want to do (besides climb out the window) is to read the executive summary upfront and then spend the rest of the time in the back of the document analyzing the exhibits. You can learn much more by studying the exhibits than by reading as far as you can in 30 minutes. (Warning: sometimes the executive summary is in the middle.)

Group cases are also becoming more and more popular.

Scenario 4: You are sitting around a table with three other candidates all going after the same job. The interviewer throws out a case to the group. How do you respond? The interviewer is most interested in how you interact with your peers. Are you kicking your competition under the table? Elbowing them in the gut? Talking over them to get your point across? If you are, then shame on you. The interviewer wants to see if you play well with others. You are going to be working as part of a team, and even though the other candidates are your competition, for this one moment in time they are your teammates and you should treat them with respect. Treat them as you would your classmates when working through a problem set. Don't be dominated by others; get your points across. Build on what others say in a positive and civil manner. Persuade them to look at a different point of view if you think they might be wrong. Don't call them out or embarrass them. It all boils down to your fit, communication skills, respect for others, empathy, and teamwork.

Scenario 5: You are shown into a conference room where three other candidates join you. The group is given a written case and 60 minutes to design a presentation. There is a computer in the room, but the only program on the computer is PowerPoint. The recruiter sits in the corner of the room and watches the dynamics unfold. Who becomes the leader and how did they become the leader? Did it happen naturally or was it forced upon the group? Who does the quant stuff? Who does the PowerPoint design? Are there discussions, arguments or fistfights? When your team is ready to present, two other consultants join in and your "team" presents the case. The only requirement is that each of you speaks for five minutes.

Now one, two, or all of you might get called back for the next round. While you act as part of a team during the presentation of the case, you are each judged individually.

How do you become a leader in a situation like that? The best way to take charge is to assign positions. Say, "Who is the finance geek?" or "Who knows PowerPoint really well?" Allocate positions based on strengths. Assign roles that include who opens the presentation, who closes, and who is the timekeeper. The downside of this is that you get stuck with whatever's left, but remember the recruiter is watching and you have already made a big impression.

(Written exercises)

McKinsey now requires that some candidates take a written exercise. “The test is testing problem-solving in a written format; folks will be surprised that the straight ‘quant’ questions are the minority. It’s not like a GRE quant test,” explains a senior McKinsey recruiter.

“The bulk of it involves making judgment calls/recommendations based on information available to you at that point,” the recruiter adds. “The exercise is supposed to feel like a case interview, but with multiple-choice responses.”

Last year the McKinsey Problem Solving Test (McK PST) contained 26 questions and you had an hour to complete it. Candidates received a bit more information about the business, the environment, and the problem with each question.

Students can’t bring in calculators or scratch paper. The test was developed internally by McKinsey and validated by Applied Psychological Techniques Inc. (APT). “It was fun, now that it’s over,” recounts a non-MBA Harvard graduate student. “There are some ratios and percentages, a couple of formulas, but nothing too overwhelming. Also, a few charts are used to present some of the information, but again fairly basic, in my opinion.”

A McKinsey recruiter said, “You need to be comfortable with calculating some percentages, basic equations, understanding relationships among data, but nothing terribly advanced.”

Some international offices have a math section that one student says is more like the GMAT than the GRE. You have 18 questions and 30 minutes to complete them. “You start with probability and it gets harder from there,” recounts a Harvard graduate student.

The McKinsey recruiter explains, “The resulting score is used as one more ‘data point’ on problem-solving for the interviewers to refer to if they have concerns or opposing reads. There is no magic or required score, and performance in face-to-face interviews is of greater importance to us.”

□ **Reading graphs**

One of the biggest changes we’ve seen in case interviewing is the increased use of graphs during the case. You will be given charts, sometimes at the outset of the case. Sometimes they slip them into the middle of the case, changing the dynamics of the question. You are expected to quickly analyze the charts, extract the most important information, and then apply it to your answer. It is easy to get overwhelmed. There are 11 different types of graphs used in consulting and case interviews, and you should be familiar with all of them.

To fine-tune your graph analytics: look at the graphs printed in *The Wall Street Journal* and *The Economist* and draw some conclusions. Then read the article and compare your thoughts with the main points of the article.

For in-depth graph analysis read *Case in Point: Graph Analysis for Consulting and Case Interviewing*.

Making slides and graphs: There is another twist: making slides and graphs. The recruiter hands you a few pages of data and asks that you create (on paper) three or four PowerPoint slides, and one should be a graph. You are then expected to present them during the case as you would during a presentation to a client.

□ **Silence**

One of the questions I am asked most often is about silence. Is it ever okay to be silent? Yes and no. The simple rule to remember is that silence is okay when you are doing something like calculating, writing down your thoughts, or drawing a graph or decision tree. You can get up to 40 seconds of silence before the "awkward" clock starts ticking and the interviewer becomes restless. It is not okay when you are just thinking while staring out the window or looking down at your shoes, particularly in the beginning of the case. If the interviewer gives you the case and you just sit there thinking, you've lost your momentum, you're sitting dead in the water.

+ If You Get Stuck

If you get stuck during a case and the interviewer doesn't ask you a question to help you along, then there a few things you can do. First, take a moment to recap where you've been. Chances are you've either gone into too much detail and are now stuck in the mud or you went off on a tangent. Recapping pulls you out of the mud and back above the trees. Remember, for the most part you want to view the case from a macro point of view. Many times, as you recap, you can see where you got off track. The second thing to do is to go back and look at the information that the interviewer gave you. Information that originally seemed irrelevant often becomes relevant as you work through the case. Third, quickly run through the Five C's in your head to see if there is something obvious that you missed. (5Cs: client, company, cost, channels, competition). Finally, if you are still stuck, ask for help. There is no shame in asking for help. If we were working on a project together, I would much rather have you ask me for help than have you waste a lot of time banging your head against a wall. But I wouldn't recommend asking for help more than once.

+ The Trouble with Math

There will be math! There are three kinds of people in the world, those good at math and those not so good. Wait, what?

Sometimes there will be a little, sometimes a lot, but nothing that you haven't seen before. The most common math you'll see in a case interview are percentages, ROI, breakevens, weighted averages, net present value, and multiplication and division with lots of zeros. The big difference is that you can't use a calculator. The two reasons they make you do math without a calculator are to see *how you think* and to see *if you think*.

How you think: I've seen students do the same math problem different ways. Do you use scientific notation? Do you turn everything into a fraction? The interviewer is curious about how you go about solving the problem. He is also looking to see if you take shortcuts. An example might be: The European pet industry was € 30 billion last year. It is expected to grow 5 percent a year, every year for the next five years. What's it going to be five years from now? When I used to give that case live, students would figure out 5 percent of € 30 billion, add them together and then calculate 5 percent of the new number, and so on for the next four years. No one wants to watch you do the same calculation three or four times. What he could have done is say: "If the market is growing 5 percent a year every year for the next five years that's 25 percent. But I need to take compounding into consideration so I know that it is going to be more than 25 percent but less than 30 percent. My best guess is around 28 percent. So, I'm going to calculate 30 times 1.28 and get € 38.4.

If you think: I don't care whether you are an applied math undergrad or have a PhD in string theory, most students have trouble with zeros. If you multiply two numbers together and the answer is supposed to be 320 million and you tell me it is 3.2 billion and 3.2 billion makes no sense at all, it's going to raise some eyebrows, because it is showing me that you're not thinking before you speak. And if you do that in something as important as an interview, what will you do in front of a client? I can't trust you, and if I can't trust you I'm not going to hire you. A good rule of thumb is that whenever you do a calculation ask yourself, "Does this number make sense?" If yes, then say it. If no, then go back and recalculate it because you know that they're going to make you recalculate. And once you say it, you can't un-ring the bell. Study the following table.

	10	100	1,000	10,000	100,000
10	100	1,000	10,000	100,000	1,000,000
100	1,000	10,000	100,000	1,000,000	10,000,000
1,000	10,000	100,000	1,000,000	10,000,000	100,000,000
10,000	100,000	1,000,000	10,000,000	100,000,000	1,000,000,000
100,000	1,000,000	10,000,000	100,000,000	1,000,000,000	10,000,000,000

There is a difference between *private math* and *public math*. With private math, you are at home with a calculator doing your math – all is right with the world. With public math, no calculator and the interviewer is sitting two feet away from you watching every digit that you write down. It is a very intimidating process. You want to get into the habit of talking your interviewer through your thought process by explaining what you are going to do, then doing it. That way if you make a mistake they can correct you immediately. If you go off and do your math by yourself and come back and say "the answer is 600 million" and the interviewer says "no it isn't" then you don't know where you made the mistake and you'll have to go back to the beginning of the calculations – and no one wants to do that. Below are some math questions to do in your head.

- A) The total widget market is $170 million and our sales are $30 million. What percentage of the market share do we hold?
- B) Our total manufacturing costs are $20 million. With that we can make 39,379 units. What is our approximate cost per unit?
- C) Our total costs are $75,000. Labor costs make up 25 percent of the total costs. How much are our labor costs?

- D) You bought a stock for $36 a share. Today it jumped 6 percent. How much is your stock worth?
- E) You raised $3.5 million for a start-up. Your commission is 2.5 percent. What's your commission in dollars?
- F) What's 7 x 45?
- G) The number of current outstanding shares for UKL Inc. is 41,084,000. Institutional investors hold 25,171,000 shares. What is the approximate percentage of shares held by institutions?

	Price	Change	Percentage Change
H)	$27.00	$0.54	
I)	$31.00	$0.62	
J)	$40.00	$1.00	
K)	$75.00	$3.00	
L)	$10.00	$1.70	
M)	$50.00	$2.50	

- N) Banana Republic makes 14 percent of Gap's estimated $16 billion in sales. What are BR's sales?
- O) Europe's population is approximately 740 million. By 2020 the European Union population is expected to drop to 700 million. What percentage change is that?

Go figure: Try to estimate some of the percentages in your head, and then work out the others without a calculator. Round off the answers as you would during a case question. (Worth noting: these are from a fifth-grade math test.)

P) 60 percent of 70 = ___ Q) 25 percent of 124 = ___ R) 68 percent of 68 = ___
S) 12 percent of 83 = ___ T) 23 percent of 60 = ___ U) 27 percent of 54 = ___

ANSWERS: A) about 18% B) about $500 C) $18,750 D) $38.16 E) $87,500 F) 315 G) 60% H) 2% I) 2% J) 2.5% K) 4% L) 17% M) 5% N) about $2.3 billion O) Europe's population drops by about 5% P) 42 Q) 31 R) 46 S) 10 T) 14 U) 15

Here are some formulas you should know inside and out:
Net Income = Revenues - expenses
Breakeven Point in Units = Fixed Costs / (Price - Variable Costs)
Breakeven Point in Price = (Total fixed cost / Production unit volume) + Variable cost per unit
Profit Margin = Net Income / Revenue
ROI = Profit from Investment / Investment Cost

Compound Annual Growth Rate = final value / the initial value. Raise the result to the power of 1 divided by the number of years.
Contribution Margin = Revenue/Unit – Variable Cost/Unit

+ Notes Design

Take notes during the case interview. While there is no standard for note-taking, the landscape format has become the norm. The first page of notes is divided into two sections – one third, two thirds. The left-hand section is where you write down the question. The problem statement for this case is that the CEO of Coors is thinking of entering the bottled water market. Is this a good idea? So you draw a line, put the object across the top, then lay out your structure. If you ask clarifying questions you can write the answers in the left-hand column underneath the original question.

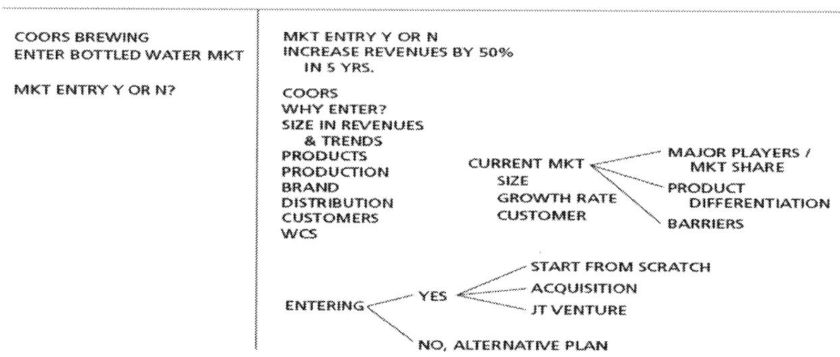

The use of plain white printer paper is fine; however, some consulting firms prefer that you use graph paper. There are several reasons for this.

- Graph paper makes it easier to draw your notes.
    - Be visual with your notes. Draw boxes, graphs, arrows, decision trees, value chains, and flow charts.
    - When appropriate, **turn your notes toward the interviewer** to explain your thought process. It makes him feel more like a team member and less like an interviewer. **This is huge so don't forget to do it.**
- Graph paper lines up your zeros. There is a lot of math in these questions and you can't use a calculator. It is not always easy to tell when you are off by a zero when your answer has eight zeros at the end of it.
- Graph paper organizes your notes. Well-organized notes make it easier for the interviewer to follow. When he isn't looking into your eyes, he's looking at your notes to see what you wrote down because he knows what you should be writing down. In

> addition, there is a good chance that the interviewer will collect your notes at the end of the interview. He uses your notes as one more data point – what did you write down? How did you write it? How did you do your math? Can he read your handwriting?

When it comes time for the case portion of your interview, rip out five pages of paper and number them (you can do this before the interview to save time and look well-organized). Remember to write on just one side of the page. Flipping pages back and forth can be disruptive and makes it hard to find important data at a glance. Using bullet points will make your notes seem better organized and make it easier to go back to find information. Star or highlight important points that you think will make the summary. This way points will jump out at you when it comes time to summarize the case.

As you fill up the pages (while leaving plenty of white space on your notes), spread your notes out in front of you. That way you can see the whole case at a glance. **You'll want to check the first page of notes from time to time.** There is a lot of important information on that first page. Some of it is immediately relevant; some is smoke put there to throw you off track. Other information will become relevant as you move through the case.

Some students use a separate sheet for their math; that way your main notes stay clean and linear. If you do use a separate sheet, make sure you label each calculation so you can tie it back into the case and not be left looking at a page full of random calculations.

Oftentimes the interviewer will hand you a chart. Always ask for permission before you write on the chart. As strange as it may seem, sometimes interviewers show up with only one copy of a chart.

(Idea box)

After hearing the initial problem statement, candidates will often think of an idea, solution, or strategy that seems inappropriate to state at the beginning of the case for fear that the interviewer might think that you are "shooting from the hip" and not analyzing the problem. Candidates write it down in their notes and then often forget about it during the case, even if it becomes relevant. The candidates wind up kicking themselves because they had the solution, but forgot about it. I tell students to draw an "idea box" on the first page of their notes. If anything pops into your head, write it in the idea box. Then you know where it is, and you'll get in the habit of checking the box when you review your first page of notes (which you should do several times during the case).

+ Summaries, Recommendations, and the Final Slide

In most case interviews you'll be asked to either summarize the case or make a recommendation. If you are asked to summarize the case, you don't get 15-30 seconds to think about it; you need to do so immediately. A summary is short, about 30-90 seconds. It isn't a rehash of everything you spoke about; it is a short recap of the problem followed by two or three main points that you want the interviewer to remember.

If you are asked to make a recommendation, you can usually ask for a moment to do your final analysis. **Put your recommendation on a separate sheet of paper** – it needs to be visual. When consultants are delivering their recommendation to a client, they usually have a PowerPoint slide behind them. This sheet of paper you're creating now should function as your PowerPoint slide. Your visual recommendation should draw the interviewer from the back of the chair to leaning over the table. If your interviewer leans forward, she'll automatically feel like a client of yours, rather than your interviewer, which is precisely what you want.

When ready, **lead with your recommendation**, state a clear "yes" or "no." Yes, they should enter the market or no, they shouldn't buy that piece of machinery. Do not say "I think." Be definitive. If your recommendation is a "no" then you should come up with an alternative plan to help the company reach its goal. Regardless of your decision, state it with confidence. Do not hedge your recommendation – you must make a decision. Hedging your recommendation is the kiss of death.

Make your recommendation: yes or no, and then tell the interviewer **why**, with the reasons behind your decision. **State and prioritize risks** based on impact, likelihood of occurrence, and the severity of the risked result if it does happen. This can often be illustrated with mini pie charts (see recommendation below). You will also want to state mitigating factors. You may not have time to draw out the mini pie charts, but that doesn't mean you shouldn't explain the likelihood of occurrence, with the severity of results and mitigating factors.

Lay out the **next steps** for the short-term and the long-term. Long-term next steps allow you to be more creative, which will separate you from the rest of the candidates. Once you lay out the next steps just add "and we can help you with that." This shows the interviewer that you understand how it all works, that consultants are always looking for more work, and that your recommendation is more likely to be successful if you are there to help make it happen. Also, offer recommendations that are realistic and able to be achieved soon – between 18 and 24 months – with reasonable budgets, and only those that will move the needle. If your idea increases profits by $10 million that's great if your company has profits of $50 million, but not so great if the company already has profits of $10 billion. Be careful of grand schemes. Most important, you need to **sell your recommendation**. You spent 30 minutes listening to the problem and suggesting a solution, but if they don't buy your recommendation the chances of your moving on are less likely.

Be prepared for the interviewers to come back at you and say, "Let me tell you why you're wrong." It doesn't matter which side you pick, they will take the other side. Now while the interviewers are giving you an earful, if you don't buy it, just say, "That is an interesting argument, but I don't find it compelling. I think my recommendation is correct and these are the reasons." That's exactly what they want you to do, defend your answer without getting defensive, and make a persuasive argument while keeping your confidence level high. However, if they come back with an argument bringing up something that you didn't yet consider, it's okay to admit you were wrong. "I didn't think about the inventory issue, and now that I'm considering it I think you are right." There is no shame in admitting you are wrong. What they don't want you to do is to change your answer because they told you you were wrong – or to defend an answer that you know is wrong just because you don't want to admit it. Corporations hire consulting firms because consultants are objective, and if you are defending an answer that you know to be wrong, you are not objective.

In some cases – particularly those that ask for a list of numbers the interviewer wants you to figure out, or those comparing two or more strategies, ideas, or options using the same criteria – you can create the "**final slide**" right at the beginning of the case. Almost no one remembers to do this, so if you do think of it, you'll score big points with the interviewer.

On a separate sheet of paper, draw a chart listing the product or markets (whatever it is that you are comparing) and below that, the criteria. As you calculate the numbers, fill them in on the final slide; this keeps all relevant information in one place and makes it easier for the interviewer to follow (think of it as a scorecard). Once all the information is filled in, you turn the final slide toward the interviewers and walk them through it. This is what you should shoot for. Similar to the final slide of a deck that a consultant would present to a client, this is the best summary.

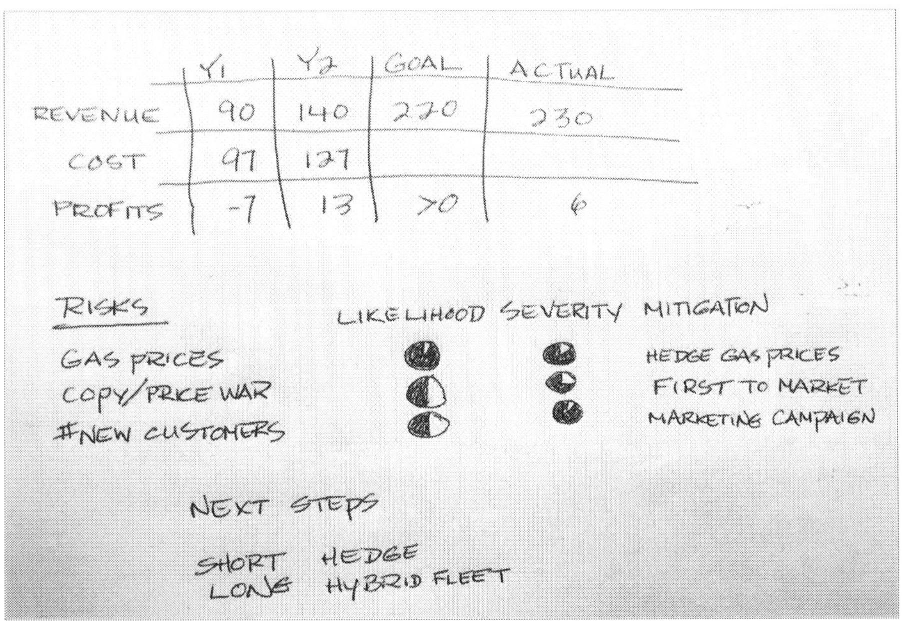

+ Case Journal

I had a student who decided she wanted to do consulting, but she had no business background. Her first attempt at a mock case interview with me was a disaster. That day she started a journal. For every live case she did with me, her classmates, and alumni (she did around 30 live cases), and with every case that she read (about 80 cases), she wrote down the problem, the solution, and most important, what she hadn't thought of. The student constantly reviewed it, so that what she didn't think of naturally soon became second nature to her. She also recorded structures, concepts, ideas, and strategies. When she had spare moments between classes or bus rides, she would flip through her journal. When she read articles in *The Wall Street Journal, Bloomberg Businessweek,* or *McKinsey Quarterly*, she would add to her journal. It never left her side.

She ended up at a top firm and took the journal with her. With every engagement she learned something new and added it to her journal. When she and her co-workers sat around brainstorming problems, she would flip through her journal and throw out ideas, which often sparked discussions and occasionally led to a solution.

I saw her five years after she had graduated and she still had her journal with her. Although it was as beaten up as Indiana Jones's journal, it held just as many treasures. She was headed to a new job and the journal was the first thing she packed.

Since then, whenever I speak at schools, I recommend creating a journal. Besides keeping all your notes in one place, it becomes a single source for case material that is also extremely helpful for your classes. If you are truly serious about case interviewing, then you will continue to read and practice all summer long. Recruiting events start as soon as you get back to campus, so if you take the time over the summer to practice, life is going to be easier in the fall.

Market Sizing → Steps

1) Clarify the question
2) Break down problems
3) Solve each piece
4) Consolidate into final result

4 : Ivy Case System

Best Case Thinking:

In my years of training students to answer case questions, I've realized that the major problem many students had was simply getting started. Sometimes they were overwhelmed, sometimes they were nervous, and sometimes they just didn't have a clue. So we developed The Ivy Case System™.

I'm sure you have heard about frameworks. A framework is a structure that helps you organize your thoughts and analyze the case in a logical manner. Often, however, you have to copy and paste from a number of frameworks in order to answer any single question. The difference between a framework and a system is that the framework is really a tool, while a system is a process. Instead of memorizing seven individual frameworks and then trying to decide which to apply, you learn a system, which already has the tools built in.

The Ivy Case System is a two-part system made up of five easy steps to get you going and four popular case scenarios, each with a collection of ideas and questions that will help you structure the remainder of your response. If you follow through the outline for each scenario, you can be confident that your response will be logical and cohesive. And because it is all based on business sense and common sense, you'll find that there is nothing in there that you don't already know ... it is just organized a little differently.

The first five steps will provide you with a quick start (no long awkward pause between question and answer). They will get you five minutes into the question, give you momentum, and provide you with enough information to decide which of the four scenarios (or which combination thereof) is most appropriate to the case question at hand.

You may want to read through the following explanation of the Ivy Case System and then check out a practice case or two to see how the system can be applied. Then it will be time to revisit the system and learn it.

The interviewer has just finished giving you the case. Here's what you do.

+ The First Five Steps

1. Summarize the question.
2. Verify the objective(s). Ask if there are any other goals or objectives.
3. Ask clarifying questions.
4. Label the case and lay out your structure.
5. State your hypothesis.

[1. Summarize the Question]

Sometimes the question is short. “How do we increase sales at the campus bookstore?” Other times the question is long and involved and is filled with data that comes at you as if from a fire hose. It’s difficult to capture all that information in your notes, so the first step is to summarize the question. That way, if you missed something or wrote it down wrong, the interviewer will correct you before allowing you to move on. It puts you and the interviewer on the same page from the beginning, thus keeping you from answering the wrong question.

Summarizing the question shows the interviewer that you listened, and it fills the gap of silence between the end of the question and the beginning of your answer. Make sure you streamline the summary; don’t repeat it back word for word. If there are numbers in the problem, always repeat the numbers because you’re not sure whether they are going to be relevant, and you want to make sure you’ve got it right.

Also, get into the habit of quantifying related numbers as a percentage, e.g., year-to-year comparisons or a change in stock price. If the interviewer tells you that the stock price jumped from $15 to $18, don’t say “It jumped from $15 to $18.” Don’t say “It jumped $3.” Tell the interviewer that it jumped 20 percent. This is the way that consultants and senior managers think, and it’s how they want you to think.

[2. Verify the Objective(s)]

You can bet that when consultants first meet with clients, they always ask about objectives and goals. What are the client’s expectations, and are those expectations realistic? In the client’s mind, **what constitutes success?** Even if the objective of the case seems obvious, there is always the possibility of an additional underlying objective. So you (the interviewee) should say, “One objective is to raise profits. Are there any other objectives or goals that I should know about?” If the interviewer says, “No, higher profits is the only objective,” you just focus on that one objective. If there is an additional objective, you may need to break the case in two and tackle one objective at a time. If you don’t ask about other objectives or goals and there is one, the interviewer will have to feed you that information during the case and you’ll lose points. By asking you might receive key information that will affect the way you lay out your structure.

[3. Ask Clarifying Questions]

These are questions to ask only when you don’t understand something or need additional information to lay out your structure. An example might be, if it’s an entering a new market case, a good clarifying question might be “Why does the company want to enter this market?” Or if you have been tasked to raise revenues by 10 percent, a clarifying question might be “What have revenues done for the last three years?” If the interviewer throws out industry jargon, slang or a string of initials or acronyms and you don’t know what they are, ask. You don’t lose any points for asking.

[4. Label the Case and Lay Out Your Structure]

This is by far the toughest part of the process, and you may want to take a moment at this point to think about structure. About 30 to 90 seconds of silence here may save wasted time later in the interview. You've decided which case scenario(s) to work with, and you have asked a few broad questions that have given you information you need to form a logical response. Because you have studied the scenarios, you can quickly go through the bullet points in your mind and decide which are the most relevant to this particular question. You then just need to tell the interviewer how you plan to proceed. Keep in mind that you are not married to your structure. Because new information is constantly added, as well as twists and turns in the case, your structure could stand through the whole case, or it might become obsolete rather quickly. A structure is – given the limited information you have – what would you analyze, and in which order, to solve this problem?

You want to make sure that your structure is MECE, or Mutually Exclusive, Collectively Exhaustive. This is a consulting term that is thrown around a lot. All it means is that there shouldn't be any overlap in your structure. For example, if you get an entering a new market question, you might want to break your structure down into three buckets: first analyze the client, then analyze the new market, then look at the different ways to enter the market. Each of those buckets is mutually exclusive of the others, but collectively exhaustive of everything we need to look at to solve this case.

Once you draw your structure, **turn your notes toward the interviewer** and walk him through your thought process. This brings him into the interview and makes him feel less like an interviewer and more like a client. Be sure to refer to the bucket headings first (in this case it would be company, market, and entering the market), then go back and talk through the bullet points you made beneath each heading.

[5. State Your Hypothesis]

Consulting firms – and only consulting firms – care about a hypothesis. They would like you to state a hypothesis within the first few minutes of the case, usually after you walk them through your structure. I know that it seems crazy to give them an answer to the case before you have any information. But the reason consulting firms like it is that when they go into a company they often don't know what the problem is, so they state an initial hypothesis and try to prove it. Chances are they are going to disprove the first five, but it narrows the scope of the problem. For example, if you get a profit and loss case, you might say, "My hypothesis is (or my thoughts are) that profits have fallen because costs have risen." That is something you can try to prove as you move through the case. If you disprove it, you'll want to update your hypothesis as you proceed through the case.

The advantages to stating a hypothesis up front are that it will help you ask the right questions, make your analysis more linear, and force you to focus on issues that you can either prove or disprove. It also helps you identify which structure to use, thus defining the starting point.

I've known plenty of candidates who received job offers without ever stating a hypothesis. Think of it as icing on the cake. If you can remember to state one, they'll love it. If you forget, though, it's not the end of the world. But because the interviews are so competitive you'll want to take every advantage. When you are doing practice cases, a simple trick to remind yourself to state a hypothesis is to lightly write the letter H in the middle of your first page of notes. That way, as you are writing out your structure, you'll see the H and be reminded to offer a hypothesis. You will get into the habit and it will come naturally to you in an interview.

In real life, consultants can take up to two days to form a hypothesis, but you have about five minutes. So, don't worry if your hypothesis is wrong. It eliminates one possibility and allows you to restate your hypothesis and focus on another aspect of the case. Think of the process as one of elimination.

+ Core to the Case

You know you are going to get a lot of cases that ask you to analyze a company (the client) and cases that ask you to analyze the market/industry. Below are two lists of core questions you should be thinking and asking about the company and market/industry. You need to learn these so you can rattle them off in your sleep. It will speed up your structure (because you won't have to stop and think) and ensure that you don't miss anything critical. You will probably add to or subtract from the list depending on the case, but it will eventually become second nature to you and thus build up your confidence.

☐ Company

- It's important to ask about the profit and revenue trends so you can get a feel for the size of the company and how it's been doing. You may even want to ask whether it is a publicly traded or private company.
- Customer segmentation is critical. You need to know who the client's customers are so you can craft a strategy.
- Characteristics and changing needs.
- Profitability of each segment.
- Product mix. What products or services does the company offer and what are the costs and margins associated with each product? Have there been any recent changes in the product mix? Product differentiation and market share.
- Production capabilities and capacity allow you to access several key areas. Does the company have the ability to expand? Are they running at full capacity now and if not, why not?

ABOUT THE COMPANY:
CORE QUESTIONS TO ASK

- Profits and revenues for the last three years?
- Customer segmentations?
    - Characteristics?
    - Changing needs?
    - Profitability by segment?
- Product mix?
    - Costs / margins?
    - Product differentiation?
    - Market share?
- Production capabilities / capacity?
- Brand?
- Distribution channels?
- WCS (What constitutes success?)
    - Which metric is used?

- Brand. How strong is its brand? Is it a market leader or has the brand faded? Oftentimes the company in the case is made up, so we have no idea about the strength of the brand.
- Distribution channels. How are the products and services currently distributed? How can the company expand its channels?
- WCS. What constitutes success? This is different from the objective. If it's an entering a new market case, the objective might be to decide whether to enter or not. While success might be defined as 10 percent of the market in three years, it is critical to understand what success means to the client and which metric is used to measure that success.

□ Market

- Market size, growth rate, and trends. Ask for three years of data. How is the industry doing overall and how is the company growing compared with the industry?
- Industry drivers. Is it brand, street cred, price, content, size, economics, technology, geopolitical events, bargaining power of buyers, bargaining power of suppliers, or distribution channels?
- Customer segmentation(s). There are often a number of segments within an industry. Which is the company going after? How big are they? How profitable are they?
- Margins. What are the typical margins within an industry?
- Industry changes. Have there been any changes within the industry, such as mergers, acquisitions, new players, new technology, or new regulations?
- Distribution channels. What are the major distribution channels within this industry? As an example, think of all the ways you can watch a movie.
- Major players and market share. Who are the competitors and how much market share do they have? Is it a fragmented market or one dominated by one or two major players?
- Product differentiation. This often ties into the one above. How do the competitors differentiate their products or services? Match it up to market share.
- Barriers. *Barriers to entry* can be access to capital, distribution channels, raw materials, technical knowledge, or human talent. Barriers could also be government regulations, customer loyalty, sticky features (making it hard to leave one product for another), or market domination by one or two major players. *Barriers to exit* could be massive investment and nontransferable fixed assets, contract requirements with

> ★
>
> ABOUT THE MARKET:
> CORE QUESTIONS TO ASK
>
> - Market size, growth rate, and trends?
> - Where is it in its lifecycle? (Emerging? Mature? Declining?)
> - Industry drivers?
> - Customer segmentation(s)?
> - Margins?
> - Industry changes
>   - M&A? New players?
>   - Changes in technology?
>   - Regulations?
> - Distribution channels?
> - Major players and market share?
> - Product differentiation?
> - Barriers to entry/exit?

suppliers, or government requirements (e.g. a company receives major tax breaks from a state government to employ a certain number of people from that state). Another barrier would be that the costs of leaving a market are higher than those incurred to continue competing in the market, barriers of emotions: we built our house on this market.

+ The Four Key Case Scenarios, Developing Your Structure

While interviewers give dozens of different types of cases, the four scenarios listed below are the basic building blocks of many of the cases. While it is unlikely that a case will fit neatly into one of these scenarios, you will find that the components that make up the various cases are tied in the scenarios below. **They are to be used to base your thinking; they will help you ask the right questions and turn the case into a well-structured conversation. They are not carved in stone, but are to be used as a guide. Each structure should be crafted based on the case.**

Be cautious of books that sell you on the fact that one structure fits all cases – it's the lazy way out. If I gave you two very different cases and you structured your thought process exactly the same way for each case, I'd show you the door. These are often just glorified cookie-cutter approaches that stifle original thought, create pedestrian answers that lack tactical or strategic brilliance, and thus make it harder to set yourself apart from the next candidate. You'll lose points for lack of creativity, imagination, and intellectual curiosity. The best interviewers use the bicameral mind – the two-lobed brain. The left side is analytical and the right side is creative.

The four key case scenarios are:

1. Profit and loss
2. Entering a new market
3. Pricing
4. Growth and increasing sales

[1. Profit and loss]

Question: Our client manufactures high-end athletic footwear. Sales are up but profits are down in the U.S. What's going on, and how do we fix it?

Profit-and-loss questions have been the most popular type of question for the last 25 years. Whenever you hear the words bottom line, profits, costs, or revenues, you should immediately think: "Profits = (Revenues – Costs)". We know that Revenue = Quantity x Price, and Costs = (Quantity x Variable Costs) + Fixed Costs.

However, I'm going to change this formula to the structure of **E(P=R-C)M**. The E represents the economy and/or environment, and M represents the market or the industry. You always want to look at external factors first, so you have an idea whether this is a company problem or an industry-wide problem.

When you get a P&L question, a good clarifying question could be, "Have are our competitors' profits also fallen?" If yes, it might be an industry-wide problem and you should take a closer look at external factors – effects from natural disasters, a rise in interest rates, or maybe a new entrant into the market. If no, it might be just our problem – increased costs, lower revenues, or outdated products. Another clarifying question could be by how much have profits fallen?

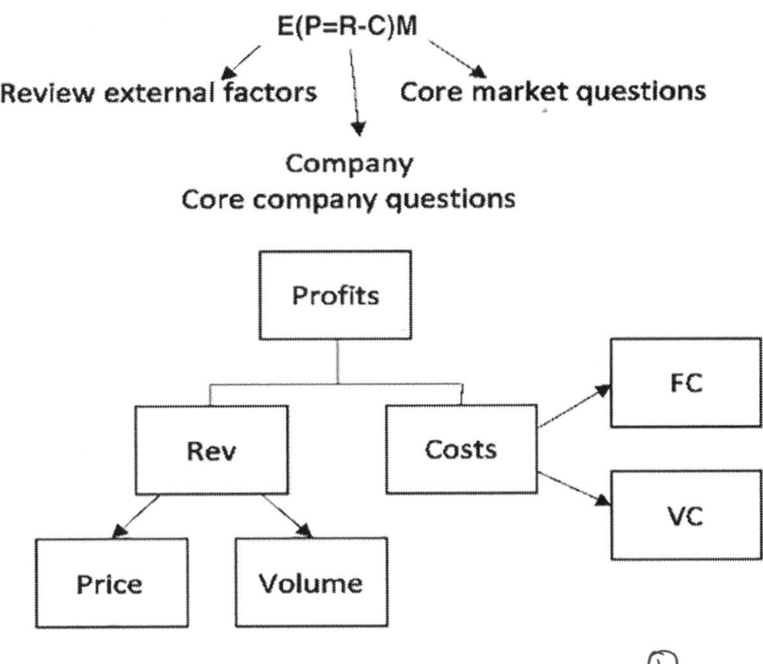

E(P=R-C)M. If you suspect that it is an industry-wide problem start by spelling out your take on external factors. I want two or three things that are important to the company inside the parentheses. If it is a retailer then we'd like to look at consumer confidence, disposable income, unemployment rate, and maybe petrol prices. If it's a manufacturer then we'll want to look at how the dollar is doing against other currencies, interest rates, petrol prices, and maybe commodities. You do this for several reasons. If you don't look at external factors then you are answering a case in a vacuum, and who lives in a vacuum? This will show the interviewer that you know what's going on outside the classroom. You should go into the interview with some key economic factors memorized, such as unemployment rate, disposable income, consumer confidence, interest rates, the dollar's strength in the currency market, and petrol prices. Those factors can be either good or bad depending on the economy and the case.

The E can also stand for the environment. In 2017 the U.S. suffered major hurricanes, tornadoes, mudslides, and wildfires. As a result of those events, some companies saw their profits drop, while others saw their profits rise. These are factors that most students don't take into consideration when analyzing a case. **Look at everything, touch on everything, analyze everything**.

The M stands for the market or industry. No one is going expect you to know what's going on in all industries. The interviewer has a lot of information to give you, but he's not going to give it to you unless you ask for it. Ask about industry trends and competitors to determine whether they are facing the same problems as the client. How has our client been doing compared with the rest of the industry? If you have memorized the industry core from the beginning of the chapter these questions will seem natural, and you'll come off projecting confidence.

Going inside the parentheses is the same as going inside the company. Start by asking questions about the company.

The company: Who are they? What do they do? What are their products? Write down the core company questions relevant to this case. Such as:

- Market leader?
- Size in terms of revenues and profits, public or private? (Ask for 3 years.)
- Products or services? Product mix? Revenue mix and trends?
- Customer segmentation?
- What constitutes "success"? (WCS?)

Review the revenue streams. Even if your hypothesis suggested costs are the problem, you need to understand your revenue streams before you can intelligently analyze the situation and cut costs. Ask "What are the major revenue streams, and how have they changed over time?" Then, when you get to costs, "What are the major costs, both fixed and variable, and how have they changed over time?" Again, it's always good to ask for trends: this is how consultants think, and it's how they want you to think.

The other parts to the profit-and-loss formula are price and volume. Price and volume are interdependent. You need to find the best mix, because changing one isn't always the best answer. If you cut prices to drive up volume, what happens to the profit and next-year sales? Do profits increase or decrease? There must be a balance. The reason behind the decision must make sense.

Once you have an understanding of the market and the company you'll need to come up with some solutions to raise profits – that, after all, is the objective. The first thing you want to do is ask for a moment to write down your thoughts. Start with headings, revenue-based strategies, and cost-based strategies. You do this for several reasons: It shows the interviewer that you are well organized and thinking ahead. It's also easier to come up with ideas when you are looking at a heading instead of a blank sheet of paper. And it keeps you from commingling your ideas. Dividing ideas into short-term and long-term solutions is also desirable, particularly if there is a time constraint to raising profits. You want to present all the revenue-based ideas first, then all the cost-based ideas. If appropriate, divide your cost-based ideas into production, labor, and finance. It will show the interviewer that you are well organized and thinking ahead.

Keep in mind that the interviewer has probably given this case ten times. He knows every possible answer you can think of, and he's grown impatient with the answers. There's a good chance he'll cut you off as soon as he knows where you're headed. This can be tough, because when you are in a pressure situation and you are cut off, it's difficult to drop that thought and come up with something new. Indeed, in my own experience, I know when I cut students off in mid-thought, they tend to pretend that they didn't hear me and keep talking. Then after I cut them off again, they panic, and then scramble as their brains shut down.

Don't let that happen to you. If you take the time to write down your answers first, and the interviewer cuts you off, just look at your notes and offer another idea. It takes a lot of the stress out of the situation and makes you look more professional.

Questions to think about:

Revenues:

1. What are the major revenue streams, and what percentage of the total revenue does each stream represent?
2. Does anything seem unusual in the balance of percentages?
3. Have the percentages changed lately? If so, why?

Costs:

1. Any major shifts in costs?
2. Do any costs seem out of line?
3. If we benchmarked our costs against our competitors' costs, what would we find?

Products:

With new products, make sure you ask about the advantages and disadvantages. Everyone forgets to ask about the disadvantages, but disadvantages can drive the case more than the advantages. Disadvantages might be things like product cannibalization, layoffs, or in the case of a new drug, side effects.

Below is a decision tree for increasing profits for a retailer. This is another example of a MECE structure for a P&L case. If it were fully fleshed out it would grow quite large. No need to write out the whole thing. They just want you to think this way.

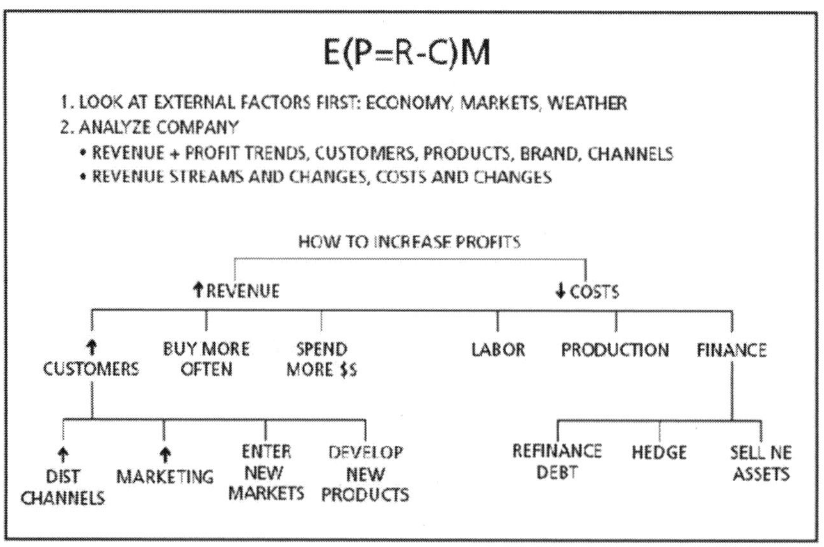

[2. Entering a New Market]

Question: Your client Company Z manufactures hair products. The company is thinking about entering the sunscreen market. Is this a good idea?

Entering a new market questions can be as straightforward as the one above, or they can involve mergers, acquisitions, joint ventures, starting a new business, or the development of a new product. So it's not just "Do we enter?" but also "How do we enter and what are the advantages and disadvantages of each strategy?"

A good clarifying question with an entering a new market question is "Why does the company want to enter this market?" Very few MBAs ever ask me this, and it is critical. With an entering a new market question, most MBAs will analyze the new market first. They want to see if the market is worth it. I think this is a mistake. They should analyze the company first, then the market. This way they can look at the new market through the company's eyes and not just their own eyes. If they don't understand the client, they really can't tell if the market is "worth it."

Your notes might include something like the following, covering the company, the current market, and how best to enter the market. This can be laid out in three buckets, or you can structure it as internal (company and how to enter) and external (market and competition). Either way, it is basically all the same information. Structure it whichever way makes you most comfortable.

Step 1: Start off with questions about the company. (Remember the core list.)

- What are the company's profits and revenues for the last three years?
- What is the company's product mix?
- If this is about a new product,

   - Will it cannibalize an existing product?
   - Is the customer segmentation(s) the same?
   - Can we use the same distribution channels?
   - Can we use the same sales force?
   - How and where will this new product be produced?
   - Will we have to hire new workers or retrain current workers?
- How strong is the brand?
- What constitutes success?

Step 2: Determine the state of the current and future market. (Remember the core list.)

- What is the size of the current market?
- What is the growth rate? (Ask for trends.)
- Where is the industry in its life cycle? (Stage of development: Emerging? Mature? Declining?)
- Who are the customers and how are they segmented?
- What role does technology play in the industry and how quickly will it change?
- How will the competition respond?

Step 3: Investigate the market to determine whether entry makes good business sense.

- Who are the competitors, and what size market share do they have?
- How do their products differ from ours?
- How will we price our products or services?
- Are substitutions available?
- Are there any barriers to entry? Examples might include lack of brand or street cred, capital requirements, access to raw materials, access to distribution channels, lack of human capital, and government policy. Also, industries dominated by a small number of big players can be a barrier.
- Are there barriers to an exit? How would we exit if this market sours?
- What are the risks? (For example, changing market regulations or technology.)

Step 4: If we decide to enter this market, we need to figure out the best way to become a player. There are four major ways to enter a market:

- Start from scratch and grow organically.
- Acquire an existing player from within the industry. (Grow inorganically).
- Form a joint venture / strategic alliance with another player with a similar interest. What can each side bring to the venture?
- Outsourcing. Have someone else manufacture the product, with the client still handling marketing and distribution.

Cost-benefit analysis. Analyze the pros and cons of each strategy. You can use this whenever you are trying to decide whether to proceed with a decision. If your answer is no, the client should not enter the market, you can stand out from the other candidates by coming up with an alternative idea to help the company reach its goal. "And we can help you with that."

Your notes might look something like this:

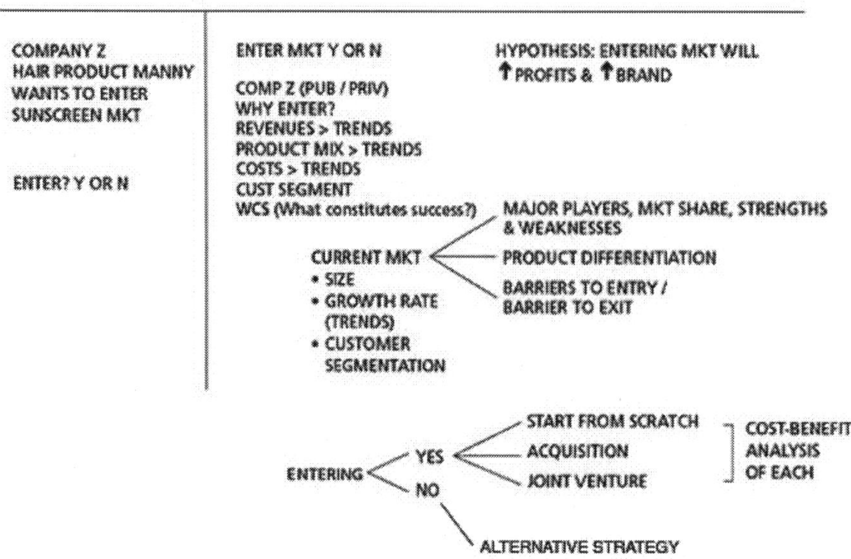

Recommendation for entering a new market: lead with the answer.
If yes, say yes, the client should do it. This is why, this is how, and these are the risks and the next steps – in both the short-term and the long-term outlook.

If no, then say no! Give the reasons for your answer, then list and prioritize the risks of not entering the market, based on the impact and likelihood of occurrence. If possible, present an alternative plan that would help the client reach the goal, and then add, "We can help you with that."

In your recommendation, DO NOT explain or even mention the options you didn't choose. Your recommendation should be linear, clear, and between 30 and 90 seconds for explanation.

M&A

Many questions about entering a new market are also merger and acquisition questions. The two most important factors about a merger are whether it increases shareholder value and whether the two cultures will mesh well. Cultural mismatch is the biggest reason mergers fail or don't live up to their potential. Larry Fink, the CEO of BlackRock says, "Buy companies with cultures your company can learn from, not just businesses that will let you cut costs."

Here are some key points about an M&A question.

- If the buyer is a private equity firm, ask "Why does the PE firm want to buy the company? What else does it own? And what does it plan to do with it (hold, flip, or break apart)?" Many students forget to ask this and they miss out on the countless synergies among portfolio companies.

- If the M&A involves one company acquiring another, ask not only "Why?" but also, "What other products do they sell?" and "What are the synergies involved?" The acquisition needs to make good business sense.

- Reasons to purchase:
    - Increase market access, boost the brand, and increase market share.
    - Diversify the company's holdings.
    - Pre-empt the competition from acquiring the company.
    - Target company is a threat.
    - Inherit management talent.
    - Obtain patents or licenses or products.
    - Gain from synergies, cost savings, cultural integration, expansion of distribution channels and customer base. Cross-sell products.
    - Gain tax advantages.
    - Increase shareholder value.

- Due diligence. Research the company and industry:
    - What kind of shape is the target company in? Management? Products? Profitability? Brand? What is the stand-alone value? What has been its growth rate? Why is it on the market? Consider all the items in the core box about analyzing a company.
    - How secure are its markets, customers, and suppliers?
    - What are the margins like? Are they high volume, low margin, or low-volume-high-margin?
    - How is the industry doing overall? And how is the company doing compared with the industry? Is it a leader in the field?
    - How will competitors respond?
    - Are there any legal reasons we can't or shouldn't acquire the target company?
    - Are there technology risks?
    - How much will it cost? Will the client overpay?
    - Does the buyer have enough cash or access to capital markets?

[3. Pricing Strategies]

Question: Company S is coming out with a new tablet. How should they price it?

Pricing questions can sometimes be stand-alone questions, but just as often are part of a larger case. Investigate the company and its objective, learn about the product or service and the competition, and then pick a pricing strategy.

Step 1: Investigate the company. How big is it? What products does it have, and is it a market leader in this field? *More important, **what is the pricing objective**: profits, market share, or brand positioning?* Is it in charge of its own pricing strategies, or is it reacting to suppliers, the market, and competitors?

The company strategy or objective is the first and most important component of a pricing case. Let's take the tablet market as an example. Apple came out with the iPad. It was first to market; the iPad's a beautiful piece of technology, but kind of pricey. We know Apple likes big margins. Apple was going for profits. Next Samsung came out with the Galaxy. Another beautiful piece of technology, but the company's margins were smaller and the price lower. Samsung was going for market share. Then the Amazon Kindle Fire was launched. Amazon sold it for what it cost them to make it. The strategy was to get as many Fires as possible out into the market, because the company makes more off the ancillary sales, the books, movies, songs, and Prime membership than it would ever make from the sale of a single device. These are three very successful companies, with three very different pricing strategies for basically the same product.

COST-DRIVEN PRICING: THE DEADLY BUSINESS SIN

Before there was Michael Porter and all the other modern-day business gurus, there was Peter Drucker (1909–2005). The following is from Peter Drucker's Wall Street Journal article "The Five Deadly Business Sins."

The third deadly sin is cost-driven pricing. The only thing that works is price-driven costing. Most American and practically all European companies arrive at their prices by adding up costs and then putting a profit margin on top. And then as soon as they have introduced the product, they have to start cutting the price, have to redesign the product at enormous expense, have to take losses – and often, have to drop a perfectly good product because it is priced incorrectly. Their argument? "We have to recover our costs and make a profit."

This is true but irrelevant: Customers do not see it as their job to ensure manufacturers a profit. The only sound way to price is to start out with what the market is willing to pay – and thus, it must be assumed, what the competition will charge – and design to that price specification.

Cost-driven pricing is the reason there is no American consumer-electronics industry anymore. It had the technology and the products, but it operated on cost-led pricing; the Japanese practiced price-led costing.

Step 2: Investigate the product. How does it compare with that of the competition? Are there substitutions or alternatives? Where is the product in its growth cycle? Is there a supply-and-demand issue at work?

Step 3: Determine a pricing strategy. There are three main pricing strategies to think about: competitive analysis, cost-based pricing, and price–based costing.

Once you have determined the company's objective, then you need to run through all three main pricing strategies.

Competitive Analysis: Are there similar products out there? How does our product compare with the competition? Do we know the competitor's costs? How are its products priced? Are there substitutions available? Is there a supply-and-demand issue? *What will the competitive response be?*

Cost-based Pricing: Take all our costs, add them up, and add a profit to it. This way you'll know your break-even point. Usually not a very good way to price anything, though, because if you misjudge the market you'll have to cut prices, which will squeeze margins – but the company needs to know what its costs are.

Price-based Costing: What are people willing to pay for this product? If they're not willing to pay more than what it costs you to make the product, then it might not be worth making. On the other hand, consumers may be willing to pay much more than you could get by just adding a profit margin. Profit margins vary greatly by industry: grocery stores have a very thin profit margin, while drug companies traditionally have a huge margin. Also consider what your product will be worth to the buyer. Compare it with other products or services in their lives. What did they pay in those cases?

In short, when solving a pricing problem, you need to look at all these strategies and see where, or if, they intersect.

NOTE: Pricing questions become more difficult/interesting when you get a case about partition pricing – meaning that you charge separately for things like delivery, shipping, installation, and warranties, versus bundling everything into one price. If you run an airline, do you advertise lower ticket prices and charge for baggage or do you advertise that bags fly free and charge a higher ticket price? If you're a large electronics store, do you include free delivery and installation on the 70-inch HDTV at a higher price? Or do you charge a lower price for the television (knowing that consumers do comparison shop on the internet even while they're standing in your store) and charge separately for delivery and installation knowing that most consumers can't get a 70-inch television into their car, never mind set it up at home. One solution might be to look at industry norms. "Do my competitors offer free shipping?" If you don't consider industry norms, you might very well be at a disadvantage when people comparison shop.

I teach at 50 schools a year. Any fee I quote includes my speaking fee and my travel expenses, combined. My competitor charges a fee and then charges travel expenses separately. My thought is that my pricing strategy makes it easier for both the school and me because I don't have to collect, copy, and submit a travel report with receipts to the school's accounts payable department. It's just one flat fee. That way I get paid sooner and don't have to wait for my credit card bill to submit my plane ticket cost. I already have an idea what my expenses will be, and that allows the school to budget in advance, which is what they like. With my way, there are no surprises. Whose way is right? Well, the norm in consulting is to charge a fee plus expenses. That might work well when you have Apple as a client, but not when a client is a cash-strapped university.

[4. Growth and Increasing Sales]

Question: BBB Electronics wants to increase its sales so it can claim it is the largest distributor of the K6 double-prong lightning rod. How can BBB reach its goal?

Increasing sales or growing the company is not the same as increasing profits. In the former case, you are less interested in costs. Still you want to have an understanding of the company and its objective, its products, and the industry.

Increasing sales can mean increasing volume, increasing revenues, or both. Say you get an increasing revenue case, and the interviewer wants you to raise revenues by 10 percent. **A good clarifying question would be** "By what rate have the revenues grown for the last three years and do you have any forecasts?"

Step 1. Learn about the company and its size, resources, and products. (You know the drill.)

Step 2. Investigate the industry: Is it growing and how is the client growing compared with the industry? Are the client's prices in line with its competitors?

Increase volume / revenues:

- Expand the number of distribution channels.
- Increase product line through diversification of products or services (particularly with products that won't cannibalize sales from existing products).
- Analyze the segments of the business with the highest future potential and margins.
- Invest in a marketing campaign.
- Acquire a competitor (particularly if the question is about increasing market share).
- Adjust prices (Take into account the price sensitivity of the customer. Lower prices to increase volume and raise them to decrease demand or increase profits per unit).
- Create a seasonal balance. (Increase sales in every quarter – if you own a nursery, sell flowers in the spring, herbs in the summer, pumpkins in the fall, and Christmas trees and garlands in the winter).

Another way for a company to grow is to find niches in developing industries with high barriers to entry. There will be less competition and more notice if someone is trying to enter.

+ Key Questions for Additional Scenarios

Following is a quick review of key questions to ask and points to consider after labeling the case.

Industry Analysis: Investigate the industry overall

- Where is it in its life cycle? (Emerging? Mature? Declining?)
- How has the industry been performing (growing or declining) over the last one, two, five, and ten years?
- How have we been doing compared with the industry?
- Who are the major players and what market share does each have? Who has the rest?
- Has the industry seen any major changes lately? These might include new players, new technology and increased regulation.
- What drives the industry? Brand/street cred, price, quality, endorsements, fads, marketing, products, size, economics, or technology?
- Profitability. What are the margins?

Suppliers:

- How many are there?
- What is their product availability?
- What's going on in their market?
- How is the supply chain? Are the companies that supply you getting what they need from their suppliers?

The Future:

- Are players entering or leaving the market?
- Are any mergers or acquisitions going on?
- Are there any barriers to entry or exit?
- Substitutions, what alternatives are there?

Developing a New Product:

Think about the product itself:

- What's special or proprietary about it? Is the product patented? For how long?
- Are there similar products out there? Are there substitutions?
- What are the advantages and disadvantages of this new product?
- How does this new product fit in with the rest of our product line?
- Can our sales force sell it?

Think about market strategy:

- How does this strategy affect our existing product line?
- Are we cannibalizing our own sales from an existing product?
- Are we replacing an existing product?

- How will this strategy expand our customer base and increase our sales?
- What will the competitive response be?
- If we are entering a new market, what are the barriers to entry?
- Who are the major players and what are their respective market shares?

Think about customers:

- Who are our customers and what is important to them?
- How are they segmented?
- How can we best reach them?
- How can we ensure that we retain them?

Funding:

- How is this product being funded? Does our company have the cash or are we taking on debt? And can we support the debt under various economic conditions?
- What is the best allocation of funds?

Consumer Adoption Rates:

How many units can we expect to sell? Sometimes you will get a case involving a new product, particularly in the high-tech field. The interviewer may ask you, "What is the market size for this product and how many units can we expect to sell the first year?" There are two things to keep in mind. First, it is very rare for a new product, no matter good it is, to capture more than 10 percent of the market its first year. It is more likely to be between 3 and 5 percent. It depends on the market, the strength of the competition, and how much better this new product is than its competitors. Second, you should take into consideration the Rogers Adoption/Innovation Curve. Draw the curve, then turn your notes toward the interviewer and walk her through your thought process.

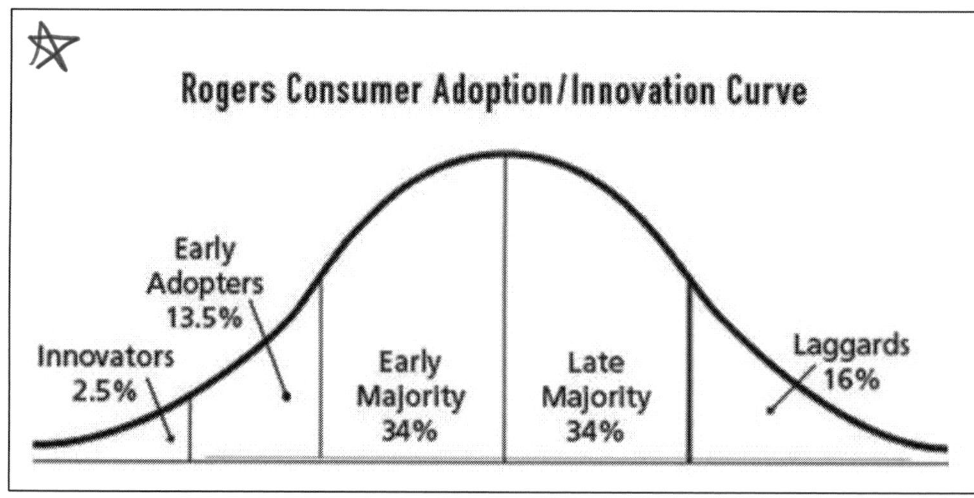

Starting a new business encompasses entering a new market as well – the first step is the same. Investigate the market to determine whether entering it makes good business sense.

- Who is our competition?
- What market share does each competitor have?
- How do competitors' products or services differ from ours?
- Are there any barriers to entry or exit?

Once we determine that there are no significant barriers to entry, we should then look at the company from a venture capitalist point of view. Would you, an outsider, invest in this start-up? Would you risk your own money? Venture capitalists don't simply buy into an idea or product they invest in:

- Management
    - How experienced is the management team?
    - What are its core competencies?
    - Have they worked together before?
    - Is there an advisory board?
- Market and Strategic Plans
    - What are the barriers to entering this market?
    - Who are the major players and what are their respective market shares?
    - What will the competitive response be?
- Distribution Channels
    - Which, and how many, distribution channels can we rely on?
- Products and services
    - What is the product, service, or technology?
    - What is the competitive edge?
    - What are the disadvantages?
    - Is the technology proprietary?
- Customers
    - Who are the customers?
    - How can we best reach them?
    - How can we ensure that we retain them?
- Finance
    - How is the project being funded?
    - What is the best allocation of funds?
    - Can we support the debt under various economic conditions?

Competitive Response

There are two sides to the competitive response coin. What will you do if a competitor comes out with a new product or service and starts to steal your market share? Or what will your competitor do if you come out with a new product aimed at stealing their market share?

- Again, you'll want to understand the situation by asking multiple probing questions, repeat the situation adding in your analysis, devise a plan, and implement it.
- If a competitor introduces a new product or picks up market share, we first want to ask questions such as:
  - What is the competitor's new product and how does it differ from what we offer?
  - What has the competitor done differently? What changed?
  - Have any other competitors picked up market share?
  - Have the consumer's needs changed?
  - Did they increase or expand into new channels?

Responses might include:

- Analyze our current product and redesign, repackage, or move upmarket.
- Introduce a new product.
- Increase our profile with a marketing and public relations campaign.
- Build customer loyalty.
- Cut prices.
- Lock up raw materials and talent.
- Acquire the competitor or another player in the same market.
- Merge with a competitor to create a strategic advantage and become more powerful.
- Copy the competitor.

When planning a product launch, or making a price change, you should take into account competitive response. Too many firms seem to have a wait-and-see attitude, which may erase much of the advantage they had hoped to gain with the new strategy.

Turnarounds

If you get a case in which the company is in trouble and you've been brought in to save it and turn it around, you might want to consider:

Gather information:

- Analyze the company and industry.
  - Why is it failing? Bad products or services? Bad management? Bad economy?
  - Are our competitors facing the same problem?
  - Do we have access to capital?
  - Is the company publicly traded or privately held?
- Possible actions:
  - Learn as much as possible about the company and its operations.
  - Analyze services, products, and finances.
  - Secure sufficient financing so your plan has a chance.
  - Review the talent and temperament of all employees, and get rid of the "deadwood."
  - Determine short-term and long-term goals.
  - Devise a business plan.
  - Visit clients, suppliers, and distributors – and reassure them.
  - Prioritize goals and get some small successes under your belt ASAP to build confidence.

Market Entry Factors to Consider → 4 main factors

i) Profitability – will it be profitable to enter this market?
└ Most important question to analyze

ii) Market growth – growing market is more attractive

iii) Competition in market already – more difficult to generate profit

iv) Barriers to entry – prevent us from getting into market or barriers, once we're in market, helps make our position defensible

└ "Are there any others you think I should be considering?"

+ 21 Ways to Cut Costs

Many case questions will ask you to come up with ways to cut costs, and it has been my experience that students tend to struggle with this request. Below are numerous ways to cut costs in the areas of labor, production, and finance. Memorize these and when you're asked, just rattle off two or three in each area.

Before you answer, the *McKinsey Quarterly* reminds us to consider the company's strategic needs and to think about the long-term consequences under a range of various economic scenarios. Do these areas "drive value" and do they help make the company "competitively distinctive"? Don't just cut equally across the board.

(Labor)

1. Cross-train workers.
2. Cut overtime.
3. Reduce employer 401(k) or 403(b) match.
4. Raise employee contribution to healthcare premiums.
5. Institute four 10-hour days instead of five 8-hour days.
6. Convert workers into owners (if they have a stake in the company they will work longer and harder and constantly think of ways to cut costs in ways they may not have done before).
7. Contemplate layoffs.
8. Institute across-the-board pay decreases.

(Production)

1. Invest in technology.
2. Consolidate production space to gain scale and create accountability.
3. Create flexible production lines.
4. Reduce inventories (JIT).
5. Outsource.
6. Renegotiate with suppliers.
7. Consolidate suppliers.
8. Import parts.

(Finance)

1. Have customers pay sooner.
2. Refinance your debt.
3. Sell nonessential assets. → divestitures
4. Hedge currency rates.
5. Redesign health insurance.

+ "If" Scenarios to Remember

(Sales Scenarios)

- If sales are flat and profits are taking a header, you need to examine both revenues and costs. Always start with the revenue side first. Until you identify and understand the revenue streams, you can't make educated decisions on the cost side.
- If sales are flat but market share remains relatively constant, that could indicate industry sales are flat – and that your competitors are experiencing similar problems.
- If your case includes a decline-in-sales problem, analyze these three things:
    - overall declining market demand (e.g., soda sales have dropped as bottled water becomes the beverage of choice)
    - the possibility that the current marketplace is mature or your product obsolete (e.g., vinyl records give way to CDs, which give way to digital)
    - loss of market share because of substitutions (e.g., video rentals have declined because there are numerous substitutions vying for the leisure dollar, such as dining out, movie attendance, pay-per-view, Direct TV, and the internet)
- If sales and market share are increasing but profits are declining, then you should investigate whether prices are dropping and/or costs are climbing. However, if costs aren't the issue, then you should investigate product mix and check to see whether the margins have changed.

(Profit Scenarios)

- If profits are declining because of a drop in revenues, concentrate on marketing and distribution issues.
- If profits are declining because of rising expenses, though, then concentrate on operational and financial issues – e.g., COGS (cost of goods sold), labor, rent, and marketing costs.
- If profits are declining, yet revenues have gone up, then review:
    - changes in costs
    - any additional expenses
    - changes in prices
    - the product mix
    - changes in customers' needs

(Product Scenarios)

- If a product is in its emerging growth stage, concentrate on R&D, competition, and pricing.
- If a product is in its growth stage, then emphasize marketing and competition.
- If a product is in its mature stage, focus on manufacturing, costs, and competition.
- If a product is in its declining stage, define niche market, analyze the competition's play, or think exit strategy.

(Pricing Scenarios)

If you lower prices and volume then rises, and you are then pushed beyond full capacity, your costs will shoot up as your employees work overtime; your profits will consequently suffer.

Prices are stable only when three conditions are met:[1]

- The growth rate for all competitors is approximately the same.
- The prices are paralleling costs.
- The prices of all competitors are roughly of equal value.

The volume (the amount you produce) and the costs are easier to change than the industry price levels, unless all parties change their prices together (e.g., airline tickets or gas prices).

The perfect strategy for the high-cost producer is one that convinces competitors that market shares cannot be shifted, except over long periods of time. Therefore, according to Henderson, the highest practical industry prices are to everyone's advantage[2] – i.e., price wars are detrimental and everyone will profit more by keeping prices high.

+ Business Case Tips

- If you ever get a case that you have already heard, as tempting as it might be to just answer it, your best strategy is to let the interviewer know. Interviewers usually can tell when someone has heard a case. You tend to do things too quickly, and your thought process is obviously different. It is hard to genuinely re-enact discovery.
- Take graph paper with you in to the interview. It helps you organize your thoughts, keeps the numbers lined up when you multiply and add, and reminds you to graph part of your answer.
- Ask for numbers. If the numbers aren't an important part of the case, the interviewer will more than likely tell you to not focus on them.
- Practice your math, particularly multiplication and percentages. Almost all recruiters will not allow you a calculator during the interview. Most students make math mistakes, and they are often off by a zero or two (see earlier discussion on this).
- Interact with the interviewer as much as possible. Remember, it should be a conversation.

A final word before you tackle the cases...

---

[1] Henderson, Bruce D. "The Product Portfolio," *Perspectives on Strategy from the Boston Consulting Group*, eds. Carl W. Stern and George Stalk, Jr. (New York: John Wiley & Sons, Inc., 19980, 21.

[2] Ibid., p.27.

Peer Advice: Here's advice from students who recently went through the process. They all received offers from BCG, McKinsey, or both.

> *"As you go through the math portion of the case, think out loud. Let the interviewer know what is going through your mind. If you are unsure of what to say, pretend the interviewer is on the telephone and you are explaining it over the phone."*

> *"For me, one of the unexpected challenges of final-round interviews was their sheer length. After five hours of intense interviews, I felt like a slouching, mumbling mess with any spark of creativity long since extinguished, and I was far more likely to make simple mistakes. Before the last couple of interviews on any given day, take a few minutes, and pause to re-energize. Splash water on your face, grab another cup of coffee, take a brisk walk up and down the hallway. Do anything that keeps your brain awake and your personality alive during that final stretch."*

> *"Motivation. Students in non-business disciplines who are looking to land a job in consulting must be able to justify their motivation for the transition. The interview process is expensive and time-consuming for firms, and interviewers are looking for clear, logical answers that will convince them of a candidate's seriousness. Additionally, candidates must be prepared to discuss how consulting fits into their long-term professional goals. Because firms recruiting outside business schools could easily fill their incoming classes entirely with business school students, the burden is greater for non-MBAs."*

> *"Preparation. Preparing for interviews in consulting should not be limited to just practicing cases. Interviews also include discussions of experiences in various environments, such as ambiguity and rancor, as well as questions related to leadership and teamwork. The candidate must be prepared not only to discuss these subjects, but also to answer subsequent questions that interviewers will ask to uncover various layers of the topic in addition to the candidate's personality. For preparation, one should practice with a group of friends. This setting, along with the resulting constructive feedback, will help one anticipate the string of questions that will inevitably be asked and improve one's communication skills. Sound preparation will give one the confidence needed during the actual interview – confidence that will create a positive impression with the interviewer. After all, while the interviewer is there to assess whether the candidate is able to structure a problem well, he or she is also judging whether or not the candidate can be put before a client."*

> *"In preparing stories for various settings, candidates must identify and select the most appropriate anecdotes. It is unnecessary for every story to portray the candidate as a hero. A failure through which one learned about one's weaknesses can be just as effective, if not more. Conversely, an experience through which one strengthened a skill or developed a new skill through perseverance will score well. Fabricating an event, however, will result in certain doom, as interviewers are adept at digging deeper into an issue and determining gaps or untruths. Therefore, a successful candidate must select and prepare honest stories that provide insight into one's personality."*

"The Ivy Case System was like a roadmap. As soon as I got a question, I was immediately able to identify what type of question it was and what types of questions to ask to tease further information out of the interviewer. This is the advantage the Ivy Case System gives you."

"Make sure you know what types of projects the country office is involved in. For example, offices in China are doing many 'market entry' projects. So it is important to understand the varieties and complexities surrounding 'entering a new market' and to practice those types of cases."

"Go through the interview process without second-guessing how you're doing. It only handicaps your performance. Prepare and then let the cards fall. Be confident. It's impossible to know what the interviewer is thinking. They may do things intentionally to throw you off. Don't let the little things, like screwing up a math problem, upset you."

Practice, practice, practice!

You can practice online interactive cases at:
www.apd.mckinsey.com Interview Prep
bcg.com Interview Prep
bain.com Interview Preparation

5 : Practice Cases

This part of the book is divided into four sections. The first is the "Anatomy" section, including a breakdown of the two most popular types of cases, profit and loss (Harley-Davidson), and entering a new market (Coors Brewing Company). Motorcycles and beer: Some might say this is a recipe for disaster, but we won't. As you go through these two cases, not only will you read the dialogue between the interviewer and the student, but you'll also read my analysis of how the interviewee is doing.

The second section is made up of five "case starts." Read the problem statement, and then take a minute to lay out your structure and make a list of questions and concerns that you would want to ask the interviewer in a real interview. Then compare your structure with mine. Remember, there are no right answers, so it's okay if our structures don't match up. Do one or two at first, then save the rest for when you feel more confident.

In the third section, you'll find seventeen dialogue cases, similar to those in the first section, but without my analysis. Read the problem statement and then jot down your structure and key issues. Study the comments or the "takeaways" at the end of each case.

Finally, you'll find the "Partner Cases." These are ten cases you and a partner can give each other. They are written so that anyone, business-savvy or not, can ask you these questions and give you solid feedback. They are arranged by difficulty.

As with all case questions, we assume facts not in evidence, as well as generous assumptions. Familiar companies are used for examples because of the power of their brand and their familiarity to the general public. The information concerning these companies may not be accurate and should not be used as reliable up-to-date data.

+ HARLEY-DAVIDSON

Interviewer: Our client is Harley-Davidson Motor Company. Its stock fell from \$54 a share to \$49 a share on news of declining profits. What's going on and how can we turn this around?

Student: Our client is Harley-Davidson. Its stock fell from \$54 to \$49 a share on news of declining profits. We need to figure out what's going on and how to fix it. Are there any other objectives I should be aware of?

Interviewer: Yes, maintaining market share.

Analysis: The student was right to summarize the case; however, she would have made a better impression if she had tried to quantify the case. Instead of saying the stock price dropped from \$54 to \$49 a share, she should have said that the stock dropped about 10 percent. Remember, so much of this is how you think – what goes through your mind when you hear some numbers.

She was also right to verify the objective and to ask whether there were any other objectives she should be concerned with. Without asking, she never would have known that maintaining market share was an issue.

Student: I have a clarifying question. What were Harley's profits over the last three years?

Interviewer: Three years ago profits were up 8 percent, two years ago they were flat, and this year they will be down 5 percent.

Student: What constitutes success to the client?

Interviewer: An 8 percent increase every year for the next five years.

Student: I just want to take a moment to jot down some notes.

Interviewer: That's fine.

The student writes on her paper E(P=R–C)M.

Analysis: This is the framework you want to use for a P&L case. Inside the parentheses is the classic "profits equals revenues minus costs." That tells us what's going on inside the company. But you want to look at external factors first. Is this a Harley problem or an industry-wide problem? She starts with the E.

Student: I'd like to start with external factors first. Can you tell me what's going on with the economy?

Analysis: The student would have made a much greater impression if she had told the interviewer about the economy, rather than asking. If you are applying for a job in business, you should know what's going on outside the classroom, particularly with the economy. The other reason to tell the interviewer what's happening with the economy is that it gives you more control over the interview. It allows you to frame the economic environment in which this case takes place. So many of these cases occur in a vacuum and you don't know what the economy is like. When you frame it yourself, there are fewer surprises. When you talk about the economy, pick out the main factors that will affect Harley's business. Let's try it again ...

Student: I'd like to start with some external factors first. I'd like to begin with the economy. I know that the U.S. is at the tail end of a recession; it is in the middle of a mortgage crisis and unemployment remains high, so people have less disposable income. Gas prices have topped $4 a gallon. I know that the U.S. dollar has been gaining strength against the euro and pound, but is still fairly weak against Asian currencies, particularly the yen. And I know that interest rates have fallen dramatically and are now close to a 30-year low. (Note: U.S. economy in 2013.)

Analysis: Much better. Do you need to go into this much detail? Yes. You'll see how everything she brought up will tie into her answer later on. Make sure that you write everything down; it will give you some place to go if you get stuck.

Interviewer: Good. What's next?

Student: I'd like to know about the motorcycle industry. Can you tell me what's been going on?

Analysis: No one expects you to know what is going on in the motorcycle industry. The interviewer has a lot of information that he wants to give the student. Sometimes it takes a series of questions from the student to extract the information. Sometimes it takes only one question, and the interviewer does a data dump. It is then up to the student to sort through what's relevant now, what's just smoke, and what might become relevant later. In this case the interviewer is going to provide a data dump.

Interviewer: I have some industry information. Last year the industry grew by 5 percent; Harley grew by 2 percent; the small, less expensive motorcycles and scooters grew by 8 percent. Female riders were up 12 percent and now make up 10 percent of all motorcycle riders, but they constitute only 2 percent of Harley riders.

I have some market share for you, but I want you to assume that each of these companies makes only one model. For Harley it is the big Harley Hog.

Student: Okay.

Interviewer: The market leader is Honda, with 27 percent; Harley, with 24 percent; Yamaha, 17 percent; Suzuki, 10 percent; Kawasaki, 8 percent; BMW, 6 percent. The remaining 9 percent is made up of two scooter companies, Vespa and Suzuki. What else do you want to know about the industry?

Student: It looks as though Harley is not growing as fast as the industry overall. That might be because it has few female riders. The trend seems to be headed toward smaller, lighter, more gas-efficient bikes. If Harley ...

Interviewer: I know where you are headed. We'll talk about strategies in a minute. Do you have any industry questions?

Student: No.

Interviewer: Do think that this is a Harley problem or an industry problem?

Student: At this point I think it is a Harley problem.

Analysis: Whenever they give you a number, like the fact that the industry grew by 5 percent, don't be happy with it. It doesn't tell you nearly enough. You always want to ask for trends. If the industry grew by 10 percent the year before, and by 5 percent this year, then the 5 percent looks very different to me than if the industry had gone from 2 percent to 5 percent. Very few students ever ask for trends. Ask for them, and you'll stand out from your peers. Again, they are trying to learn how you think, and if you don't ask for trends, you're not thinking like a consultant.

Interviewer: What's next?

Student: I'd like to look inside the parentheses to see what's going on inside the company. I'd like to start with the revenues first. What are the major revenue streams and how have they changed over time?

Interviewer: Okay. I'm going to give the four major revenue streams for Y1 and Y2. The four major revenue streams are domestic motorcycle sales, international motorcycle sales, replacement parts, and garb.

Student: "Garb" being merchandise?

Analysis: If you ever get a phrase, industry jargon, or a string of initials that you don't understand, ask for clarification. You don't lose any points for clarification questions up front.

Interviewer: Yes, garb is merchandise. For Year 1, domestic motorcycles made up 45 percent, international 40 percent, replacement parts 10 percent and garb, 5 percent. For Year 2, domestic motorcycles made up 35 percent, international 40 percent, replacement parts 15 percent, and garb 10 percent. I'd like you to look at those numbers and how they changed over the last year, and in four or fewer sentences tell me what's going on with Harley customers.

While the interviewer was providing those numbers, the student was making a chart, including the following:

Revenue Streams	Y1	Y2
Domestic	45%	35%
International	40%	40%
Replacement Parts	10%	15%
Garb	5%	10%

Student: It looks as if Harley customers are buying fewer new bikes, fixing up their old bikes, and buying some garb to make themselves feel good and look bad.

Interviewer: (smiles)

Analysis: She did a great job. She kept it to one sentence and added a little humor to the interview as well.

Interviewer: Okay, good. Let's talk about costs.

Student: Before we do, can I ask about volume? Do we have any numbers on volume of bikes sold?

Interviewer: We do. In Year 1 Harley sold 350,000 bikes and in Year 2 it sold 330,000 bikes.

Student: Thanks.

Analysis: Good move on the student's part. Volume is part of revenue, so asking for that number was appropriate and she scored some points.

Student: What are the major costs, both fixed and variable, and how have they changed over time?

Interviewer: The only cost you need to worry about is the cost of steel. We are in the middle of a steel contract that expires in 24 months. We currently have a good deal, but we are concerned about getting slammed with high steel costs in 24 months as the economy improves. I just want you to keep that in the back of your mind.

What I'd like you to do now is to come up with some short-term strategies that will help turn Harley around. By short-term, I mean 18 months or less.

Student: Okay. The first thing they should do is market to women.

Interviewer: What would they market?

Student: They could design a new bike ...

Interviewer: It is going to take more than 18 months to design, manufacture, and distribute a new bike. Let's leave that for the long-term.

Student: They could market the Hog to women.

Interviewer: They'd have to be pretty big women. The Hog is a hard bike to handle. That's one reason only 2 percent of Harley owners are women.

Student: Then they could market the garb. Women like to look ...

Interviewer: What else?

Student: They could raise the price of garb and the price of replacement parts. We know that people are going to continue to buy those items.

Interviewer: What else?

Student: I'm not sure. They could lay people off?

Interviewer: Are you asking me or telling me?

Analysis: Whenever you are answering a P&L case and they ask you for strategies, you want to do two things: (1) write revenue-based strategies and cost-based strategies on your paper, and (2) ask for a moment to jot down some ideas.

By writing revenue-based strategies on your paper, you are showing the interviewer that you are well organized and thinking two steps ahead. It is easier to think of some ideas if you are looking at a heading on a piece of paper rather than at a blank page. It also keeps you from ping-ponging back and forth between revenue-based and cost-based ideas. You want to present all the revenue-based ideas first, and then the cost-based ideas.

The reason to ask for a moment to note down a few ideas is that it allows you to think of ideas in any order, but present them in the right order. It also gives you some place to go. Keep in mind that the interviewer has probably given this case ten times. He knows every answer that you can think of, and he's heard them all before. There is a good chance he will cut you off as soon as he knows where your answer is headed. It is very difficult for people to drop a thought and then come up with a new thought right away. When cut off in mid-thought, people tend to panic, scramble, and then shut down. They can't think of another idea to save their lives.

If you take the time to jot down some ideas and you are cut off, then you can just look at your notes and offer another idea. It takes a lot of stress out of the process and makes you look more professional.

Also, if you hit a wall and can't think of anything, go back and look at your first page of notes. Remember, the student told us a couple of great things about the economy: Interest rates are way down and the dollar is still down against the yen.

Let's take it from the top.

Interviewer: Come up with some short-term strategies.

Student: Can I take a moment to jot down some ideas?

Interviewer: Absolutely.

The student notes revenue-based and cost-based strategies on her paper, then writes out a few ideas.

Student: Okay. I'd like to break these down by revenue-based and cost-based. I'll start with revenue-based. Harley can raise the prices of its garb and replacement parts because we know people will buy them anyway. We can also increase international distribution channels.

Interviewer: Where?

Student: In Asia, where the dollar is still weak.

Interviewer: Okay, what else?

Student: Because interest rates are so low, we can offer financing packages and give high trade-in values to encourage customers to buy new bikes.

Interviewer: What else?

Student: On the cost side, because interest rates are so low, we can refinance our corporate debt.

Interviewer: Okay, good.

Student: And we can consider laying people off. You said the volume dropped from 350,000 bikes to 330,000. That's about a 5 percent drop.

Interviewer: We are considering changing prices. I have some data. I want you to run the numbers and then tell me what you want to do, and more important, why you want to do it. If we leave the price the same, Harley will sell 330,000 motorcycles and make a net profit of $10,000 each. If we discount the price, Harley will sell 440,000 motorcycles and net $7,000 each. And if they raise the price, they will sell only 275,000 motorcycles but net $12,000 each.

Analysis: The student should take some time here to run the numbers. You are better off taking a little extra time and getting the right answer, rather than rushing through and getting the wrong answer. Before you give your answer, ask yourself if the number makes sense. If it doesn't, go back and figure it out. You can't un-ring the bell. I'd hate to see you lose a great opportunity over a silly math mistake.

Remember, silence is okay as long as you are doing calculations, writing notes, or drawing a chart.

Student: If we keep the price the same, then our net profit will be $3.3 billion. If we lower the price, our net profit will be $3.08 billion, and if we raise the price, our net profit will also be $3.3 billion.

Interviewer: So if we raise the price or leave it alone, we'll make the same net profit. What do you want to do, and why?

Student: I'd like to keep the price the same. You said market share was a key objective, and if we raise the price, we are going to sell 55,000 fewer bikes. That's about a 5 percent drop, which will probably lower our market share. If we sell more bikes, we'll sell more garb, and eventually more replacement parts. And even if we cut production, we will still probably have a lot of Year 2 inventory left over. What do we do with it when the Year 3 models come out? If we sell it at a discount, we'll probably cannibalize our Year 3 sales.

Interviewer: That's all very interesting, but let me tell you why you're wrong. If we raise the price, we'll have lower labor costs because we'll be able to lay people off. In addition, the higher price will enhance the brand. As far as your other concerns go, you told me that you plan to increase international distribution channels where the dollar is still weak. If we do that, any extra inventory can be shipped overseas and sold at the new higher price. Garb sales tend to be higher when you enter a new territory. So market share shouldn't be an issue. Besides, how do you measure market share? Is it number of units sold or total revenues?

Analysis: Ouch. The interviewer got right in her face even though she'd given a well-thought-out answer. *Luckily she knows that this "let me tell you why you're wrong" business is just a test.* She keeps her emotions in check and does what the interviewer wants her to do: stick with and defend her answer.

Student: You make an interesting argument; however, I don't find it compelling enough. I can't believe that you can do all that within an 18-month period. Therefore, I think the best option in these economic conditions would be to keep the price the same.

Interviewer: Okay, good. Give me two long-term, revenue-based ideas and two long-term, cost-based ideas.

Student: Can I take a moment to make a couple of notes?

Interviewer: Certainly.

Student: [30 seconds later] ... Okay. On the revenue-based side, the first thing I'd do is come up with a new bike that is geared not only toward women but also to younger men. This will give us something besides garb to market to women. I'd also look to see if we can acquire a scooter company. We couldn't put the Harley name on it, but we could take advantage of the fastest-growing segments of the market, women and scooters. Besides, there will be a number of synergies we would be able to take advantage of. On the cost side, we're concerned about the price of steel. We can buy some steel futures to hedge against a steel increase. We could stockpile some steel at the current price, and because we are developing a new bike, we can make more parts from composites instead of steel. We could modernize the plant with new technologies and maybe have some parts made overseas.

Interviewer: Good. Why don't you take a moment and summarize the case for me.

Student: Our client is Harley-Davidson. Its stock dropped around 10 percent on news of declining profits. We looked at external factors first and determined that it was more of a Harley problem rather than an industry problem. Harley is out of step with the two fast-growing segments of the industry, women and scooters. So we came up with some short-term and long-term strategies on both the revenue and cost sides. An example of a short-term, revenue-based strategy is offering low financing to customers. On the cost side, we could refinance our debt. In the long term we could produce a new bike geared toward women and younger men, and acquire a scooter maker. Also on the cost side, we could hedge steel prices and have certain new parts made out of composite instead of steel. If Harley follows these strategies as well as some of the others we talked about, it should be on its way to higher profits in 24 to 36 months.

Analysis: She came on very strong at the end. The turning point was when she defended her decision to keep the price the same. That gave her additional confidence, and it showed through the rest of the interview.

+ COORS BREWING COMPANY

Interviewer: Our client is Coors Brewing Company and for the last 50 years it's been advertising the fact that a key ingredient in Coors beer is Rocky Mountain spring water. The CEO calls you in to his office and says that Coors is considering entering the bottled water market. I want you to analyze the market, identify any key issues, and make a recommendation.

Student: So our client is Coors and it's thinking of entering the bottled water industry. Besides conducting an industry analysis and identifying major issues, are there any other objectives I should be concerned with?

Interviewer: Yes. The CEO told the board of directors that he would increase revenues by 50 percent in five years or he would resign.

Analysis: It was important that the student asked about other objective, or he would never have learned about the needed 50 percent increase in revenues. If he hadn't asked about this, the interviewer would have had to feed him the information during the case, and he would have lost points.

Student: I'm assuming that's overall company revenues. So my initial hypothesis is that by entering the bottled water industry, Coors will increase overall company revenues by 50 percent. I just want to take a moment to draw out my notes.

Analysis: Because this is an interviewee-driven case, he put forth a hypothesis within the first five minutes of the case. He also took time to lay out his structure. Once he's done, he turns his notes toward the interviewer and walks her through them.

COORS BREWING
ENTER BOTTLED WATER MKT

MKT ENTRY Y OR N?

MKT ENTRY Y OR N
INCREASE REVENUES BY 50% IN 5 YRS.

HYPOTHESIS: ENTERING THE H2O MKT ↑ SALES & PROFITS BY 50% IN 5 YRS.

COORS
WHY ENTER?
SIZE IN REVENUES & TRENDS
PRODUCTS
PRODUCTION
BRAND
DISTRIBUTION
CUSTOMERS
WCS

CURRENT MKT
SIZE
GROWTH RATE
CUSTOMER

MAJOR PLAYERS / MKT SHARE
PRODUCT DIFFERENTIATION
BARRIERS

ENTERING
YES
START FROM SCRATCH
ACQUISITION
JT VENTURE
NO, ALTERNATIVE PLAN

Student: First I'd like to look at Coors, then the water market and finally the best ways for Coors to enter the market. And if we decide that Coors shouldn't enter the market, I'd like to come up with an alternative plan, which will help the company reach its goal of increasing revenues by 50 percent.

I'd like to start by looking at the company. Why does it want to enter this market? If it needs to increase revenues by 50 percent, I need to know what its revenues are today. I'd like to know what its product line looks like and get an understanding of its production process. Is bottling beer similar to bottling water? Branding is also important. Will it call this Coors water or will they use another name? Next is distribution. I'll assume that it currently has beer distributors all around the United States; will it use those same distributors to distribute their water? Will the customer segmentation be similar? I'm betting a lot more people drink water than beer. And finally what constitutes success in the mind of the client? What percentage of the bottled water market does Coors expect to capture in five years?

Next, I'd like to look at the bottled water industry. What were its revenues last year and how has it been trending over the last three years? Do we have any forecasts? I'd like to know who the major players are and what market share they have? How do their products differ from Coors'? Are there any other companies that sell Rocky Mountain spring water? Then the last thing I'd like to know about the industry is whether there are any barriers to entry or barriers to exit.

Finally, I'd like to think about how best to enter the market. Coors can start from scratch and grow organically; it can buy its way in or it can do a joint venture. I'd like to look at the advantages and disadvantages of each.

Analysis: He did a great job. By turning his notes toward the interviewer he brought her into the case and made her feel more like a client and less like an interviewer.

The student started off analyzing the client company. Many students make the mistake of starting off with the water industry. It's important to understand why Coors wants to enter. He also made a pretty exhaustive list of company issues that he wanted to investigate, particularly what constitutes success in the eyes of the client. It's critical to know this, so you have a goal and can reality-test the client's response.

Next he asked for all the important industry information. And finally he laid out options on how to best enter the market.

Interviewer: Sounds good. Where do you want to start?

Student: Why enter the water market?

Interviewer: The CEO has a goal of increasing company sales by 50 percent in five years. He will never make it with beer alone. Assuming the beer market to be a zero-sum market, beer sales have been flat and are forecasted to remain that way for the next five years. Any new product would only cannibalize sales from an existing product.

Student: What were its revenues last year?

Interviewer: $5.2 billion.

Student: So it would have to increase its revenues by [quick calculation] $2.6 billion for a total of $7.8 billion.

Interviewer: That's right.

Student: I know it produces Coors and Coors Light; what other products does it have?

Interviewer: Besides those two, it has Keystone and Keystone Light. That's the beer you buy when you have only $1.50 left to your name. It also produces Killian's Irish Red and Blue Moon.

Student: No non-beer products?

Interviewer: Assume no. You asked about brand and distribution channels and we'll talk about them in a little bit. Who do you think drinks Coors?

Student: Blue-collar beer drinkers, construction workers, college students, and sports fans, mostly male.

Interviewer: Okay. In your notes you also asked what percentage of the water market did Coors expect to get in five years. It expects 10 percent. What else do you want to know?

Student: I want to know about the bottled water industry, growth trends, major players, market share, product differentiation, and barriers.

Interviewer: Last year, the bottled water industry did $11 billion in revenues. It's forecasted to grow 5 percent a year, every year for the next five years. Flat water makes up 96 percent of the market compared with sparkling water's 4 percent. The three major players are Coke, Pepsi, and Nestlé. Assume that together they share 60 percent of the overall water market. There are about a dozen other players, some international and some regional. Some of the regional players produce private-label water as well as producing under their own names. They make up 36 percent of the market. The final 4 percent is the sparkling water. The major players there are San Pellegrino, Perrier, Voss and Poland Spring Sparkling.

Also, assume that there are three levels of water. The premium level consists of brands like Fiji, Evian, and San Pellegrino, to name a few. The big three, Coke, Pepsi, and Nestlé, dominate the national mid-level water market. This is where Coors wants to enter, at mid-level. The lower tier is made up of regional waters, which are usually priced lower. What's next?

Student: I just want to take a minute and figure something out. Coors needs $2.6 billion in five years. It thinks it can take 10 percent of the market in five years. Is 10 percent of the bottled water market greater than or equal to $2.6 billion? If the market was $11 billion last year and it is growing 5 percent a year for the next five years, we need to figure out what the water revenues are five years from now.

[The student writes down A = 11b (1+.05)5, but then thinks better of it.]

Student: If the industry is growing at a rate of 5 percent a year for the next five years, that's 25 percent. However, we need to take compounding into consideration. So I know that it's going to be more than 25 percent but less than 30 percent. So my best guess is around 28 percent. So $11 billion times 1.28 equals ... [writes out the calculation] around $14 billion. Ten percent of that is $1.4 billion, so that's going to be short by $1.2 billion.

Analysis: He almost made the math more complicated than it needed to be. Interviewers make you do math without a calculator for two main reasons: to see how you think, and to see if you think before you speak. No interviewer would want to sit there and watch that student struggle with the exponents or do the same calculation over and over again if he had decided to take 5 percent of 11 billion, then 5 percent of that number, and so on.

The other concern would be if he had trouble with the zeros and came up with $140 billion instead of $14 billion; $140 billion doesn't make any sense, and even if he caught his mistake right after he had said it, you can't un-ring a bell like that. You're not thinking before you speak and if you do that in an interview, what are you going to do in front of a client? I can't trust you. And if I can't trust you, I'm not going to hire you.

Interviewer: What percentage of the bottled water market would we need to get in order to reach the goal of $2.6 billion?

Student: Well, 10 percent is 1.4, and 20 percent is 2.8, so a little less than 20 percent. Around 18 percent.

Interviewer: Good. There is no way we're getting 18 percent of the bottled water market in five years. We'll be lucky to get 10 percent. What's the quickest way to increase market share?

Student: Lower prices.

Interviewer: What's the quickest way to increase market share?

Student: A marketing campaign?

Interviewer: What's the quickest way to increase market share?

Student: An acquisition?

Analysis: He lost his confidence. The interviewer asked him a question, didn't like the answer, and asked him the same question two more times. While the student was confident about his first answer, he stumbled when he was asked again and again. If you take this whole case interviewing process and boil it down, the two most important things are structure and confidence. Usually one follows the other.

Interviewer: Good. Say that Coors is going to buy a regional player called Bulldog Water, out of Athens, Georgia, with 4 percent national market share. Now, Bulldog's water source is Athens tap water, and Coors' water is Rocky Mountain spring water. Two very different water sources about 2,000 miles apart. So Coors will run two separate companies, which is fine. Coors will be in the middle tier and Bulldog in the lower tier. Besides the increase in market share, what are two other advantages to buying Bulldog?

Student: Expertise. Coors is new to the water ...

Interviewer: Good. What else?

Student: Production facilities ...

Interviewer: Coors isn't going to ship water by tanker 2,000 miles to save on production costs. What else?

Student: Distribution channels. They ...

Interviewer: Good. Coors can piggyback on Bulldog's distribution channels.

Analysis: The student handled that well. He was cut off in the middle of answers and was able to come up with additional answers.

Interviewer: Before, you asked me about branding. Should Coors call its water Coors Water or something else?

Student: What will be the market acceptance of a beer company selling water? That's the question. Is the Coors name too closely associated with beer? I'm betting that it is. Water is seen as pure and healthy, beer is not. I don't think mothers would like to see their kids drinking Coors. Besides that, Coke, which is one of the best-known brands in the world, didn't call its product Coke Water; they called it Dasani.

Interviewer: Coors ships beer to independent beer distributors all over the U.S.; should they use their beer distributors to distribute water?

Student: Yes. It will save on shipping and the cost of building a new network.

Interviewer: Let me tell you why you're wrong. Water is sold in three times as many places as beer. You can't buy beer in a vending machine; you can't buy it at McDonald's and you can't buy it at school. If Coors wants 10 percent of the water market, it has to have its product in every possible venue. Besides, I don't want a beer truck pulling up in front of an elementary school and unloading water. It sends a bad message. And my last point is that if Coors is interested in increasing revenues, why are you focusing on costs?

Student: Those are all valid points. I think you're right. They should build a new network of distributors.

Analysis: Interviewers will often take the other side of a question to see whether you can defend your answer without becoming defensive, and then come back with a persuasive argument. In this case the student was wrong and he knew it. There is no shame in admitting you are wrong. It is better to admit it than to come back with a weak case just because you don't want to admit you are wrong.

Interviewer: Okay, so say Coors calls its water Rocky Mountain Spring Water; it builds a new network of distributors, it comes out with a national marketing campaign, maybe even gets a celebrity spokesperson and offers an introductory low price. How will Coke respond, or will it?

Student: To quote Churchill, I think Coke will try to strangle the baby in the cradle. Coors is too much of a ...

Interviewer: Wait a minute. You're comparing Coors to fascism?

Student: The quote was about Bolshevism: Strangle Bolshevism in its cradle.

Interviewer: Are you sure? I was a history major at Williams.

Student: Positive. Coke will respond, and quickly. It won't want Coors to get a foothold in the market and start stealing market share.

Analysis: The case almost went off track there, but the student kept the focus. It would have been easy to go off on a tangent about Churchill or World War II, but he took control and steered it back.

Interviewer: Say Coors does all that. We are still $1.2 billion short. How are we going to close the gap? And keep in mind that we already spent our allowance and can't buy another company, and the margins aren't there for exporting.

Student: [Thinks for a minute.] Coors spent a lot of time, effort, and money building a new brand. They spent a lot of time, effort, and money building new distribution channels. And they did it all for one bottle of water. They've done all the hard part. So now they increase their product mix. They could add flavored waters, but also Rocky Mountain Spring lemonade, iced tea, green tea, and maybe sports drinks. Not only under the Rocky Mountain label, but under the Bulldog label as well.

Interviewer: Excellent. Let's say we did all that and we figure that we will be $50 million short of our goal. You have a meeting with the CEO. What are you going to tell him?

Student: I'd like to take a moment. Because if I go in now, I'm going to have to tell him that we'll be short of his $2.6 billion revenue increase. I'd like to think about how I can go in and tell him yes to everything. First, the economy will be in better shape five years from now. So most of that $50 million will come from increased beer sales. Second, we can look at other alcoholic products, such as vodka, tequila, or alcopops – like Mike's Hard Lemonade. I'd also like to point out that the original assignment was to analyze the bottled water industry and determine whether it was a good idea for Coors to enter. The water takes us 95 percent of the way there. Do we throw the baby out with the bathwater even if we are $50 million short?

Interviewer: So what's your recommendation?

Student: Yes, we enter the water market. We do it under a new brand, Rocky Mountain Spring; we do it by acquiring Bulldog Water for its market share, expertise, and distribution channels. We build a new network of distributors and then introduce additional products to the mix, such as lemonade and iced tea.

Interviewer: Good.

Analysis: He came on strong in the end. The interview was starting to get away from him, and he was just answering questions instead of driving the question. He was creative in coming up with additional products for both of the water companies. But what clinched it was the fact that he was determined to go in to the meeting with a "yes" and a way to get there. Most students would have left it at "It looks promising but we're going to be $50 million short."

In addition, he stated his recommendation first, then backed it up with a plan. He got beat up along the way, but he kept his cool and regained control of the interview. Still, he didn't enumerate the risks associated with his recommendation. It is important to state not only the next steps, but also the associated risks.

+ Case Starts

Many people struggle with getting started: thinking about the key issues, asking the right questions, and crafting their structure. This section was designed to help you with your case starts.

Some cases, referred to as interviewee-driven cases, are very vague and broad. "Here's my problem. What do I do?" With cases like these (more common to BCG and Bain & Company), you need to take great care in drawing your structure. Also, your structure should be "hypothesis-driven." A hypothesis is the assumed answer, and hypothesis-driven means you need to consider the case from the answer.

Other cases are interviewer-driven: "Here's my problem. I want to you to determine market size, price, break-even, and profits." In these cases the interviewer has given you a laundry list of information to determine (more common to McKinsey). **Keep in mind that you don't necessarily have to answer the questions in the order in which they are given. Answer them in the order that makes sense to you.** One mistake candidates often make is to quickly jump into calculating the market size. **Always lay out your structure before you figure out the market size.** When the interviewer gives you a list of issues, you can often take that opportunity to quickly draw up a final slide. It will act as your structure, a scorecard for the interviewer to follow, and your summary.

Keep in mind that some frameworks are as simple as short-term and long-term, and internal and external. Take a step back and look at the big picture. Don't try to force it and don't use the same structure all the time. I've seen many students use P = R – C as their structure for every case. To me that is the same as using one of the cookie-cutter frameworks like the 5Cs or 4Ps. These students have, in fact, turned the profit formula into a checklist. By doing so, they'll lose points for lack of creativity, imagination, and intellectual curiosity.

With all cases, you should summarize the case, verify the objective, ask clarifying questions, and then lay out your structure. (See the "The First Five Steps" section in the Ivy Case System chapter.)

To get the most out of this chapter, read the case out loud, pretending it is a real interview. Make an audio recording of yourself as you work through the first few steps, summarize the case, verify the objectives, **and ask key questions**. Write or draw out your notes as you would in a real interview, and then compare your notes with those found on the following pages. It's okay if they don't match up. Remember, there are no right answers; the interviewer is looking to see how you think, how you structure your thoughts, and how you communicate. Play the case start back, and listen to the speed, tone, and confidence level of your voice. At first you're not going to be happy, probably downright embarrassed, but the more you practice the stronger you become.

+ CASE STARTS – CASES

CS1: Power plants, chemical, paper, and textile factories have polluted about 70 percent of China's lakes and rivers. Water quality is a major concern for Chinese consumers. They are turning toward bottled water as a safer alternative. The cities continue to grow, as does the bottled water market. Nestlé wants to know how best to grow its market share.

CS2: Hacker Guard is the industry leader in the U.S. identity-theft monitoring market. It wants to do an IPO but has seen inconsistent profits and losses six out of the last ten quarters. How can it stabilize the turmoil and increase its profits? (The interviewer hands you a chart.)

CS3: A Hong Kong company is acquiring a U.S. video game maker. What considerations should be made?

CS4: The CEO of a large Italian electronics firm has come out with a new computer tablet, which is much like the iPad. How should it price its product?

CS5: Our client is a global automaker headquartered in Detroit. Its motor parts division, with 20 percent industry market share, carries almost 500,000 parts, options, and accessories for vehicle customization. The client has not been profitable for several years and the CEO suspects that the company's high degree of vertical integration is hurting them. The client makes about 80 percent of its own parts, compared with 40 percent at its primary competitors. The CEO has asked for our help. How would you approach this issue?

CS1: CHINA WATER

Power plants, chemical, paper and textile factories have polluted about 70 percent of China's lakes and rivers. Water quality is a major concern for Chinese consumers. They are turning toward bottled water as a safer alternative. The cities continue to grow, as does the bottled water market. Nestlé wants to know how to grow its market share.

Summarize the case. China's drinking water, particularly in the cities, is horrible. The bottled water market is growing and Nestlé wants to increase its market share. Are there any other objectives I should be concerned with?

Assume no.

Lay out your structure. First, you should ask about Nestlé and its position in the Chinese bottled water market; current market share; growth rate and WCS (what constitutes success in the mind of the client). What percentage of the market is the company hoping to get and is that realistic? How many brands does it sell under? What is its pricing strategy? How is it priced compared with the market leaders?

Second, investigate the Chinese water market: growth rate, major players and their market share, changes in the industry (mergers? new players? new technology?) and barriers to expansion. Are there restrictions on foreign companies holding more than a certain percentage of market share? Are the home delivery and retail markets growing faster than the office delivery market?

Third, I'd like to investigate several key growth strategies that will serve as a foundation; increase distribution channels (other-people stores, Nestlé stores, home delivery, and street carts); increase and diversify product line (more brands, more types of water e.g. vitamin water, flavored water); invest in a major marketing campaign; acquire competitors; and create seasonal balance (e.g. Vitamin C water in winter).

And fourth, I'd like to know about Nestlé's market share in other key water markets, including North America and Europe. How are those markets growing and would it be wiser to allocate more resources there or in China?

Your notes should look something like this:

CHINESE DRINKING WATER
IS POLLUTED

BOTTLED WATER MKT ↑

NESTLE WANTS TO ↑
MKT SHARE

GROW MKT SHARE

NESTLE

CURRENT MKT SHARE
GROWTH RATE
WCS
BRANDS
PRICING STRATEGY

GROWTH STRATEGIES

↑ DISTRIBUTION CHANNELS
- OTHER STORES
- NESTLE STORES
- HOME DELIVERY
- STREET CARTS
- OFFICE DELIVERY

↑ PRODUCT LINE
↑ BRANDS, TYPES OF WATER
↑ MKTG CAMPAIGN
ACQUIRE COMPETITOR
CREATE SEASONAL BALANCE
↑ PRICES?

CHINESE H_2O MKT

SIZE
GROWTH RATE
MAJOR PLAYERS / MKT SHARE
Δ'S IN INDUSTRY
(MERGERS, NEW PLAYERS,
NEW TECH?)
BARRIERS – GOV'T REG
MARKETS
HOME, OFFICE, RETAIL

ALTERNATIVE MKTS:
N AMERICA, S AMERICA,
EUROPE, ASIA

FYI – China's bottled water industry will climb to $25 billion by 2020, up from $16 billion in 2017 and $1 billion in 2000. North America will increase 18 percent by 2020, to $30 billion, and Europe will remain flat. Nestlé's current Chinese market share is 1.7 percent. Its Chinese water revenues climbed 7 percent last year. The market leader is Hangzhou Wahaha Group, with 14 percent market share.

CS2: HACKER GUARD

Hacker Guard is the industry leader in the U.S. identity-theft monitoring market. It wants to do an IPO but has seen inconsistent profits and losses six out of the last ten quarters. How can it stabilize the turmoil and increase its profits? (The interviewer hands you a chart.)

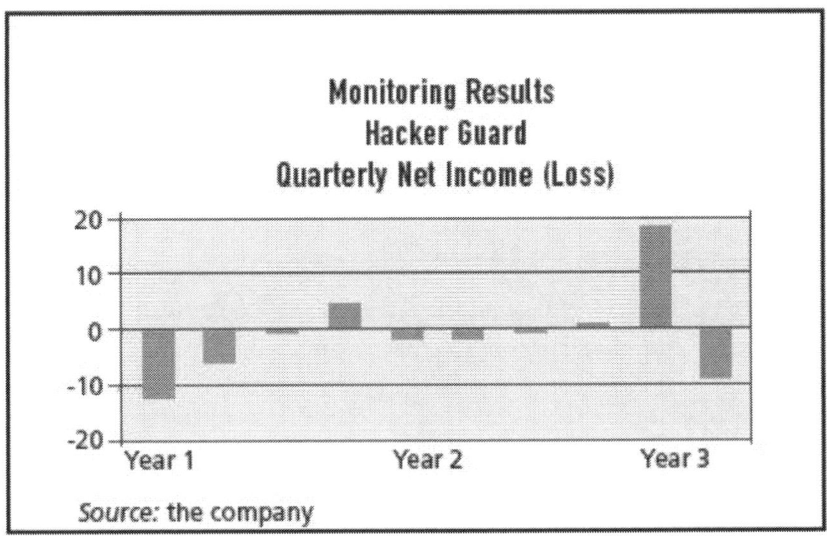

Summarize the case. Hacker Guard wants to do an IPO but needs to stabilize its P&L statement. We need to figure out why this is happening and come up with ways to increase profits. Besides identifying the problems and increasing profits, are there any other issues I should be concerned with?

Assume no.

First, take a minute to study the chart. What does it tell you? There doesn't seem to be any pattern to the swings and some of them are sizeable. What would cause Hacker Guard to lose $12 million one quarter and make $18 million in another quarter?

Lay out your structure. Because this is a P&L problem, immediately lay out the P&L framework and then build on it. E(P=R-C)M is the initial framework. To start, look at external factors. Is this just Hacker Guard's problem or are all companies in this space having a similar problem? Touch on a few things in the domestic economy: the unemployment rate, interest rates, and anything else that might affect the disposable income of a U.S. household.

Next, look at the identity-theft industry. What market share does the company have? What are the industry revenues and what have the trends been in the last three to five years? Are other firms' P&Ls all over the place or is it just Hacker Guard's? Were there profit spikes at the same time with all firms, meaning something happened in the market, such as a large corporate breach like those at Sony, T.J.Maxx or Equifax?

Once you have an understanding of the industry, look inside the company. Start with the revenue streams. What are the major revenue streams and how have they changed over time? Customer segmentation: Who are its clients? Middle-class households? How many clients does it have and how much do they pay per month or per year? How long do customers stay? Is there a contract like that for a cellphone? What is its churn rate? How does that compare with churn rates for others in the industry and for other industries such as cellphones?

Next up are its costs. What are its major costs and have they changed over time? Can we benchmark them to the competitors? Were there any large purchases like an acquisition or major upgrades to the company's computer system?

Your notes might look something like this:

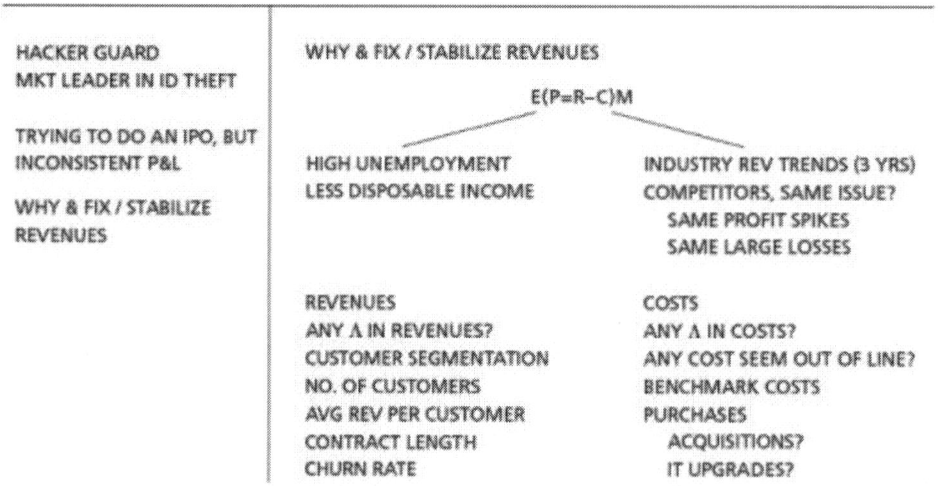

HACKER GUARD
MKT LEADER IN ID THEFT

TRYING TO DO AN IPO, BUT
INCONSISTENT P&L

WHY & FIX / STABILIZE
REVENUES

WHY & FIX / STABILIZE REVENUES

E(P=R–C)M

HIGH UNEMPLOYMENT
LESS DISPOSABLE INCOME

INDUSTRY REV TRENDS (3 YRS)
COMPETITORS, SAME ISSUE?
SAME PROFIT SPIKES
SAME LARGE LOSSES

REVENUES
ANY Δ IN REVENUES?
CUSTOMER SEGMENTATION
NO. OF CUSTOMERS
AVG REV PER CUSTOMER
CONTRACT LENGTH
CHURN RATE

COSTS
ANY Δ IN COSTS?
ANY COST SEEM OUT OF LINE?
BENCHMARK COSTS
PURCHASES
ACQUISITIONS?
IT UPGRADES?

CS3: HONG KONG VIDEO GAMES

A Hong Kong company is acquiring a U.S. video game maker. What considerations should be made?

Summarize the case and verify the objective. This is a pretty short case, so instead of repeating the question, just ask, "Besides determining the key factors to this acquisition, are there any other objectives I should be concerned with?"

Assume no other objectives.

Lay out your structure. This is a merger and acquisition case. Break it into five main buckets: company, current market analysis, due diligence and risks, costs, and exit strategies.

Your notes might look something like this:

HONG KONG COMPANY

IS BUYING US VIDEO GAME MAKER

WHAT ARE THE KEY ISSUES?

KEY ACQUISITION ISSUES

HONG KONG COMPANY
WHO ARE THEY?
PE FIRM?
COMPETITOR?

WHY BUY?
- STRATEGIES
- PATENTED TECH
- ↑ MKT SHARE
- COST SAVINGS SYNERGIES

WHAT ELSE DOES IT OWN?

COSTS
FAIR VALUATION?
CAN THEY AFFORD IT?

CURRENT MKT
SIZE & GROWTH RATE
PLAYERS AND MARKET SHARE
PROD DIFFERENTIATION
CUSTOMER SEGMENTATION
Δ IN INDUSTRY – MERGERS, EXITS, NEW PLAYERS

DUE DILIGENCE & RISKS
- ECONOMY
- MARKET LEADER?
- SECURE
  - CUSTOMERS, SUPPLIERS, DISTRIBUTORS AND TOP MANAGERS
- CULTURAL MIX
- MARGINS
- COMPETITIVE RESPONSE

EXIT STRATEGIES
- SELL
- SPIN OFF AND TAKE PUBLIC
- CLOSE DOWN AND SELL ASSETS

Company. I'd first ask about the Hong Kong Company. Who are they? Is it a private equity firm or a competitor? Why does it want to buy this company? Is it for access to the U.S. market? A special patented technology? To increase its market share? Or to take advantage of cost-saving synergies? What else does it own? Does it own other gaming companies?

Industry. What's the current industry like? Is it growing and what are the trends and forecasts? Who are the major players and what market share do they have? How are their products different from those of the targeted company? What is the industry segmentation and have there been any changes taking place in the industry? Mergers? New players?

Due diligence. I'd want to look at the overall economy. Is the targeted company an industry leader? How secure are its customers, suppliers, distributors, and top management? Will the cultures of the two companies mesh well? Are the margins what we anticipated? What will be the competitive response to our buying this video game maker?

Exit strategies. What's the game plan if this fails? Do we sell, spin off the company and do an IPO, or do we break it up and sell off the pieces?

CS4: ITALIAN COMPUTER TABLET

The CEO of a large Italian electronics firm has come out with a new computer tablet, which is much like the iPad. How should it price its product?

Summarize the case and verify the objective. Ask if there are any other objectives – such as the reason the CEO wants to enter this market.

Lay out your structure. Your notes might look something like this:

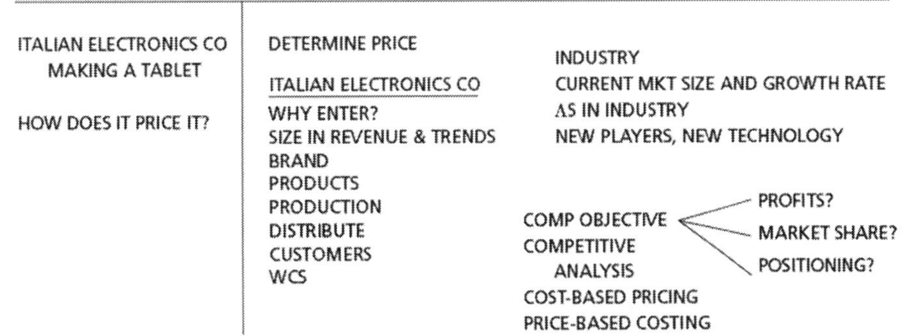

First, I'd like to know about the company. Why does it want to enter this market? How big is the company revenue-wise and what have the trends been? Does it have a well-known brand? What other products does it have? Where is the production of the product taking place? Does it have established distribution channels? Does this fit in with its current customer segment? And what constitutes success in the mind of the client?

Second, I'd look at the industry: current size, trends, and forecasts. Are there any significant changes in the industry, such as new players or new technology? Remember how HP came out with a tablet, pulled it three weeks later, and came out with another one a year later?

Third, I'd look at four pricing strategies. The first one is **company objective**. This ties in with "what constitutes success" in the mind of the client? Is it looking for profits and wanting to price the tablet at a premium (like Apple)? Is it looking for market share (like Samsung) and thus pricing it a little lower? Or is it interested in market positioning (like Amazon), selling at around cost and hoping to make profits on the ancillary products? The second is **competitive analysis**. Who is our competition, how do their tablets differ from ours and how much do they charge? Are there any substitutions? How will the competitors respond to our entering their market? Third is **cost-based pricing**. What does it cost our client to manufacture, distribute, and market? Make sure all those costs are baked into your number. What sort of margin does the company make on its other products? The fourth is price-based costing. What is the market willing to pay? Is it more than our costs?

CS5: GLOBAL MOTOR CARS

Our client is a global automaker headquartered in Detroit. Its motor parts division, with 20 percent industry market share, carries almost 500,000 parts, options, and accessories for vehicle customization. The client has not been profitable for several years and the CEO suspects that the company's high degree of vertical integration is hurting it. The client makes about 80 percent of its own parts, compared with 40 percent at its primary competitors. The CEO has asked for our help. How would you approach this issue?

Summarize the case and verify the objective. Repeat the question to make sure you and the interviewer are on the same page. Then verify the objectives. In this case the objectives are to come up with a strategic plan to make the company profitable. While you might think that this is a P&L case, I'd approach it a little differently.

Lay out your structure. Your notes might look something like this:

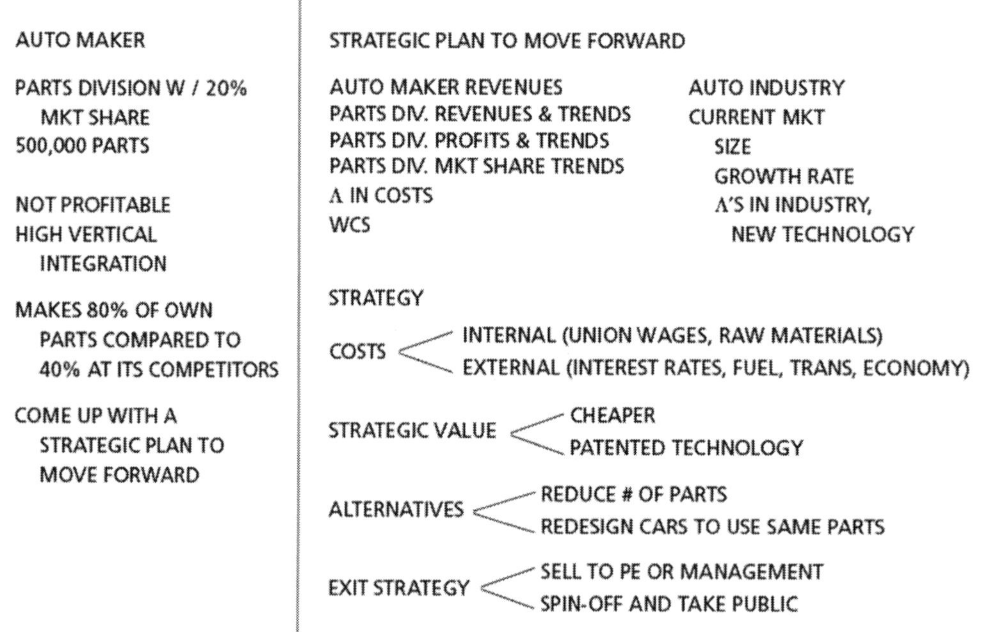

Ask questions about the company and the parts division. What are the overall company revenues and what have the trends been? What are the parts division revenues and their trends, and what percentage of the overall company revenues do they account for? Has the parts division been gaining or losing market share over the last three years? Have there been changes in costs? What constitutes success in the mind of the client?

Ask questions about the industry. What have been the overall trends for the auto industry? Have there been any changes in the parts industry, new players, or new technology? Strategies. I'd break this down into four buckets: costs, strategic value, alternatives, and exit strategy.

Costs. I'd look at both external costs (the overall economy, interest rates, fuel costs, transportations costs, etc.) and internal costs (union wages, raw materials, etc.).

Strategic value. What is the true strategic value of making our own parts? It might have been cost-saving initially, but that may have changed. Is there a patented technology that only our cars have?

Alternatives: This could mean reducing the number of individual parts per car, or having new models using as many common parts as possible. This is tricky; some believe this is what got GM in trouble because all its cars seemed the same. Would it be cheaper to buy our parts from another vendor?

Exit strategy. Does the company sell its parts division to a private equity firm, to management? Does it spin the parts division off from the automaker and make it its own company? What would the company get for it and what would it do with the money?

+ Case Practice

While nothing beats live practice, the next best thing is reading as many cases as possible. This builds up an archive in the back of your mind and allows you to draw from one case to help you answer another. The best way to use this section is to read the case, then write out your structure. Your answer and my answer will probably not match up. There is no way for you to predict the added variables and twists and turns in the case. Once you draw your structure, sit back and read the case, making notes in your journal of anything you may not have thought about. Then reread it. You'll pick up more the second time through.

+ Case List

+ THE SHOW'S OVER – NETFLIX

Interviewer: Our client is Netflix. The company wants us to develop a game plan for how and when it should shut down its DVD-by-mail membership services.

Student: Besides coming up with a game plan to shutter its DVD-by-mail service, are there any other objectives I should consider?

Interviewer: No.

Student: I have two clarifying questions. Why do they want to shut it down?

Interviewer: Why do you think?

Student: I can think of a number of reasons. It's not profitable anymore. The technology is becoming obsolete. It wants to consolidate its customer base to streaming. Maybe to reduce its footprint and focus on its core business. Or perhaps it needs warehouse space for other projects.

Interviewer: All good reasons. Then why do you think Netflix hasn't shut it down already?

Student: Because it is still profitable.

Interviewer: What's your other clarifying question?

Student: Is there any particular event or number that would trigger the shutdown?

Interviewer: It wants to shut it down while it is still profitable.

Student: Okay. Can I have a second to write out my thoughts?

Interviewer: Sure.

The student takes two minutes to draw out three buckets.

Student: I'd like to break this down into three buckets. Current status, how to shut it down, and when to shut it down.

Under current status, I want to know how the program works, the different pricing options, the number of members, and the membership trends. The revenues and profits for the last three years for both DVD-by-mail and domestic streaming. The margins. The percentage of revenues that the DVD rentals make up of Netflix's total domestic revenues, and how that has changed over time. Have we consolidated or closed any of the warehouses?

Under how to shut it down I have five areas to consider: customers, staff, the warehouses and equipment, the DVDs, and barriers to exit.

Customers. Is it a shrinking customer base? Where are they going to go? Can we convert them to streaming? How can we make up the lost revenue from the program? What are the steps we could take to unwind the business, such as not renewing or signing up new memberships?

Staff. Can we transfer or reassign workers to other areas? How many workers would we have to lay off and what would that cost, in terms of dollars and company morale?

Warehouses. What to do with the warehouses? Do we sell, rent, repurpose or hold on to them, basically land-bank them?

DVDs. What do we do with the DVDs? Sell them, destroy them, give them away? Or is there an overseas market we could sell them into?

Barriers to exit. Non-transferable fixed assets or basic emotion.

Interviewer: Basic emotion as a barrier to exit?

Student: This is where the company started, how it built its house.

Interviewer: Interesting.

Student: And finally, when?

- If R=C can we calculate the time when it will no longer be profitable?
- If it needs resources currently allocated to the DVD program to fund other projects or develop new content.
- Can we encourage members to leave, either by limiting new titles or raising prices? What would be the consequences of either move?

Interviewer: You wanted prices and membership. The price per plan for DVD-by-mail varies from $4.99 to $14.99 per month according to the plan chosen by the member. DVD-by-mail plans differ by the number of DVDs that a member may have out at any point.

The interviewer hands the student a chart.

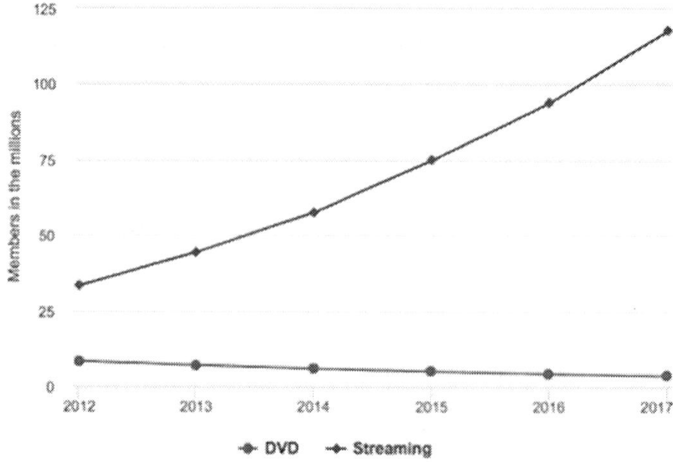

Student: Wow. The DVD-by-mail program is bleeding members. But I'm also thinking that each member must be profitable, maybe even more profitable than the streaming member. Otherwise Netflix would have shut it down by now. Any information on the profit margins?

Interviewer: Now what do you think?

He hands the student the chart.

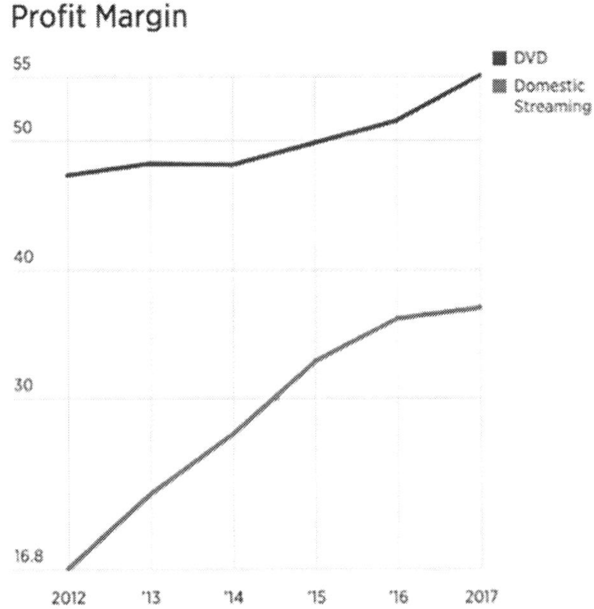

Student: Profit margins are 55 percent for DVD members. That's surprising. It looks like the streaming member profit margins are around 37 percent, which is also very good. What surprises me is that the profit margin for the DVDs has been going up even as the number of members has fallen.

Interviewer: Why is that?

Student: It means costs are going down. And a major cost in this case is shipping. I would assume that there is a decrease in the DVD usage by paying members, kinda like that gym membership I never use. Other costs, primarily those associated with processing and customer service expenses, probably decreased because of lower operation expenses resulting from the decline in DVD shipments.

Interviewer: Anything else?

Student: Yes. There was probably a decrease in content expense. Fewer members means fewer copies of the movie are needed. Also, if fewer DVDs are mailed out, that means Netflix can reduce the number of warehouses and staff.

Interviewer: It has reduced the number of warehouses – from 50 to 17 – which has led to longer delivery times, with fewer DVDs and fewer warehouses. How do you think Netflix decides who gets the new DVD first?

Student: First come, first served?

Interviewer: Are you asking me or telling me?

Student: Telling you.

Interviewer: Well you're wrong. Traditionally Netflix gave priority to subscribers who rented the fewest number of discs in a given period, with the rationale that because they paid the same price for the service but used it less, they should have high priority to get the disc they wanted. But this doesn't work anymore. Can you tell me why?

Student: Because this group would probably be slower returning the DVDs.

Interviewer: Right! What's next?

Student: I think there are probably a number of subscribers who don't realize that they're still paying for the service. What kind of numbers are we talking about? How much profit did the DVD program bring in last year?

Interviewer: Around $250 million.

Student: That's money that could be funneled toward building content on the streaming side.

Interviewer: When it does shutter the service, what should Netflix do with all the DVDs?

Student: I can think of a few ideas. Netflix could send them to its best DVD customers if they sign up for the streaming service. It could donate them to libraries across the country or sell them online either in the U.S. or abroad. Or simply destroy them so they don't end up on the black market.

Interviewer: I want you to look at my last chart, take two minutes and make a recommendation about when Netflix should shutter its DVD-by-mail service.

He hands the student the chart. All numbers are in millions.

Domestic DVDs	'17	'16	'15	'14
Membership	3.4	4.1	4.9	5.7
Revenue	462	542	645	765
Cost of Revenue	250	262	323	397
Contribution Profit	250	280	322	368
Contribution Margin	55%	52%	50%	48%

The student takes two minutes to run some numbers and finalize his recommendation.

Student: Netflix should not shutter the DVD-by-mail program for at least five years. It's losing around 17 percent of its customer base per year; however, cost reductions far outweigh the loss in revenue while increasing profit margins are feeding the bottom line. The risks are that it will reach a point where expenses can't be reduced any further and profits will be reduced to a point that it is not profitable or can't make a meaningful contribution to the bottom line. In the short-term, the next steps would be to continue cutting content and adjusting the algorithm that determines which subscribers get new releases first. In the long-term I'd recommend revisiting this issue in three years to reassess the situation. And we can help you with that.

(Case Takeaways)

- The student's structure was good and complete. It wasn't a traditional structure but one crafted to the situation, as it should be. He would have looked ridiculous if he used the one-structure-fits-all approach.
- He didn't state a hypothesis.
- The student handled it well when the interviewer threw his question back at him and when the interviewer told the student he was wrong.
- His recommendation was straightforward, definitive, and no-nonsense.
- His math was solid during the analysis of the last graph.

+ JAMAICAN BATTERY ENTERPRISE

Interviewer: Our client is the Jamaican Battery Enterprise. Currently, they sell car batteries throughout the Caribbean, Africa, and Central and South America. Over the past two decades they have been eyeing the Cuban battery market. However, Cuban Battery Enterprise, a state-owned battery company, currently has 100 percent of the secondary market. The reason they have 100 percent of the secondary market is that the Cuban government imposes a 50 percent tariff on the manufacturing costs and shipping costs on all imported batteries.

The Cuban government has just announced it will be lowering the tariff on batteries by 5 percent a year for the next 10 years until the tariff reaches zero.

The Jamaican Battery Board of Directors wants to know the size of the Cuban market and if, when, and how they should enter it.

Student: The board of directors of the Jamaican Battery Enterprise wants to know the size of the Cuban market and if, when, and how they should enter it. We know that the Cuban battery market is now dominated by the Cuban Battery Enterprise because of a 50 percent tariff on the manufacturing and shipping costs on all imported batteries. But we also know that the government is lowering the tariff by 5 percent a year for the next 10 years until the tariff reaches zero.

Interviewer: Yes, that's right.

Student: I'll assume that the objective is to gain market share and be profitable. Are there any other objectives I should know about?

Interviewer: No.

Student: What is the market share that they would like?

Interviewer: One hundred percent.

Student: Let me rephrase. What is the market share that they can reasonably expect to gain and under what timeframe?

Interviewer: Twenty-five percent within five years of entering.

Student: Let's start by estimating the size of the Cuban secondary car battery market. I'll assume that there are 10 million people in Cuba.

Interviewer: That's a little low but a good figure to use.

Student: I'll also assume that disposable income is limited and that only one in ten households has a car. So if we estimate that the average Cuban household is made up of five people ...

Interviewer: Where did you get five from?

Student: I'm assuming that there are two generations living in a number of the homes.

Interviewer: Okay.

Student: So, if there are 2 million households and if only one in ten has a car, that means that there are 200,000 cars. I would also like to add in another 10,000 vehicles, including taxis, trucks, and government vehicles.

Interviewer: So 210,000 vehicles.

Student: Yes. I'll also assume that Cubans keep their cars for a long time and that the average car needs a new battery every three years.

Interviewer: Three years? What were you thinking when you made that assumption?

Student: I was assuming that this is a monopoly in a communist country, thus the quality of the battery might not be competitive with a Jamaican Battery, which probably lasts five years.

Interviewer: Go on.

Student: So, 210,000 vehicles will need a new battery every three years. But there are two factors we need to figure in. First, let's say that half of the 10,000 "other" vehicles we mentioned are government or military vehicles. So we need to subtract 5,000 from the total. Now it is 205,000 divided by every three years, which equals around 68,000 batteries. Also, the number is going to be reduced over the long run because our batteries will last five years, not three. I'm not sure how to factor that in.

Interviewer: That's okay. It's just important that you brought it up.

Student: If we want 25 percent of that market, we're talking 17,000 batteries a year.

Interviewer: Okay, what's next?

Student: I'd like to know some costs and prices. What are our costs and prices compared with theirs?

Interviewer: Prices are irrelevant, but costs aren't. It costs the Cuban Battery Enterprise $12 to produce a battery. Their raw material costs are 20 percent, their labor costs are 50 percent, and their overhead and all other costs are 30 percent.

Student: It costs us $9 to produce a battery. Our raw material costs are 20 percent, our labor costs are 25 percent, and all other costs, including overhead and marketing, are 55 percent. It costs us $1 to ship it to Cuba.

Let me just write this out.

Cuban Battery Enterprise	Jamaican Battery Company
Production costs: $12	Production costs: $9
Raw material 20%	Raw material 20%
Labor 50%	Labor 25%
All other costs 30%	All other costs 55%
Shipping costs $0	Shipping costs $1
Tariff $0	Tariff $5
Total cost $12	Total cost $15

That means it costs us $9 manufacturing plus $1 shipping, which equals $10. Add in the 50 percent tariff and we're talking $15 a battery.

We now need to figure out when we will be competitive. In five years the tariff will drop from 50 percent to 25 percent, which is half. So, it will still cost us $10 to manufacture and ship the battery; however, the tariff will be only $2.50. That makes our total cost $12.50. So I would say, based on sheer numbers, we can enter and compete during Year 6. But if we can market and explain that, for a little bit more, our battery will last five years instead of three years, then we might be able to charge a premium, and that could justify entering the market in Year 5.

Interviewer: Let's switch hats for a second. You now are advising the Cuban Battery Enterprise. What do you advise them?

Student: My first step is to approach the government and try to get them to reconsider lowering the tariff.

Interviewer: Their minds are made up. The tariff will be reduced.

Student: Next, I would want to find out why our labor costs are so high.

Interviewer: Why do you think?

Student: The two things that jump to mind are technology and medical costs. Maybe our technology is old and our manufacturing process is very labor intensive.

Interviewer: Yes, that's part of it. What else?

Student: We are in a communist country where healthcare is free. That's the hidden cost in everything that's done – every service and every manufactured item. Even a country like Canada, with its national healthcare program, has higher prices. If the Canadian dollar wasn't so weak compared with the U.S. dollar, the Canadians would price themselves right out of the market in many items.

Interviewer: We'll save that discussion for another time.

Student: Well, we can't do much about the healthcare costs, but we can upgrade our technology. The upgrade would also make our batteries more competitive and able to last five years instead of three years.

Interviewer: Say we upgrade our technology and are now able to make a world-class battery for $9 each. How would that change things?

Student: Well, the tariff becomes moot in the sense that we can be competitive without it. This is good, but we still have a perception problem. I think we need to launch a marketing campaign to show the Cuban public that we have a new battery that is world class. I'd also like to review our customer service and our distribution channels. These are key functions that are often overlooked in a monopoly environment.

Interviewer: Good point. Our customer service is pitiful and our distribution channels are restricted to two major warehouses, one in Havana and the other in Nuevitas. You said that you would launch a marketing campaign, and I'll assume that there will be a customer service aspect to that. What would you do about the distribution channels?

Student: I'll make two assumptions. First, I'll assume that we have at least two years before the Jamaican Battery Enterprise enters our market. Second, I'll assume that other non-American battery companies will also enter our market, probably about the same time and with a strategy similar to the Jamaican company's.

Interviewer: Both fair assumptions.

Student: First, I would go to every gas station on the island, both in the cities and in the countryside. I would front each one the cost of the batteries, give them a nice display rack, free logo t-shirts, and maybe some cash. In return, they would have to sign an exclusive agreement to sell only our batteries.

Let me ask you this: Does the government make its own tires? And if yes, how's the quality?

Interviewer: Yes, they do, but the quality is poor. However, based on your advice, they will also upgrade their technology and launch a marketing plan because the tire tariff is also being eliminated.

Student: So, you know what I'm getting at. We can open a service store where residents can get both a new battery and new tires, and maybe an oil change. We can snap up all of the best locations before the foreign competitors come into our market.

Interviewer: We're switching hats again. You are now back to advising the Jamaican Battery Enterprise. You have seen that the Cuban Battery Enterprise has upgraded its plant, increased its distribution channels, formed a joint venture with the Cuban Tire Enterprise, and launched a nationalistic marketing campaign. Do you now enter the Cuban battery market, and if so, how?

Student: Whenever you enter a new market, there are several things you need to examine. Who are the major players? What size market share do they have? How are their products or services different from ours? And are there any barriers to entry? The major player is the Cuban Battery Enterprise. They now have 100 percent of the market. Two years ago, their products were inferior, but today they are very similar. The tariff was a barrier to entry, but now it looks as if access to distribution channels could be a threat.

I've learned that there are three main ways to enter a market. Start from scratch, buy your way in, or form a joint venture. I'd like to do a quick cost-benefit analysis of each. Starting from scratch would be a fine strategy if we can define our distribution channels. If the Cuban company has all the gas stations tied up and has built tire and battery stores, then our distribution means are limited. Plus, selling 17,000 batteries a year might not justify an investment of building our own battery stores.

The second strategy is to buy our way in. Because this is a communist country, there isn't a lot of buying opportunity. If we were going to buy anyone, it would have been Cuban Battery Enterprise, and we should have bought it when it was a mess and not a formidable competitor.

The third way is to form a joint venture. If I work under the assumption that there are no independent battery distributors, then my first choice is to form a joint venture with one of the tire companies that are entering the market. My guess is that there will be several tire companies and battery companies jumping in, so we need to be part of that coalition.

Interviewer: So it all boils down to ...

Student: So it all boils down to distribution channels.

Interviewer: Great job.

Type of Case: Strategy / entering a new market / market-sizing

Comments: This was a long case and one that you'd get in the final rounds, where you have about an hour to answer it. It had a market-sizing component to it, but probably the hardest thing was the switching of the hats. It forced the student to come up with counterstrategies to the strategies he had just developed.

Most students would have tried to figure out the reduction in tariff fees year by year, but this student saved time and impressed the interviewer by picking a point in the middle and working from there. He made the math simple and was able to do the calculations in his head.
The student was very well organized – he even wrote out the costs and percentages in a little chart. This impressed the interviewer and made everything easy for the student to find when flipping back through his notes.

+ FLATLINE

Interviewer: Our client is a one-billion-dollar U.S.-based medical device manufacturer with products strictly in the cardiovascular space. Their most profitable product – in terms of margin – is an artificial heart valve for a procedure called Transcatheter Aortic Valve Replacement (TAVR), which is used to treat severe aortic stenosis, a disease that affects individuals over the age of 85. TAVR is used by only a few hundred specially-trained doctors. Revenues associated with this device totaled $250M last year, but profits have remained flat over the past two years. The CEO has asked us to investigate why profits have been flat, determine whether there is any upside, and brainstorm about how we can increase profits.

Student: Could I have a few minutes to restate the case facts as well as my understanding of our objectives? The CEO of this medical device manufacturer wants us to explain why profits have remained flat for a high-margin product that generates about $250 million in revenues annually, or about 25 percent of the company's revenues. He also wants us to determine whether there is any upside, what that upside is, and how we can capture it. Are there any other goals that we should be concerned with?

Interviewer: No.

Student: I have one clarifying question. What constitutes success here? Is it a certain increase in profits? And what is the timeframe?

Interviewer: The timeframe is ASAP. There is no one particular profit goal, although this is a high-margin product and he's expecting significant profits.

Student: I'd like to take a minute to structure my thoughts here.

[Student takes 60 seconds to draw out his notes and then turns them toward the interviewer.]

Okay, I don't see any external factors at play here, but I'll want to take a look at the market. And because the primary goal is to increase profits, our framework requires us to explore revenues and costs because profits equals revenues minus costs. Revenues, in turn, are price times quantity. Costs can be broken into fixed and variable. I'd like to explore these five levers.

Interviewer: That looks like a good framework.

Student: I'd like to start by looking at the price. How do our prices compare with our competitors' prices?

Interviewer: Actually, our client is the only manufacturer of a device for TAVR. There are two other competitors on the horizon, though; one is about 12 months away from launching its product and the other is about 16 months away.

Student: That's a great place to be. What opportunity do we have to raise our prices? Given that the audience is over the age of 85, I assume Medicare pays for it. Is the device fully reimbursable or partly reimbursable by Medicare?

Interviewer: Great question. Medicare fully reimburses for the TAVR procedure because it's safer and more effective than alternative procedures. It's also less expensive than the alternative because there is less readmission and fewer complications, which drive up the cost. But they've set a cap and we've hit it.

Student: If Medicare is reimbursing fully, I don't think it's a good idea for us to raise our prices above the cap. Let's look at quantity. How many devices do we sell annually? You mentioned there are only a few hundred doctors who are trained in the procedure. I suspect the number of devices is therefore limited because of the number of trained doctors.

Interviewer: Exactly. Here's a chart of the number of devices we sold last year.

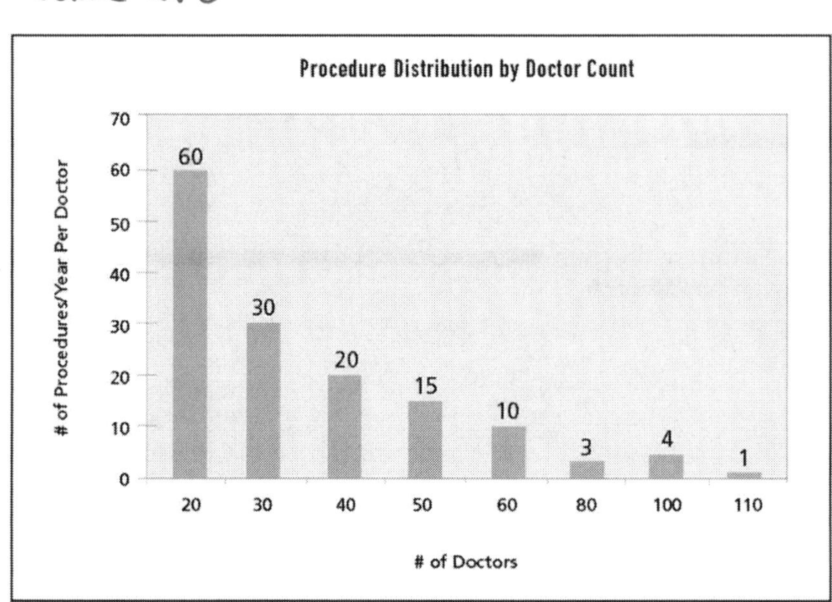

Student: Thank you. Is it accurate to say that one procedure equates to one device?

Interviewer: Yes, that's correct.

Student: If I'm interpreting this correctly, 20 doctors performed 60 procedures each, 30 doctors performed 30 procedures each, and so on. Is that correct?

Interviewer: Yes. So how many devices did we sell last year?

Student: Okay, if I multiplied out the number of procedures by the number of doctors and add it all up, I get the number of procedures.

[The students walks the interviewer through the math of 20 x 60 = 1,200 plus 30 x 30 = 900, plus 20 x 40 = 800, etc. Then he adds them all up.]

That makes 5,000 procedures or devices. Based on revenues of $250M, that's $50,000 per device.

Interviewer: That's correct. What else does this chart tell you?

Student: It appears that there are a lot of procedures performed by a few doctors and a lot of doctors who perform very few procedures. It's quite skewed.

Interviewer: Exactly. Why do you think that is?

Student: I think this might be a function of two things: the geographic distribution of 85-year-olds and the availability of trained doctors in those geographies.

Interviewer: That's probably true. So what do you want to do?

Student: Let's table quantity for a second and focus on costs. Has anything changed on the cost side that could be affecting our profits?

Interviewer: Actually, we've already compressed both fixed and variable costs as much as possible. There really isn't any more room there.

Student: Okay, then it looks like we need to focus on quantity. Has anything changed in the population of 85-year-olds over the past two or three years?

Interviewer: Assume that the inflow and outflow of individuals has remained constant.

Student: Is it possible that we've fully penetrated the market? How many 85-year-olds are there in the U.S. and where are they distributed?

Interviewer: Good question. Here is a chart that shows the distribution by city.

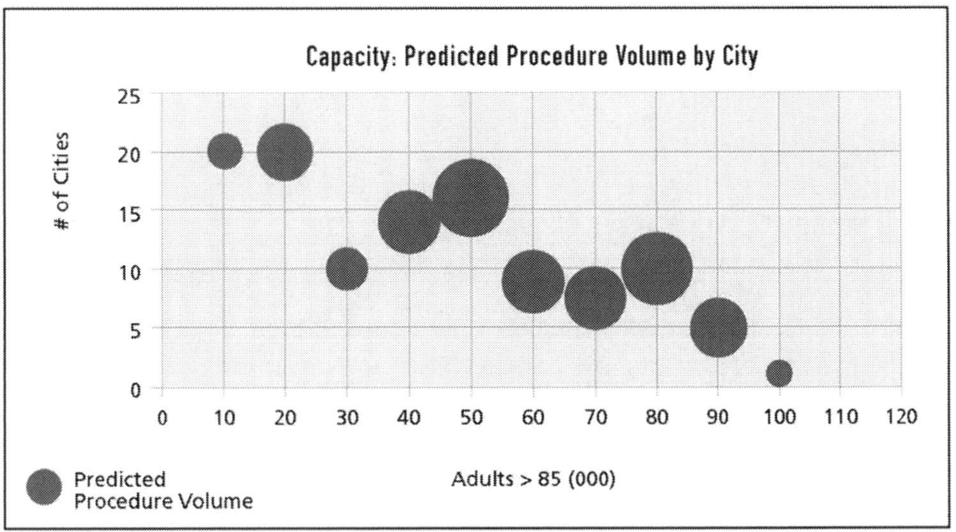

Student: Interesting. So this shows the number of cities that have our population. In other words, there are 20 cities that have 10,000 people over the age of 85, 20 cities with 20,000 people, and so on. Is that correct?

Interviewer: You're correct. What else does this chart tell you?

Student: As one would expect, as the population of adults over 85 goes up, the number of cities with that population goes down. This tells us the population, but it does not tell us the number of devices we can expect. What do the sizes of the bubbles mean?

Interviewer: Another good question. That information was deliberately left out. The size of the bubble indicates the ratio of devices per some number of 85-year-olds. Based on condition prevalence, we've seen 10 devices per 10,000 85-year-olds.

Student: That's just the number I needed to calculate the predicted number of devices we should be selling. I'll start from left to right. There are 20 cities with 10,000 people. We expect 10 devices in each of these cities for a total of 10 x 20 = 200 devices.

[The student takes two minutes to write up the chart, walking the interviewer through the calculations. He turns the chart toward the interviewer.]

Here is a chart with that data:

A > 85 Pop. (000)	Total # Cities	Predicted Procedure Volume
10	20	200
20	20	400
30	10	300
40	14	560
50	16	800
60	9	540
70	8	560
80	10	800
90	5	450
100	1	100

Student: If I add up the predicted procedure volume, I get 4,710 – which is lower than the 5,000 devices we're already selling.

Interviewer: What do you make of this?

Student: There are two things that could explain this. First, the ratio you mentioned (10 devices for every 10,000 85-year-olds) might not be accurate. Secondly, it's possible that there are some cities where we've been able to exceed this ratio. Have we analyzed what our penetration is in the cities where doctors have performed the procedure in terms of devices per 10,000 targets? That is, are we above or below the 10 per 10,000 ratio?

Interviewer: Great question. We looked at this and came up with the following. What does this tell you?

[Interviewer shows the student this chart.]

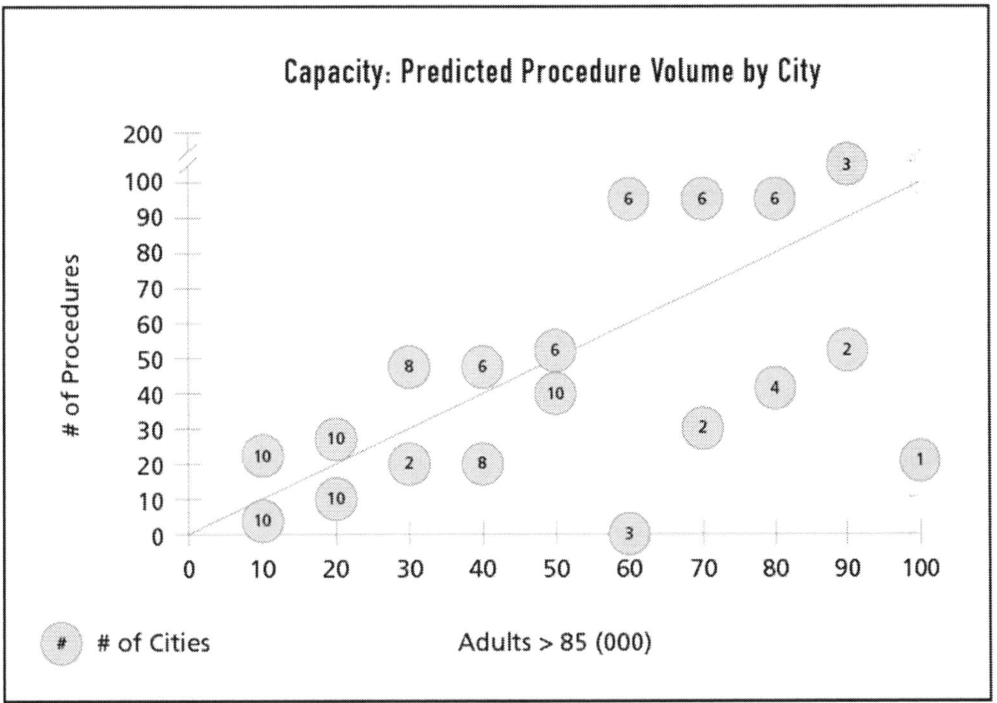

Student: Interesting. At first glance, it seems as if the diagonal line is our 10 devices per 10,000 ratio. My hypothesis was correct. There are some cities where we are above that ratio, or over-penetrated, and some cities where we are below that ratio, or under-penetrated. For example, there are six cities with 60,000 85-year-olds where we've done 100 devices each, and three cities where we're doing zero devices. Is it safe to assume that there are sufficient doctors in those geographies?

Interviewer: Yes, assume that the supply of doctors is evenly distributed per 10,000 85-year-olds nationwide. How would you calculate headroom?

Student: I would calculate headroom by "moving" all the under-penetrating cities up to the line.

Interviewer: Based on this information, what's the headroom for growth?

A > 85 Pop. (000)	Total # of Cities	Predicted Procedures	Cities Below Predicted Volume	Avg. # of Procedures/City	Upside (# of Procedures)
10	20	200	10	5	50
20	20	400	10	10	100
30	10	300	2	20	20
40	14	560	8	20	160
50	16	800	10	40	100
60	9	540	3	0	180
70	8	560	2	30	80
80	10	800	4	40	160
90	5	450	2	50	80
100	1	100	1	20	80

Student: Based on this, the headroom for growth is another (he adds up the last column) 1,010 devices. In terms of dollars, it's $50,500,000. On a revenue base of $250 million, that's a 25 percent increase in revenues.

Interviewer: Great. How would we accomplish this upside?

Student: I would start by looking at what we did in the geographies where we've over-penetrated. For example, did we do any marketing in those geographies?

Interviewer: Actually, we partnered with hospitals in those geographies on outreach efforts to encourage the elderly to come in and get tested for aortic stenosis. That way, we could get them the procedure quickly. Can you think of other things we can do to drive procedures?

Student: One thing I would do is focus on educating referring physicians. Because someone would go to a specially-trained doctor only after seeing a referring physician, it's important to educate them on this procedure.

Interviewer: So can you sum things up for the CEO?

Student: We have an opportunity to increase revenues by 25 percent or approximately $50 million. Two ways we can achieve this growth are by increasing patient outreach efforts in cities where we are under-penetrated and by increasing awareness among referring physicians.

(Case Takeaways)

This was a math-heavy case. The student...

- quantified related numbers as percentages.
- walked the interviewer through his calculations.
- was able to draw conclusions from the graphs.
- built tables based on the graphs.

He also picked up that there was information missing from a graph. He verified that he was reading the graph correctly, and his summary was short and to the point.

+ BLADE TO BLADE

Interviewer: Our client is a small privately-held lawn mower manufacturer in lower Alabama. The company makes low-end mowers, the type marketed to low-income households. It has 1 percent of the national market. There are 25 national competitors.

Like the rest of the industry, the company's sales have been flat. But its bigger problem is that the company it has been purchasing its engines from for the last 40 years suddenly called up and said it was filing for bankruptcy and closing its doors.

The client has looked around for another engine manufacturer, but the only one it could find is charging 40 percent more than what our client has been paying. The reason for this is that the engines it uses involve a side-mounted engine rather than the flat-top engine most other mowers use. They've been using this side-mounted engine for 40 years. It's inexpensive and reliable, a real workhorse. You know the old saying, "They don't make things like they used to." Well, this engine is "like they used to." In addition, the side-mounted engine has become our client's signature over the years.

Here is a chart of the lawn mower industry. As you can see there are 25 competitors, and 23 of them make up 98 percent of the market.

Lawn Mower Industry		
18 %	5	
40 %	8	
40 %	10	
2 %	X	Y
	ENG	

Our client is Company X. Its biggest competitor is Company Y. Together they share the lowest 2 percent of the market. Company Y buys its engines from the same engine maker (ENG), so it is in the same boat. X and Y have been competing against each other in this market for the last 40 years and there is no love lost between them. If both mowers were in the room you couldn't tell them apart, except one has a big X on it. These are basic mowers. You pull the cord to start it, push it, and the grass blows out the side. It's one step above Fred Flintstone pushing Dino around the front yard.

If the client raises its price by 12 percent, that increase will push it up into the next level where there are already ten companies fighting over a 40 percent market share. More important, there are big names in that group, including Honda, Lawn-Boy, and John Deere. Their mowers have a lot more bells and whistles than ours. We can't compete in that market without drastic redesign and upgrades.

I know I have given you a lot of information, but just one last thing: The client uses "just in time inventory," which is normally a good thing; however, because it didn't see this bankruptcy coming, it has only enough engines on hand for one month as it heads into its busy season. What does it do?

Student: That was a lot of information. Let me make sure I got it. Our client is a privately-held lawn mower manufacturer in lower Alabama. It has 1 percent of the national market. Its engine supplier suddenly filed for bankruptcy, which left our client in a position of low inventory heading into its busy season. The only alternative engine is 40 percent higher than what the client has been paying. However, if it raises its prices, that action will push it into the next tier where it will have to compete directly with the likes of Honda and John Deere. So its objective, I imagine, is not only to survive this crisis but also to maintain or increase sales and market share. Are there any other objectives I should be concerned with?

Interviewer: No.

Student: Can I ask a few clarifying questions?

Interviewer: Certainly.

Student: What are its margins?

Interviewer: Twenty-five percent.

Student: What is the manufacturing cost of the mower and what percentage does the engine account for?

Interviewer: You can assume that it costs us $100 to manufacture and we sell it to the distributor for $125. The cost of the engine makes up 60 percent of the cost of the mower. The other parts – the wheels, shell, and handle – make up 25 percent, and labor accounts for 15 percent.

Student: If the engine makes up 60 percent of the cost of the mower, that's $60. If that component were to jump up 40 percent, that means [student does a quick calculation on his graph paper – 60 x .4 = 24] ... that means the engine would jump $24, for a total cost of $84, which would make our new mower cost $124. That takes quite a bite out of our margins if we can't raise our prices.

Interviewer: You can see their dilemma.

Student: This mower is manufactured in Alabama, so I'll assume our labor costs are reasonable. I don't think we'd gain anything by moving the operation to China or Mexico. Where do we buy the other parts?

Interviewer: In Alabama. This company supports the surrounding communities. You can assume that buying the wheels from Mexico isn't going to solve this problem.

Student: Do you mind if I take a moment to lay out my structure?

Interviewer: Go ahead.

Student: One last question. How much does the flat-top engine cost compared with the old side-mounted engine?

Interviewer: The price is the same, although some would argue that the quality isn't as good.

The student draws a line down the middle of his page and starts writing.

Student: I want to divide this into short-term solutions and long-term solutions. In the short term, the company has several options. It can buy the new engine and raise its prices, but that would pit it against Honda, so that's not ideal. It could close its doors and liquidate the company, or even sell its company to Honda, who wants to enter this lower market. Again, not an ideal solution. It could eat its margins for the busy season, and then switch to the flat-top engines when things slow down. Do you know how long it would take to redesign the mower and retool the factory?

Interviewer: Eight weeks.

Student: Another short-term solution would be to buy the engine company out of bankruptcy. If we can get it up and running again quickly, we'd be able to save our busy season.

Interviewer: Interesting. What would you want to know before you bought the company?

Student: The first thing I'd like to know is why they went bankrupt.

Interviewer: They went bankrupt for two reasons. Bad management and $2 million in debt. The engine company itself was a cash cow, always has been. It too, has 25 percent margins. However, the owner took out all the cash and signed a big loan to start a new company in another industry, which failed. Now it can't pay back its loan and the bank won't extend it because of the company's bad credit history and the tight credit markets.

Student: Do we have $2 million in cash reserves?

Interviewer: No, we have $1 million. But the bank is willing to take 40 cents on the dollar based on the value of the company, and it values the company at $2 million. So you get the building and the equipment, which is ten years old and has about two to three years of life left on it. The owners would have been better off investing in new equipment than in racehorses or whatever they threw their money at. With new equipment, they could have built the side-mounted engines for less and built other engines as well.

Student: So the bank will take $800,000. I'm concerned about laying out 80 percent of our cash reserves for an acquisition. How's our bank credit?

Interviewer: It's good. If we put $500,000 down, we could take out a loan for the rest. What else would you need to know?

Student: I'd need to know if there are any new engine suppliers on the horizon.

Interviewer: Assume no; what else?

Student: Would we be able to get the workers back, particularly the floor supervisors? And if so, will the cultures of the two companies mesh well?

Interviewer: This is lower Alabama and they were just laid off, so we could get the workers back. And on one side you have guys building engines and on the other side guys making lawn mowers. They probably play in the same softball league and drink out of the same keg. What else?

Student: Is the side-mounted engine the only product we make? And are the engine company's suppliers in good shape? While there is nothing to indicate that they are in trouble, we need to find out. This is an old design and some of the parts might be tough to find.

Interviewer: Good. Yes, we have only that one product and the suppliers are in good shape. What else?

Student: We would need to review an exit strategy. What happens if this fails and what happens if we are successful? While an exit strategy might not be that critical, in this case it is something you want to think about.

Interviewer: Okay, good. Anything else?

Student: One last thing, competitive response; 98 percent of the industry isn't going to care one way or the other. We need to think about Company Y. How would it react? Would it still buy its engines from us? Do we even want them to buy their engines from us?

Interviewer: Okay, assume that the engine company and Company Y have been doing business for close to 40 years. There hasn't been a contract between the two of them in 30 years. Thus, we are under no legal obligation to sell to it. We can if we want to, but we don't have to. What would you do with Y and why would you do it?

Student: The way I see it, we have three options. First, we can cut Company Y off completely, forcing it to buy its engines from the other guy at a 40 percent premium. That might force it up to the next tier if it raises its prices, and we can gobble up its market share, or it might eat its margins for a while and then switch to a top-mounted engine. It would have little choice. It can't live on 1 percent margins.

Second, we can sell to it but increase the price by 30 percent. It would continue to buy our engines but that would still cut deeply into its margins, and I think that it would buy from us to get through the busy season, then switch to the flat-top engine. The third option is to sell to it at a 5 percent increase. This would keep it buying from us. This is important because we just laid out $800,000 for this engine company and can ill afford to cut off half our revenue stream. It would also keep Company Y from manufacturing a flat-top mower. This is good because we would still be supplying engines to this entire sector of the market, and it would also keep us from having to produce a flat-top mower ourselves. If we did this, I'd probably insist on a two-year contract. But before I did anything, I'd like to run the numbers. We know the engine company's margins are 25 percent. Do we know how many engines they sell in a year?

Interviewer: Good questions. But I don't want to get into that. Say we continue to sell to them for the next two years. What additional steps would you take to ensure company X's success?

Student: Do we know how much the new equipment would cost and what the building is worth?

Interviewer: No.

Student: Well, I'd probably buy the new equipment, if that would allow us to cut our manufacturing costs and to expand our product line. I'd set the new equipment up under the same roof as the lawn mower production. This would allow us to sell the old equipment and the building and put the proceeds toward either buying the new equipment and/or paying down the $300,000 we owe to the bank. There would be some synergies and cost savings we could take advantage of.

Interviewer: Give me three ways to cut costs in this case, besides moving everything under one roof.

Student: Now that we have the new equipment, we can produce other engines to sell, as well as help our own company expand our product line. We could build weed-whackers and leaf blowers. We could even create some seasonal balance to our production line by building engines for snow blowers.

Interviewer: Okay, that's one. What else?

Student: We could cross-train the workers to build both engines and lawn mowers. Also, we could retool the assembly line to be able to quickly switch from one product to the other as demand dictates. The third way is to go back down the supply chain and renegotiate with our suppliers. Maybe sign longer contracts or get bulk discounts if the engines and mowers share parts. In addition, interest rates are at a near-40-year low, so maybe we could refinance our debt.

Interviewer: Nice. Can you summarize the case for me?

[The student starts to summarize almost immediately.]

Student: Our client is a small, privately-held lawn mower manufacturer. It has learned that its engine supplier is closing down and is left without a suitable alternative. We investigated several short-term strategies, the best of which was to buy the engine company out of bankruptcy. We've verified that Company Y will remain a customer, while identifying a number of ideas to make our company more productive, including consolidating production space and workers. We also identified several cost-cutting measures, including reducing inventories and refinancing our debt.

Interviewer: Okay, good.

Type of Case: Merger and acquisition
Comments: The student did very well. The opening prompt was long and involved and the student did a great job summarizing the question. He asked some good questions up front, quickly realizing that cost-cutting wasn't going to solve this problem. He broke the problem down into short-term and long-term solutions. Once he did that, he was quick to realize that this was a mergers and acquisitions question. He asked a lot of good questions about the engine company, and he analyzed the Y situation by laying out his three options rather than just automatically cutting Company Y off, which would have been an emotional response.

+ DISPOSABLE REVENUES

Interviewer: Our client is a leading disposable consumer goods manufacturer that makes disposable plates, cups, bowls, utensils, and napkins. Each of these categories has seen growth over the past four years with the exception of the cups category. There, revenues have been flat over the past two years. The head of the business unit has hired us to determine the reason for the decline and recommend ways to arrest the decline and drive growth once again.

Student: I'd like to reiterate the facts of the case as well as my understanding of our objectives. Our client manufacturers disposable products and while the other categories are growing, the cups segment has been flat for the past two years. They want our thoughts on why this is happening and recommendations on what can be done to return the category to positive growth. Is that correct?

Interviewer: Yes, that's correct.

Student: Okay. Can I take a minute to think about my approach?

Interviewer: Sure. [Student takes 30 seconds to write out her thoughts.]

Student: To understand what may be happening, I'd like to start by examining the industry – including our competitor set. I'd then take a closer look at the cup category to see whether there are sub-segments within it and what might be happening there. Last, I would like to explore our options for shifting direction.

Can you give me a picture of the competitive landscape? That is, how many competitors are there and what are their revenues over the past few years? How has the cup segment been doing over the last three years? Any changes in the industry, mergers, new technology? Are all disposable distribution channels the same? If cups and plates use the same distribution channels and plates are growing, then channels probably isn't the issue – but it never hurts to take a look. Also, how are the competitors' cups different from ours?

Interviewer: Take a look at this graph and tell me what you think.

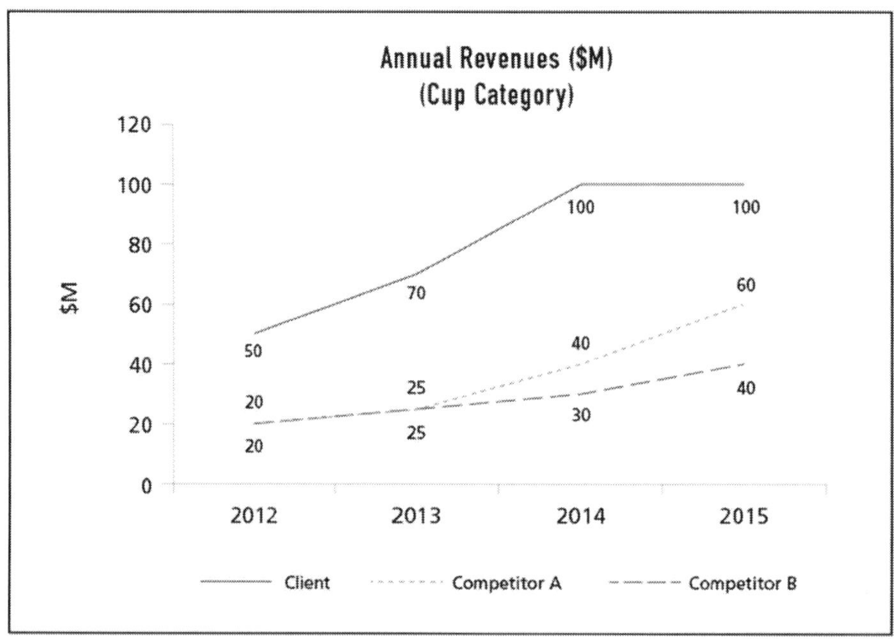

Student: Thanks. Based on the graph, there is nothing systemic that could be impacting our sales growth. It's clear that the cup category is growing, as evident by the growth in total sales from $90M in 2012 to $200M in 2015. Moreover, it appears that the category's growth is being driven by Competitor A and B's sales – and not our client's. That is, while our sales have flattened after 2014, our competitors' sales numbers have accelerated. In some ways, their growth is coming at our client's expense. So, while it's clear that our client still enjoys category leadership, its share is dwindling.

What can you tell me about our competitors' cups? Are they superior in quality? Do our competitors have better distribution channels? Better pricing? Is there anything about them that would encourage a consumer to purchase a competitor's cup rather than ours?

Interviewer: Good questions. Actually, there is nothing unique about our competitors' cups. They are virtually identical to our client's cups in terms of quality, pricing, and appearance, and all three competitors have the same distribution channels.

Student: Okay. Cups come in all sizes. How many different sizes are there? Is there growth in all sizes?

Interviewer: All good questions. Cups come in three distinct categories based primarily on size and material. The "Casual" category consists of the traditional 8-ounce paper cup. Next is the "Party" category, which includes both 12-ounce and 16-ounce cups that are usually red in color and made of plastic. The third category is called "Special" and the cups there are also red and made of plastic, but just larger in size – usually 20 ounces. This chart illustrates our client revenues each year in the various categories. Are there any immediate conclusions you can draw from this?

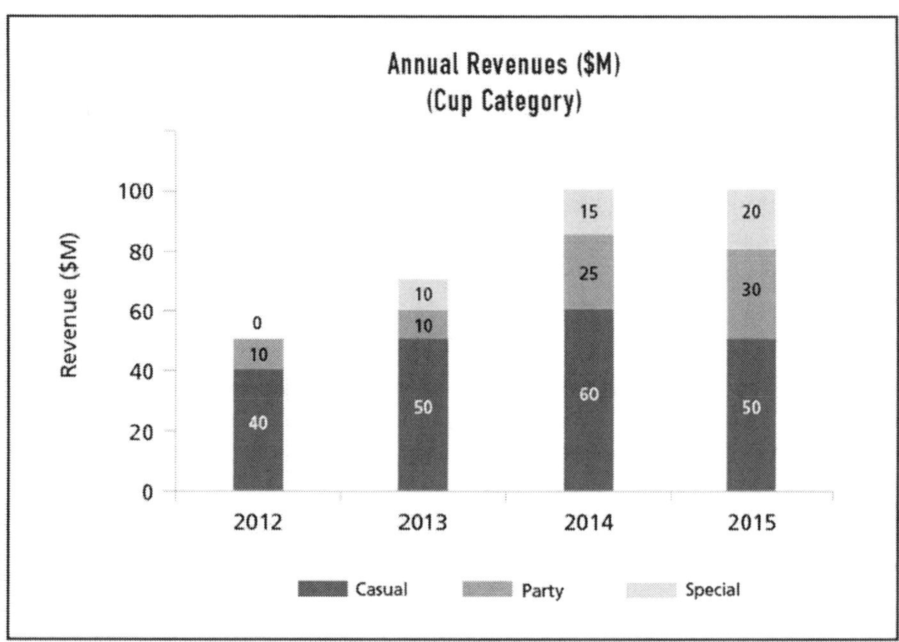

Student: There are a couple of conclusions I can draw from this. First, there is a seismic shift in what's driving our growth. From 2012 to 2014, there was steady growth in the Casual category, but from 2013 onward, growth is largely the result of the Party and Special categories. Next, the decline in the Casual category revenues from 2014 to 2015 leads me to believe that there is something going on with consumption patterns. In other words, people need and want bigger cups as evident by the growth in the Party and Special categories. To validate this inference, I'd have to see how revenues trended in these categories for our competitors.

Interviewer: Okay. That's a good idea. Here's a table with this data.

	Competitor A			Competitor B		
	Casual	Party	Special	Casual	Party	Special
2012	0	20	0	0	20	0
2013	0	25	0	0	25	0
2014	0	40	0	0	30	0
2015	0	60	0	0	40	0

Student: I think my inference might be correct. Neither competitor offers a cup in the Casual category – perhaps because they might have anticipated growth coming in the Party size. What's interesting to me is why neither offers a cup in the Special category. Based on our client's growth, there appears to be an opportunity there.

Interviewer: You bring up a good point. What do you think our client should do?

Student: Well, I think there are several things. In terms of manufacturing, I think they should investigate phasing out the Casual offering and ramping up production of the Party and Special category cups. They will have to understand the economics of the decision.

Interviewer: That's an interesting strategy since casual cups are still the client's biggest revenue source, although shrinking. And if they phase out casual cups one of the competitors will pick up the market. But let's explore the economics of that decision since you brought it up. What data would you need to evaluate whether the client should completely replace Casual cups with the Special cups rather than taking a gradual phase-based approach?

Student: I would first like to understand our cost structure: fixed and variable. How many 8-ounce cups do we sell annually? What is the unit price for the 8-ounce and the 20-ounce cups? Last, I'd like to know if I should assume the same volume of the larger cups, or does shelf space dictate a smaller quantity?

Interviewer: All great questions. First, the fixed costs would remain the same at $10M. The variable cost for the Special cup is 3 times the variable cost for the Casual cup ($0.001 vs. $0.003). The smaller cup has a unit price of $0.02 whereas the larger cup has a unit price of $0.05. Assume that because the Special cup is larger, replacing the Casual cups with the Special cups cuts the volume of Special cups by half.

Student: This is very helpful. So based on this information, since we did $50M in revenues in 2015 for the Casual cups, we sold 2.5B cups ($50M / $0.02). Our total cost of producing these was $10M (fixed) + 2.5B x $0.001 (variable) = $12.5M. The total cost of producing the Special cups requires determining the quantity of cups we can shelve. You said we can shelve only half the number of Casual cups, so that means 1.25B cups (2.5B / 2). So, our total cost of producing these will be $10M (fixed) + 1.25B x $0.003 (variable) = $13.75M. It looks like making the replacement could increase our costs by $1.25M ($13.75M - $12.5M).

Let's look at the revenue side. With 1.25B cups at $0.05, that means we would achieve $62,500,000 in revenues. In other words, our revenues would increase from $50M to $62.5M. So making the switch from Casual to Special makes sense from an economics perspective.

I think another key consideration is distribution. We have to consider what the shift in mix will mean in terms of distribution. I know in retail, shelf space is critical. Would retailers allow our client to swap out the Casual cups for Party and/or Special cups? Stepping back a bit, where are consumers even purchasing the larger cups?

Interviewer: These are good questions. Let's assume that the economics of manufacturing are not an issue. Let's focus on distribution. Here is a graph that shows distribution by category by distribution channel for 2015.

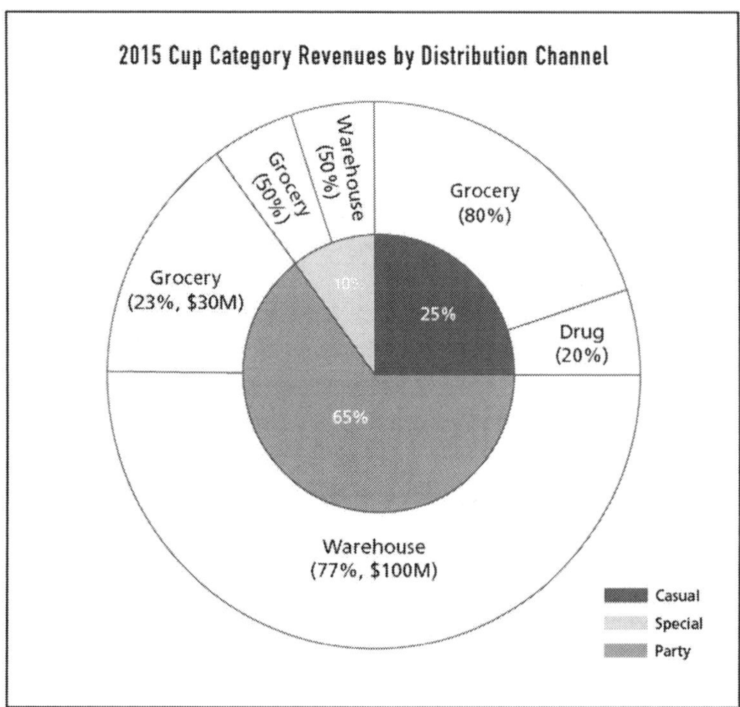

Student: This is interesting. *[She takes a minute to make her own chart and turns it toward the interviewer.]* So based on the graph, the underlying data looks like this:

2015 Revenues ($M)			
	Casual	Party	Special
Grocery	40	30	10
Drug	10	0	0
Warehouse	0	100	10

One obvious conclusion is that Party cups are bought either in the grocery or through the warehouse channels, which makes sense given the quantities usually needed for a party and the value proposition of warehouses selling large quantities of most products. Because our client is the only competitor with Casual cups, our client exclusively has shelf space in the Drug channel and sizeable distribution in Grocery. It might be possible for our client to swap out the Casual cups for Party or Special cups in the Grocery and Drug channels. Is that a possibility?

Interviewer: Sure. What else would you like to know before you sum things up?

Student: I would like to know our shelf space in the warehouse channel. One way would be to know what percent of the $100M of Party revenues is our client's and what percent is our competitors'. Knowing this would allow us to estimate what share we have to take.

Interviewer: Why don't you sum things up? What is your recommendation to our client?

Student: I would recommend that our client reduce or eliminate manufacturing of Casual cups and accelerate manufacturing of Party and Special cup sizes, given consumer demand and revenue growth. We've seen that replacing the Casual with Special cups generates an incremental $12.5M in revenues. To support growth in these categories and maximize their chances of success, I'd leverage our current distribution channels and expand our shelf space through promotions, better pricing, and better cup design.

(Case Takeaways)

- The math wasn't hard, but could easily be overwhelming when doing public math without a calculator. She handled it well and walked the interviewer through her calculations.
- She brought up distribution channels as part of her initial structure and then dismissed it, only to find that it was a big part of the solution.
- When the interviewer had some concerns about eliminating the casual cups altogether, she held her ground and did her analysis.
- She did a good job analyzing the graphs, even drawing the analysis in her own chart and turning it toward the interviewer and walking him through it.
- Her summary was short and to the point

+ POWERSPORTS POWERTHROUGH

Interviewer: The client is the number three player in the North American powersports industry. It makes mainly snowmobiles, motorcycles, and ATVs. Over the past year its stock fell from $40 to $25 and net income was down 18 percent while gross profits were down 13 percent. What's going on? How do we fix it?

Student: Just to make sure I got this right: Our client is the number three player in the North American powersports market. Its stock fell from $40 to $25, which is a drop of a little less than 40 percent. Its net income was down 18 percent and gross profits fell 13 percent. We've been tasked to figure out why and fix it.

Interviewer: That's right.

Student: Any other objectives or goals I should consider?

Interviewer: No.

Student: Are our competitors having the same problem?

Interviewer: Yes.

Student: Has our market share stayed the same?

Interviewer: Increased, actually.

Student: My initial hypothesis is that industry revenues have dropped because of external factors, which is also the cause of the client's falling gross profits and that the CEO gave modest guidance during his quarterly analyst call, which expedited the stock's decline.

Interviewer: Interesting. Why modest guidance?

Student: Because if the entire industry is having this problem it's probably external factors causing this drop, and that won't change overnight.

Interviewer: Point taken.

Student: Can I have a moment to think about my structure?

Interviewer: Certainly.

The student takes a minute to write out his structure and then turns it toward the interviewer. He writes E(P=R-C)M

Student: I'd like to look at external factors first, economic factors, as well as changes in the industry. Then I'd like to look at the company – its product mix, revenues, and costs for the last three years, and then come up with a plan to raise revenues and profits, both in the short term and long term.

Interviewer: Talk to me about the external factors first.

Student: The overall worldwide economic slowdown. The strengthening U.S. dollar and falling Canadian dollar played roles. Consumer confidence is down. The weakening oil markets combined with an unseasonably warm winter, I believe, constrained demand for off-road vehicles and snowmobiles.

Interviewer: Wouldn't lower gas prices be good for ATVs and snowmobiles?

Student: Yes, in the consumer market. But I'm betting that this company sells a lot of ATVs to oil companies, which have been hurt by the drop in oil prices and were forced to lay off part of their workforce and curtail cap-X spending. And if workers are laid off, they're not going to buy a new snowmobile or motorcycle.

Interviewer: Okay, what's next?

Student: Let's touch on the market. You said not only that the rest of the industry is having the same issues, but also that our market share has increased. That means to me that we are either making acquisitions or gaining market share organically, maybe as a result of a player exiting the market.

Interviewer: All our businesses increased market share despite a weak powersports industry. We've made acquisitions in accessories such as helmets, trailers, goggles, and gloves. But we also gained organically in the snowmobile and motorcycle markets.

Student: You said our net income was down by 18 percent. How'd the industry do overall?

Interviewer: Down 25 percent.

Student: Next I'd like to focus on the company. Do you have any information on the product mix and their revenues for the last three years? As well as overall profits?

Interviewer: This is what I do have. *[The interviewer hands this information to the student.]* Take a minute and look this over and tell me what you think.

Y2 Performance Summary (in thousands)			
Reporting Segments[3]	Y2	Y1	Change
Sales Off-Road Vehicles / Snowmobiles	862,032	1,051,801	(18%)
Motorcycles	162,558	122,219	33%
Global Adjacent Mkts (other products & channels)	81,028	100,980	(20%)
Total Sales	1,105,618	1,275,000	(13%)
Gross Profit	310,274	367,573	(16%)
Gross Profit as % of Sales	28.1%	28.8%	-77bps
Operating Expenses	169,072	176,927	(4%)
Operating Expenses as % of Sales	15.3%	13.9%	141bps
Operating Income	159,160	210,000	(24%)
Operating Income as % of Sales	14.4%	16.5%	-207bps
Net Income	110,682	135,397	(18%)
Net Income as % of Sales	10%	10.6%	-60bps

Student: ATV and snowmobile sales are crushing us. Not only are they down 18 percent, but they also make up around [*quick calculation*] 80 percent of the revenues. While motorcycles are up 33 percent, they make up only about 15 percent of sales. That's nice, but it's not going to move the needle much. The other interesting thing is that while the company's operating expenses were down 4 percent it's probably only because our sales are down and the client probably reduced production.

Interviewer: The client has been reducing costs across the board for the past three years. I can tell you right now, there's not much there to fix.

Student: Can you give me the breakdown between ATVs and snowmobiles?

Interviewer: Of that 80 percent of revenues, 90 percent is ATVs and 10 percent is snowmobiles.

[3] Reporting Segment sales include their respective parts, garments, and accessories (PG&A) related sales.

Student: So ATVs make up 72 percent of all sales and we sell twice as many motorcycles as snowmobiles. I imagine we have excess inventory on hand. Have they reduced their prices?

Interviewer: The short answer is "no." They have run promotions but are reluctant to cut prices. Neither have the competitors, but I think if one does it they all will, and it will cause a price war.

Student: The volume and the costs are easier to change than the industry price levels, unless all parties change their prices together.

Interviewer: That's called price fixing and is illegal.

Student: I was thinking more along the lines of airline and gas prices. Regardless, unless the industry prices go up, it will hurt everyone in the long run.

Interviewer: Fair enough.

Student: What were the revenues the year before?

Interviewer: Motorcycles were up 67 percent but overall revenues were up just 5 percent. All businesses increased market share in North America for last year despite a weak powersports industry. What about moving forward? We need to fix this.

Student: External challenges will continue to restrain growth and profitability in the short run. However, if gas prices go up and next winter is snowy, our stock might get a dead cat bounce.

Interviewer: A dead cat bounce?

Student: It's a finance term that means a temporary recovery from a ...

Interviewer: I know what it means. Give me some solutions.

Student: Can I take a moment ...

Interviewer: Knock yourself out.

[Student takes 60 seconds to collect his thoughts and lay out his ideas as bullet points.]

Student: We were tasked to increase stock price and profits both in the short and long terms. As far as increasing the stock price, most would advise a stock buyback program. The stock is down over 40 percent and is probably a very good deal. But this would only increase the price in the short run.

I think the cash on hand would be better spent making acquisitions, not just a competitor, but suppliers as well. The company needs to aggressively manage costs and this is one way to do it. In addition, I would continue to introduce more products, particularly accessories, which also builds brand. I'd also continue spending ad dollars on the motorcycles since that is the fastest growing segment.

Another thing we could do is to offer consumer financing, either at zero or 1 percent. Offer more for trade-ins as well. We determined that it was important not to drop prices, but we still have a lot of inventory on hand. I would do venture selling, trade our inventory for stock in oil companies that are down but not out, firms that might be a target of a takeover or who have the resources to ride out the oil price downturn. Their stock is even more depressed than ours. There is a chance they will fold, but in the long term I think it is worth the risk, and if they are bought out or turn it around, we would have made a larger profit while protecting our prices. We would need to do our due diligence.

Interviewer: Interesting. Okay, summarize the case for me.

Student: We were tasked to figure out why our stock and profits were falling and come up with some solutions to turn the company around. It was quickly determined that external factors were hampering our profits. While much of that was out of our control, we decided to be proactive by using our cash to make acquisitions in a depressed market and to exchange excess inventory for stock in oil companies, thus maintaining our prices and reducing inventory.

(Case Takeaways)

- The case had a nice conversational tone.
- The student quantified related numbers as percentages.
- He stated his hypothesis up front after learning that competitors were having the same problem.
- Many students don't look at external factors and answer the case in a vacuum. This case was all about external factors; remember to always at least touch on them.
- His analysis of the chart was good. He didn't repeat the obvious; he quantified the numbers as percentages and based his analysis on that. He also dug a little deeper wanting to know the breakdown of ATVs and snowmobiles.
- His idea to trade excess inventory for stock was different and interesting. Certainly something that no one else brought up.
- His structure was good, his confidence level was high throughout, he defended his answer, and he went beyond the expected answer, showing his creativity.

+ SNOW JOB

Interviewer: Snow Shovels Inc. (SSI) imports and distributes snow shovels. The snow shovel market is relatively stable. As expected, sales depend on demand, and demand depends on weather. SSI has to order its shovels four months in advance. How many shovels should they order?

Student: SSI imports and distributes snow shovels. They have to order their product four months in advance. They want to know how many shovels they should order.

Interviewer: Yes.

Student: Besides deciding how many shovels to order, are there any other objectives I should be concerned about?

Interviewer: Yes. The goal is to maximize profits with the lowest level of risk and the least amount of inventory on hand.

Student: What areas of the country does the company cover?

Interviewer: Just Wellesley, Massachusetts.

Student: I'd look at expanding into other areas.

Interviewer: No. They want to focus on just their little corner of the world.

Student: Maybe we can increase their distribution channels. How many distribution channels do they have?

Interviewer: Good question, but not relevant to what I'm looking for in this question.

Student: How many did the company order last year?

Interviewer: Two thousand.

Student: What was the weather like last year?

Interviewer: Cold, with lots of snow.

Student: Did they have any inventory left over from the year before?

Interviewer: Yes, 500 shovels.

Student: Is it fair to assume that they sold all 2,500 shovels this past year?

Interviewer: Yes.

Student: So there is no leftover inventory?

Interviewer: That's right. SSI hates to carry over inventory.

Student: Could we have sold more? Were there orders left unfilled?

Interviewer: Yes. It's fair to say that if it's a cold winter, SSI will sell 3,000 shovels. If it's a mild winter, they will sell only 1,000.

Student: Do we know what the forecast is for the coming winter?

Interviewer: There is a 40 percent chance that it will be a cold winter, and a 60 percent chance that the winter will be mild.

Student: Okay, let me get this straight. There is a 40 percent chance of a cold winter, in which we could sell 3,000 shovels. There's a 60 percent chance of a mild winter, in which we would sell 1,000 shovels. And SSI hates to carry over inventory. How much do we pay for the shovels and what do we charge?

Interviewer: We buy them for $10 and sell them for $20.

Student: So we make $10 a shovel. Let's figure that 40 percent of 3,000 equals 1,200 and 60 percent of 1,000 equals 600. If you add them together, that equals 1,800 shovels.

Interviewer: That's it? That's your answer? Why does everyone come up with 1,800 shovels? I've given this case five times today, and everyone has come up with 1,800 shovels. Think about the information I gave you. Think about the objective.

Student: I'd like to look at the estimated value. If we order 1,000 shovels and assume that no matter what kind of winter we had, we would still sell 1,000 shovels, then the estimated value would be ...

# Ordered	# Sold	Income	Costs	Net	Times %	Expected Profit
1,000	1,000	1,000 x 20	1,000 x 10	10,000	100%	$10,000
						$10,000

If we order 2,000 shovels and there is a 60 percent chance of a mild winter in which we would sell only 1,000 shovels, and a 40 percent chance of a cold winter in which we would sell all 2,000 of them, the value would be ...

# Ordered	# Sold	Income	Costs	Net	Times %	Expected Profit
2,000	1,000	1,000 x 20	2,000 x 10	0	60%	0
2,000	2,000	2,000 x 20	2,000 x 10	20,000	40%	$8,000
						$8,000

If we order 3,000 shovels and there is a 60 percent chance of a mild winter in which we would sell only 1,000 shovels, and a 40 percent chance of a cold winter in which we would sell all 3,000, the value would be ...

# Ordered	# Sold	Income	Costs	Net	Times %	Expected Profit
3,000	1,000	1,000 x 20	3,000 x 10	(10,000)	60%	$(6,000)
3,000	3,000	3,000 x 20	3,000 x 10	30,000	40%	$12,000
						$6,000

Based on the numbers above, and assuming that you're relatively risk-adverse, I would have to suggest that you order 1,000 shovels. You are pretty much guaranteed a $10,000 profit. If you order 3,000 shovels, you have only a 40 percent chance of making $12,000 and a 60 percent chance of losing $6,000.

Interviewer: Good point. Can you graph it?

Student: Sure. It would look like this.

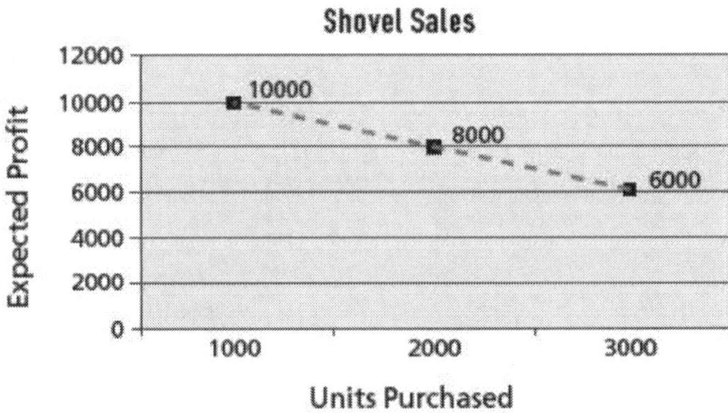

Student: One last question. In this case, we assumed that the leftover inventory is a loss in the current period. It's really an asset – unless they plan to throw it away.

Interviewer: Good point. You're right, but in this case we don't want to deal with it.

Type of Case: Strategy

Comments: This case is all about risk. The student tried to come to a fast answer, then pulled back and quickly re-thought this strategy based on the interviewer's reaction. Estimated value may not be common knowledge to a lot of non-MBAs, so go back and re-read the answer. Note: I've given this case 40 times to students, and only two got the correct answer. On a scale of 1 to 10, this is probably a 9.

+ MUSIC TO MY EARS

Interviewer: Our client is the leading manufacturer of musical instruments and is best known for its grand piano. The piano sells for $200,000. Alicia Keys, Billy Joel, and Elton John all play and record on our client's piano. The company also manufactures a slew of other musical instruments, everything from cellos and violins to saxophones and drums. These are also kind of pricey but nothing close to the piano – that's in the stratosphere by itself. The CEO called us in because he's thinking about entering the U.S. high-end headphone market. He's talking about over-the-ear headphones like Beats. He wants us to analyze the market and then make a recommendation on whether the company should enter.

Student: So the leading manufacturer of musical instruments is considering entering the high-end U.S. headphones market. We've been asked to analyze the market and then make a recommendation. Are there any other objectives?

Interviewer: Yes. He's looking to get 5 percent of the high-end market within a year after entering the market. It could be 5 percent of the number of units sold or 5 percent of the industry revenues. Either one is fine with him.

Student: I have one clarifying question: Why does he want to enter this market?

Interviewer: He wants to enter because the musical instrument market is growing at 2 percent a year and the headphones market is growing at 75 percent a year; it's forecasted to continue that growth for the next several years. He thinks it's time to diversify his product line and that his brand is strong enough to make the jump from one industry to another.

Student: I'd like to take a moment to lay out my thoughts.

[Student takes 90 seconds, draws out his notes, and then turns the notes toward the interviewer.]

I'd like to start off by looking at three different areas. First I'd like to look at the company, then the high-end headphones market, and finally the different ways for the company to enter the market.

Interviewer: Sounds like a plan.

Student: Let's start with the company. I'd like to know how big they are, and what were their revenues and profits for the last three years? Next I'd like to know more about their products, specifically, do they make electric guitars and pianos, or are all their products acoustic? Do they have any experience with electronics? Next, I'd like to investigate the brand. When consumers hear the company's name, what type of music do they think of, thus what is their current customer segmentation? Finally I'd like to look at the company's current distribution channels. How and where are their products sold, and does this match up to distribution channels used by the major brand headphones sellers?

Next, I'd like to look at the high-end headphones market. What's the current size of the market and what's its growth rate? How many different customer segments make up the market? Have there been any major changes in the industry, mergers, or new technology? I know that Apple bought Beats in 2015. And I know that wireless headphones are all the rage. Again I'd like to see if the distribution channels match up. And finally, I'd like to know who are the major players, what market share do they have, and how will our product differ from what's out there.

The last area to investigate is how best for our client to enter this market. I can think of four possible entry strategies. They can grow organically, make an acquisition of an existing player, form a joint venture, or outsource to a third party.

My hypothesis is that the company should not enter this market because it's very competitive, brand-driven, and dominated by some major players. But we'll see.

Interviewer: Okay. Let me answer some of your questions. Our client's revenues were $850 million last year with profits of $175 million.

Student: That's just a little more than 20 percent profit margin. Is that normal in the musical instrument industry?

Interviewer: It's toward the high end. Our client makes only acoustic instruments.

Student: So no electronic experience.

Interviewer: No.

Student: That means they don't have the knowledge, capacity, or capability to make headphones.

Interviewer: Correct, they don't yet. Addressing your other questions, consumers think of classical music when they hear our client's name, despite the fact that Alicia Keys and Billy Joel favor our products. What else did you want to know about the client?

Student: Distribution channels and customer segmentation.

Interviewer: They have five superstores where you can buy all their instruments. But most of their products are sold through independent and chain music stores. Their customers are all musicians, mostly professional. They also sell to orchestras, schools, universities, and concert halls.

Student: If we are going to get 5 percent of this market, we need to go way beyond our current distribution channels and customer base. What about the market?

Interviewer: I'm going to do a little data dump here. I want you to analyze the information and then give me at least five takeaways. We know that the high-end headphones market is growing at 75 percent a year. Say high-end headphones are any headphones that sell for $100 or more. The market leader is Company A and they have 60 percent of the market, and we'll say they did $400 million in sales. Company B has 20 percent, and the remaining 20 percent is made up of 24 other players from C to Z. And you have some big-name brands in there as well. The last bits of information are some prices. We'll assume that each of these players has only one headphones product in the high-end category just to make life easier. Company G sells its headphones for $100, Company C is $125, Company A is $225, and Company B is $425.

Student draws this chart and then takes a minute to analyze the information.

Company	Price	Market Share
A	$225	60
B	$425	20
C – Z	$100 – ?	20

Student: Given what you told me, my first takeaway is that there is no way our client is getting 5 percent of the market in units. You have two major players with 80 percent and 24 other players fighting over the remaining 20 percent. We have neither the brand recognition nor the street "cred" to elbow out 5 percent. The client might still get 5 percent of the overall industry revenues; that's a possibility but it seems unlikely. My second takeaway is that this market isn't that price sensitive. Consumers are willing to pay for brand and/or quality. Number three, I'd like to figure out the size of the market. You said Company A has 60 percent of the market and that they did $400 million in sales. So if I take 400 and divide it by .6 I get ... 666. I'm going to round down to a market size of $660 million. If the market size is $660 million and we're going after 5 percent, the client is looking for sales of around $32 million.

Interviewer: What else?

Student: I'd like to compare that $32 million with the $850 million the client did in revenues last year to see what kind of revenue bump this would provide. So 10 percent is 85 million; 5 percent is around 42 million, so it's got to be around 3 percent. Not much of a bump. We could probably get that a variety of ways without the risk. But the rub is, the headphones market is growing at 75 percent. It makes it intriguing.

Interviewer: Anything else?

Student: One last thing. We did $850 million in revenues last year. The total high-end headphones industry was only $660 million. We're bigger than that entire industry.

Interviewer: That's right. What's the first thing that goes through your mind when you hear that?

Student: That the market's not big enough for us.

Interviewer: What's the second thing that goes through your mind?

Student: Acquisition.

Interviewer: Good. Earlier you laid out different ways for the client to enter the market. Go through them and give me the pros and cons of each.

Student: Can I take a minute to write down my thoughts?

Interviewer: No, I want you to list them off the top of your head.

Student: The first way for us to enter is to produce it in-house. The pros are that we would have total control over the design, process, and quality. Another pro would probably be a high margin in the long run. The cons would be that we don't have the knowledge, talent, or capability to manufacture the headphones, nor do we have the correct distribution channels. I think the biggest con would be time to market. This market's on fire and ...

Interviewer: What's next?

Student: Acquisition. The pros are that the company we purchase has everything we don't have, an existing product, manufacturing, market share, customer base, distribution channels, and industry knowledge. We probably couldn't afford to buy any of the big brands, so we'd have to go for a smaller player, which would mean the client wouldn't get the 5 percent it's looking for. We'll probably end up over-paying because the market is growing so fast. And we'd want to make sure that the company has a quality product that we'd feel comfortable putting our name on.

Interviewer: What's next?

Student: Wait. Most important, we need to make sure that the cultures of the two companies will mesh well, otherwise it could be a bloody nightmare. We're talking about an old-school company that crafts pianos by hand and a young electronic company working with plastics. I can't imagine two company cultures being further apart.

Interviewer: Okay, good. Next?

Student: A joint venture or strategic alliance. The pros would be similar to an acquisition; the cons would be loss of control – and we'd have to do $64 million in sales to reach our goal. Finally, outsourcing. The pros would be we'd have an expert producing the product for us, and the initial costs would be lower. It would be easy in and easy out if necessary. If for some reason it failed, we could exit the market gracefully. The con would be loss of control. We are basically turning over our brand to a third party and we'd still have to find new distribution channels.

Interviewer: We need to make a recommendation to the CEO. What do you tell him?

Student: Can I take a minute ...

Interviewer: No. He just walked into the room and is expecting an answer.

Student: My recommendation is that we not enter this market; 80 percent of the market is dominated by two major players. You have 24 other companies fighting for the remaining 20 percent. There are going to be others entering this market as well. We'd never get the 5 percent you want. We don't have the brand recognition nor the customer base needed to make this successful. Plus it represents only a 3 percent increase in revenues. I'd do two things instead to get that 3 percent increase. I'd come out with a lower-price line of instruments so more people can get into the brand. And I'd work to get rid of the classical music label, make it known that your instruments play more than just classical music. Maybe sign Alicia Keys to be a spokesperson. That will expand your customer base and increase your brand recognition. I know some purist might object, but in 1965 Bob Dylan walked out on the stage at the Newport Jazz Festival with an electric guitar for the first time, and although he got booed it worked out pretty well for him in the long run.

Interviewer: Let me tell you why you're wrong. I'd enter the market. I'd outsource it to company B, the one with the highest quality. The problem with Company B is that we'd have to charge $500 a pair, otherwise the company wouldn't manufacture for us because it would cannibalize its own brand. But I have no problem charging $500 a pair, in fact I'd charge $800 a pair, because we're the Ferrari of pianos. We need to be the Ferrari of headphones, otherwise it would hurt our brand. If we sold them for $800 we'd have to sell only 40,000 pairs to hit that $32 million target. That's a little more than 3,000 a month. And our existing client base is high-end consumers who could drop $800 on a pair of headphones and not think twice about it. You said the 3 percent or $32 million isn't much, but it turns into $56 million and then $98 million within three years. Finally I'd make the ear cups partially out of wood. We're woodworkers, right? We could make something that looks sleek, sophisticated, and sexy well worth $800.

Student: I think your strategy is brilliant, except for two things. Who buys headphones? For the most part it's young people maybe ages 12 – 32. Some can't afford $800 for a car, let alone a pair of headphones. And if they did pay $800 they'd expect the headphones to last at least five years, which is a lifetime to someone in their twenties. I don't think your market is sustainable and it certainly won't grow at 75 percent like the lower end of the market.

Interviewer: While I find your argument somewhat persuasive, I still want to participate in the growth of that market.

Student: Then I suggest you buy the underlying stock of company A. That way you can participate in the growth, no one is going to give you a hard time for going outside your core business, you can hedge your downside, and your investment is more liquid.

Interviewer: Okay, that was productive. Many thanks for coming in today.

(Case Takeaways)

- Ask about the company before the market in an entering-a new market question, so you can analyze it through the company's eyes and not just through your eyes.

- Always ask why they want to enter. This is an important clarifying question.
- Run out the numbers. The student not only figured out the size of the total market, he also figured out the 5 percent and then compared that with the company's revenues. Very few students ever run out these numbers. You need to do it to put things in perspective.
- Look at the big picture. I've given this case live over 200 times and *only two people* mentioned that the instrument company is bigger than the entire high-end headphones industry.
- The interviewer cut him off and wanted to move on, but he held his ground to get a key point in.
- Try to go beyond the expected answer. Adding a lower-priced product line and having Alicia Keys as spokesperson is a fairly common "don't enter" answer. However, he put a memorable twist on it with the Bob Dylan anecdote. His parents must have been hippies.
- The student defended his answer without getting defensive, and came back with a decent rebuttal.

+ IN THE RED

Interviewer: Our client is the number one player in the DVD rental kiosk market. They place kiosks in front of CVS, Wal-Mart, 7-Eleven, and multiple grocery stores and fast-food restaurants. Over the past seven years the client has installed more than 40,000 DVD rental kiosks, but this year for the first time, they are uninstalling more than 500 units. Last year the company's revenues rose by 3 percent to $2 billion, and it is projected to stay flat this year and then forecasted to decline for the next several years. The board of directors want to get ahead of this trend, so they've hired you to increase revenue 10 percent in the short term and then 5 percent a year for the next four years.

Student: Let me make sure I've got this right. The market leader in the DVD rental kiosk industry has installed 40,000 kiosks over the past seven years. Recently they've uninstalled 500 kiosks or about 1 percent of their machines. Although the company's revenues were up 3 percent last year to $2 billion, they've seen their sales flatten and are now facing declining revenues for the next several years. They've asked us to come up with a five-year plan that will increase revenues by 10 percent in the short term; that's $200 million and 5 percent a year for the next four years. Are there any other objectives I need to consider?

Interviewer: No.

Student: I have a clarifying question. What were the company's revenues for the last five years?

Interviewer: I have the last three years. Three years ago they were up 41 percent, last year they were flat, and this year revenues were up 3 percent.

Student: Why did they uninstall 500 kiosks?

Interviewer: They were unprofitable. The volume dropped. When the client puts a kiosk in front of a store, they need to pay that store rent, and they need to pay a licensing fee to the movie studios.

Student: Interesting. I'd like to investigate that more, but first I'd like to take a moment to write out my thoughts.

Interviewer: Fine.

[Student takes 90 seconds, draws out her notes, and then turns the notes toward the interviewer.]

Student: Let me show you what I have so far. I've broken it down into three buckets, the company, the movie rental industry, and ways to increase revenues. The client wants to raise its revenues by 10 percent this year. We know that revenue equals price times volume. Its revenues went from growing 41 percent to flat, and then up 3 percent. I want to know what happened. Next I'd like to look at their product mix and their distribution channels. Do they do any online streaming or downloading, or is it strictly kiosk-based? I'd also want to look at their pricing; when was the last time they raised their prices and what was the result? I'd like to review their costs ...

Interviewer: Why do you want to look at costs? This is a revenue case, not a profit case.

Student: Okay. Next I'd want to look at the industry. What are the industry drivers and what are the growth rates and trends for the last three years? Have there been any changes in the industry, mergers, or new technology? We need to look at the competition; are our direct competitors having the same issue? We should also analyze substitutions like Netflix, HBO, Amazon, and Hulu – places that stream video and offer downloading; piracy is an issue as well.

In my third bucket I'd like to explore ways to increase sales, not only through the traditional methods of increasing marketing, but maybe changing the product mix.

My hypothesis is that sales have gone flat because the physical DVD industry is in decline. I'd like to start with the company. Why did revenues go from climbing 41 percent one year to flat the next?

Interviewer: That was the last year the client installed new kiosks.

Student: Then why did the client's revenue go up 3 percent this year?

Interviewer: A change in product mix. We reduced the number of Blu-rays because they weren't selling, and increased the number of video games. What's nice about video games is that customers usually hang onto them for multiple nights, compared with just one night for movies.

Student: Can you tell me about their current product mix?

Interviewer: The client rents three items. DVD movies, Blu-ray movies, and video games. The DVD movies make up 70 percent of our sales and we charge $1.20 a night. Blu-rays make up 5 percent of our sales and we charge $1.50 a night. And video games make up 25 percent of our sales and they rent for $2 a night.

The student made this chart:

DVD Movies	$1.20	70%
Blue-ray	$1.50	5%
Video Games	$2.00	25%

Student: I'd like to go for the low-hanging fruit first. When was the last time we raised our prices and did we see much fallout? Did we lose many customers?

Interviewer: It's been almost three years since we raised them from $1 to $1.20 and we saw very little fallout. Say we decide to raise the price of a DVD from $1.20 to $1.50. How much additional revenue would that bring in? Assuming little customer fallout.

Student: Well, raising prices from $1.20 to $1.50 is a 25 percent increase. If the DVDs make up 70 percent of our revenues, that means 70 percent of $2 billion – which is $1.4 billion. We take the $1.4 billion and multiply it by .25 and we get $350 million. Which far exceeds the $200 million we need for a short-term gain of 10 percent. That buys us some time.

Interviewer: What's next?

Student: I'd like to stay with the product mix for a moment. Maybe there are other items we can sell through the kiosks. Are they retoolable?

Interviewer: Yes, to a certain degree.

Student: Who's our client base?

Interviewer: Who do you think?

Student: My guess is that it's made up of several demographics, low-to-middle-income families, gamers – so males between the ages of 12 and 32, the elderly, and people who live outside the infrastructure of the internet, where it might take them two weeks to download a movie.

Interviewer: Spot-on. What other products would you place in the kiosks?

Student: If that's our demographic... Let me think. Low-to-middle-income families. I'm thinking young kids. I saw an ad for Fatheads the other day – you know, the wall decals of famous athletes. While those are far too expensive, I'm thinking autographed color photos of Disney characters. Maybe even headphones or earbuds with Disney characters. When I was a kid we had educational computer games like Freddie Fish and Spy Fox. We could add those as well, which would extend rental times. For the gamers, maybe we can rent a controller. That way they can play against a friend. I'd want to be careful not to sell anything that the 7-Eleven we're sitting in front of might also sell, but that might prove tough. We want something that will raise the purchase price, maybe some sort of electronics such as a phone charger, earbuds, and other similar electronics. Can we put in more video games as well?

Interviewer: We've hit a limit with the number of video games we can rent. There are only so many titles. And while people will rent an old movie, they won't rent an old video game. Okay, in the short term we'll raise our price for DVD rentals and change the product mix. What's next?

Student: What can you tell me about the industry? What are the industry drivers? I assume our direct competition is having the same issues.

Interviewer: The industry drivers are distribution channels and content. The overall home entertainment industry is flat. We know that distribution channels are changing; digital downloads, both rentals and purchases, are up 46 percent. Subscription streaming, Netflix, and hulu are up 32 percent. Kiosk rentals are down 3 percent. There are three major players in the kiosk market; our client has 80 percent, Company B has 15 percent and Company C has 5 percent. And subscription rentals, such as physical rentals from Netflix, are down 19 percent. Netflix is trying to get customers away from physical DVDs and into streaming.

Student: So other kiosk players are facing the same problems. I might want to go after the disenfranchised Netflix customers who want to stick with DVDs but feel neglected. Maybe increase marketing overall.

Interviewer: In the short term your plan is to raise the price of the DVDs, change the product mix, and increase marketing. How about the long term?

Student: We need to reinstall the 500 kiosks. They're not making any money just sitting around. You said we uninstalled them because of low volume. Let's reinstall them in high-traffic areas. Subway or tube stops, train and bus stations, and domestic airports.

Interviewer: Give me the pros and cons of putting them in airports.

Student: For the pros, we can charge airport prices, maybe $3 a movie. Travelers can rent in one city and return in another. While there is internet on airplanes, it's not often strong enough to stream. People still need to bring their content with them for the most part. The cons are that many laptops don't have a CD drive any longer. So we might have to start putting content on flash drives if we can figure out a way for customers not to copy it. Another con is that planes show movies; some like JetBlue and Virgin even have DIRECTV. There's a lot of competition for people's time and attention. Most travelers come prepared; they bring a book or have already downloaded a movie.

Interviewer: Other long-term ideas?

Student: Have we thought about digital downloads, going head-to-head with Amazon and Apple?

Interviewer: Too expensive and we'd get eaten alive. It's a very competitive market.

Student: Okay then, are all the kiosks in the U.S.?

Interviewer: Yes.

Student: Then I'd look at other countries, perhaps Canada and Mexico. Their internet infrastructure probably isn't as good as in the U.S. They like American movies.

Interviewer: Give me the pros and cons of placing our kiosks in Brazil.

Student: I've never been to Brazil, but I would think that the pros would be a large population, low-income compared with American standards, so they might not have computers, but probably do have DVD players. Weak internet infrastructure would be another pro. It would also be a good distribution channel for local filmmakers. But I see many more cons. First they speak Portuguese, so movies would need to be dubbed. I don't believe many Brazilians carry credit cards, which would be essential. Piracy is an issue. Why pay a dollar to rent a movie when you can buy one for 50 cents? While servicing the kiosks in the cities might not be a problem, the more rural locations would be.

Interviewer: How would we get around the servicing issue?

Student: Some sort of service contract with a local company or – you know Coke is everywhere that we would be. Why not do a joint venture with Coke? They could purchase part of the international company and use the DVDs as a promotion.

Interviewer: Okay, summarize the case for me.

Student: The client's revenues have flattened, the industry has matured, and substitutions have hurt sales. We were tasked to develop a five-year plan, first to raise revenues by 10 percent the first year and then 5 percent every year after. We looked at the company, its pricing strategy, and its product mix – resulting in raising DVD prices by 25 percent and bringing in $150 million more than was requested. We changed and expanded the product mix. We looked at the industry, saw that our competitors are having the same issues, and we validated our hypothesis that the DVD market has matured and is in decline. In the long run we recommended expanding internationally and forming a strategic alliance with Coke. This will get the client through the next five years; however, they need to diversify their business model to secure long-term growth and survival.

Interviewer: Good. End of case. Thanks for coming by.

(Case Takeaways)

- The student's structure was good, but she should have divided into short-term and long-term solutions right up front.
- She asked about costs in a revenue case and was quickly corrected. She rolled with the punches and just moved on as if nothing had happened, which was the right thing to do. It's never bad to ask about costs, just be prepared to move on.
- Her clarifying questions were solid. Whenever you get a revenue case, always ask what the revenues did the previous three years. Consultants like to put things in perspective, which is why they always ask for trends, and why they quantify related numbers as percentages.
- She stated her hypothesis right after laying out her structure.
- In a revenue case it's not bad to write out revenues equals price times volume. It shows that you look at both sides of the equation. When I gave this case live, less than 40 percent of the students thought about raising the price.
- Her public math was solid. She walked the interviewer through her calculations as she did them.
- When she was coming up with ways to change the product mix, she thought about it by customer segmentation, which showed she is incredibly well organized.
- She didn't commingle or bounce back and forth between pros and cons.
- The student was able to go beyond the expected answer by coming up with creative options for new products and the idea of a joint venture with Coke.

+ RED ROCKET SPORTS

Interviewer: The Red Rocket Sports Company designs and markets apparel and footwear products under many brand names. All products are produced using similar manufacturing processes. Additionally, these products share similar distribution channels and are marketed and sold to similar types of customers. Take a look at the numbers below and tell me what's going on with Red Rocket Sports and where they should be concentrating their efforts. I'll be back in 30 minutes for your analysis.

Net Sales	Y3	Y2	Y1
Footwear	$2,430,300	$2,226,700	$2,050,000
Apparel	$1,355,000	$1,258,600	$1,050,000
Total	$3,785,300	$3,485,300	$3,100,000
Net Sales	**Y3**	**Y2**	**Y1**
US	$2,070,060	$2,020,000	$1,807,650
UK	$474,700	$444,700	$415,800
Europe	$810,400	$695,500	$607,400
Other	$430,140	$325,100	$269,150
Total	**$3,785,300**	**$3,485,300**	**$3,100,000**

(TAKE 30 MINUTES TO DO YOUR ANALYSIS, THEN READ ON)

After 30 minutes the interviewer comes back into the room and the candidate presents his findings to the interviewer.

Interviewer: Take me through your analysis.

Student: The first thing we need to look at is the yearly percentage changes by type of product and by area. *[Pulls out handmade chart.]* These numbers are estimated but should be pretty accurate.

	Y2/Y3	Y1/Y2
Product: Footwear	10%	10%
Apparel	10%	20%
Market: U.S.	2%	12%
UK	7%	7%
Europe	15%	15%
Other	30%	20%

There are a number of things we can infer from this chart:

- Footwear has grown consistently by about 10 percent over the last two years.
- Apparel growth has slowed, from 20 percent in Y1/Y2 to just under 10 percent in Y2/Y3.

- The U.S. market has had dramatic declining growth – from 12 percent to 2 percent, although it is still by far our biggest market.
- The UK growth has remained steady, at approximately 7 percent.
- The same is true for the European market, with a consistent growth rate of 15 percent.
- The most promising markets are the "other" markets, which I'll assume are Asia and Latin America. They grew by around 20 percent in Y2 and by just over 30 percent in Y3. At this rate, they will bypass the UK in total sales by next year. I believe that the "other" markets represent the highest area of potential growth.
- The action is in apparel, despite the slowdown in Y2/Y3.

Next, I looked at what part of the business each product line and market represents.

	Y3	Y2	Y1
Product: Footwear	65%	65%	65%
Apparel	35%	35%	35%
Market: U.S.	55%	60%	60%
UK	12%	12%	15%
Europe	20%	20%	20%
Other	11%	8%	8%

What this chart tells us:

- Footwear represents two-thirds of our sales and has remained as such over the last few years.
- The U.S. is by far our biggest market, making up more than half of our sales, but that number is inching down.
- The UK has inched down as well – declining from 15 percent to 12 percent. Europe has hung in at 20 percent.
- The "other" markets have inched up, now representing 11 percent of sales.

Our traditional markets in the U.S. and UK are mature, while the "other" markets have the highest growth rate. However, the traditional markets still represent the bulk of our business – over two-thirds of sales. And apparel sales have driven the growth rates over the last two years despite the slowdown in Y3.

Interviewer: How can you say that? Why do you have so much confidence in apparel?

Student: You need to look past the percentages and focus on the numbers themselves. Sales went from $3,100,000 in Y1 to $3,785,300 in Y3. That's an increase of $685,300. Of that number, apparel accounted for almost half, despite representing only 35 percent of sales.

Interviewer: Okay, so what should Red Rocket do about this?

Student: Action 1: Concentrate efforts on growth areas, particularly in "other" markets:

- Increase the product line, particularly in apparel.
- Increase distribution channels.
- Reinforce the sales force.
- Launch a major marketing campaign.

Action 2: Secure our traditional markets to maintain business:

- Launch marketing campaigns to boost sales in mature markets.
- Focus on best-performing distribution points and best-performing stores.

Action 3: Investigate market trends to anticipate future changes:

- Talk to industry analysts and get their opinion of the trends.
- Elaborate our strategy of product/market effort, based on info from experts.

It's easy to graph these recommendations in a 2x2 matrix.

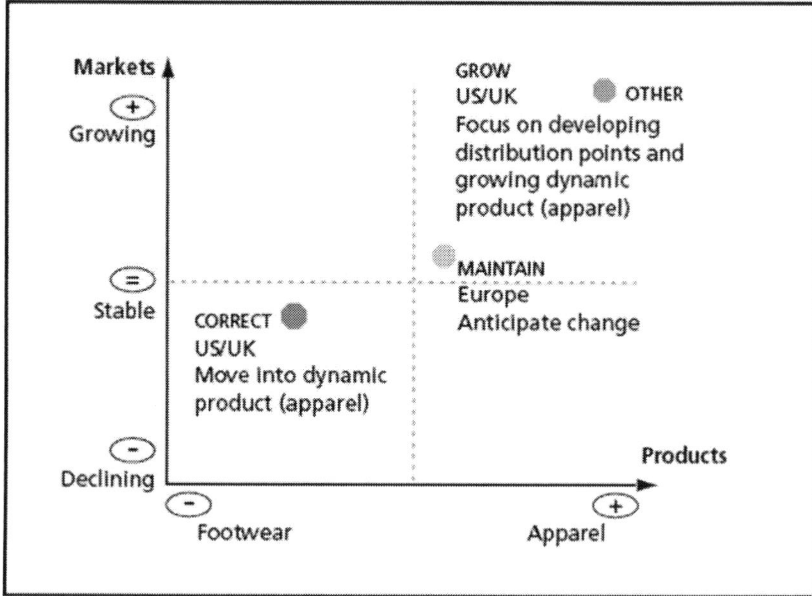

Type of Case: Company analysis
Comments: The student used charts and bullet points to make her presentation. She eyeballed the numbers because of the time constraint and the absence of a calculator. Remember, consultants use charts, graphs, and PowerPoint slides to get their points across with clients – you need to do the same.

+ COKE

Interviewer: The Coca-Cola Company is trying to boost profitability domestically by raising its prices. It's focusing on the grocery store market, where the volume is high but the margin is low. What are the economics of raising the prices, and is this a good idea?

Student: So, Coke plans to increase profitability by raising prices. It wants to know if that's a good idea.

Interviewer: That's right.

Student: I know that raising profitability is its main objective. Are there other objectives that I should be aware of?

Interviewer: It doesn't want to lose market share.

Student: Are we just focusing on Coke and not any of its other brands?

Interviewer: You can think of all Coke products as one product, Coke.

Student: What's Coke's current market share?

Interviewer: Not relevant to the question.

Student: How much does it cost to make a can of Coke?

Interviewer: Not relevant to the question.

Student: How many cans does Coke sell to U.S. grocery stores and at what price?

Interviewer: Coke sold 100 million cans at 23 cents each to grocery stores last year. If prices remain stable, it expects volume growth of 6 percent. It wants to raise the price to 27 cents per can and forecasts volume growth of only 1 percent.

Student: Let's see. First I can multiply and then find the difference:
100,000,000 cans x .27 x 1.01 = $27,270,000
100,000,000 cans x .23 x 1.06 = $24,380,000
Difference = $ 2,890,000

So even though Coke would be selling 5 million fewer cans, it'd be making more of a profit, about $3 million more.

Interviewer: Profitability would be boosted by what percent?

Student: I can take 27 minus 24 equals 3 divided by 24 equals approximately 12 percent. By raising prices and selling less, Coke can boost its sales by approximately 12 percent.

Interviewer: To maintain market share, Coke needs to stir up consumer demand with a major marketing campaign to raise brand awareness and focus on lifestyle issues. Knowing that, if you were Pepsi, what would you do?

Student: Pepsi has three choices. It can follow Coke's lead and raise its prices to match Coke's; it can leave prices the way they are; or it can take advantage of the price change and lower its price.

If Coke spends a fortune marketing its product and does its job and gets people into the stores, Pepsi can snatch sales away at the last minute with a lower price. We are talking grocery stores here. Women do most of the buying in grocery stores and are often price conscious. If they saw two brand-name colas, Pepsi and Coke, and Coke sold for $2.99 a 12-pack compared with $2.59 for a 12-pack of Pepsi, then most shoppers would choose the one on sale or the one with the lower price.

Pepsi might even want to lower its price so it could increase its market share.

In sailing, if you are behind, you're not going to catch up with or beat the opponent by sailing the same course. You have to take a different tack. If Pepsi lowers its prices and cuts marketing costs, it can steal customers away from Coke, through in-store promotions and point-of-contact displays.

Interviewer: So, if you were Pepsi, what would you do?

Student: Let's run some numbers. How many cans does Pepsi sell to grocery stores?

Interviewer: Pepsi sells 80 million cans at 23 cents apiece. If Pepsi follows Coke and raises its prices, its volume will drop from 6 percent to 3 percent. If Pepsi keeps its price the same, its volume will increase from 6 percent to 12 percent.
If Pepsi lowers its prices to 21 cents, Pepsi's volume will increase from 6 percent to 20 percent.

Student: Okay, let me run some numbers.

80,000,000 x 1.03 = 82,400,000 x .27 = 22,248,000
80,000,000 x 1.12 = 89,600,000 x .23 = 20,608,000
80,000,000 x 1.20 = 96,000,000 x .21 = 20,160,000

I'd follow Coke's lead.

Interviewer: Even if you knew that Coke's volume would rise from 1 percent to 3 percent?

Student: Yes.

Interviewer: Interesting. Thanks.

Type of case: Strategy based on numbers.

Comments: It's a straightforward case once you have the numbers. The student should have figured out the percentage change without the interviewer having to ask her for it.

+ THE UP-IN-SMOKE CIGARETTE COMPANY

Interviewer: The Up-in-Smoke Cigarette Company, which manufactures cigarettes, is considering outsourcing its distribution truck fleet to an independent company. To continue providing this service in-house, they would have to significantly upgrade their fleet to conform with new regulations requiring commercial trucks to provide electronic records of their itineraries – including average and maximum speed, time driven continuously, and the length of driver breaks.

The chief operating officer (COO) has hired you to help her decide: Should they outsource, or should they upgrade the fleet and continue doing distribution in-house?

Student: Our client is a cigarette company that is trying to decide whether to outsource its delivery function. They've asked us to determine whether it is best to outsource the work or keep it in-house. Are there any other objectives we need to focus on?

Interviewer: No. Do you have a problem with having a cigarette company as your client?

Student: It wouldn't be my first choice, but no.

Interviewer: We don't always get to pick our clients. If this might be a problem, then tell me now.

Student: It's not a problem.

Interviewer: Okay, then proceed.

Student: To help the COO decide, I will consider two main factors: the economics of such a move and the associated risks.

Under the economic factors, I will compare the needed investments in the truck upgrade with the potential costs or savings from outsourcing.

Under the risks, I will look at both the internal and external risks. Internally, I will look at the cultural impact and impacts on labor – including the potential of a strike. Externally, I will look at the bigger macroeconomic risks – cost of gasoline, government regulations, and future flexibility versus competition.

Interviewer: Okay, good. Where would you want to start?

Student: I would like to start with the economics of the problem. I would like to figure out the costs for both outsourcing and keeping it in-house. Also, I would like to know the estimated investments and the company's required payback period.

Interviewer: It would cost the company about $1 million to upgrade its fleet, including trade-ins on the old trucks. Essentially, it would have to buy new trucks, as the current trucks are old and the COO figures they are due for replacement soon anyway. The company requires a four-year payback on all its investments. For detailed information on the costs associated with both in-house deliveries and outsourcing, please take a look at the following table.

	In-house	Outsource
# of Deliveries	400	400
Average Cost of Delivery	?	$2,400
Labor Costs	?	N/A
Insurance	$200	$100
Gas	$200	N/A
Maintenance (per delivery, includes oil change, tires, etc.)	$100	N/A
Cost per Delivery	?	?

Student: In order to determine the difference between outsourcing and in-house deliveries, I need to determine the labor cost per delivery. Can you tell me more about labor costs? How many full-time drivers do we have and how much do we pay them on average?

Interviewer: We have 10 full-time drivers that we employ for $5,000 per month, including benefits.

Student: Great. That means the salary costs are 10 drivers times 12 months times $5,000 per month, which is $600,000 per year. We divide $600,000 by 400 deliveries and we now know that the labor cost per delivery is $1,500. When we add the additional costs, we have the total in-house cost per delivery of $2,000. In the case of outsourcing, the total cost is $2,500.

Overall, our client would save $500 per delivery or $500 times 400 deliveries, which equals $200,000 per year with in-house distribution.

However, when we compare that with the required investment of $1 million, we get a payback of five years, which is longer than the required payback of our client.

Interviewer: How'd you get five years?

Student: I divided 1 million by 200,000 and got five.

Interviewer: Okay, good. What's your final recommendation?

Student: Just looking at the economics of the move, I would recommend outsourcing the delivery to the independent company. However, I would like to analyze some of the risks involved.

As I mentioned initially, the internal risks are worth analyzing. For example, I would like to consider the potential impacts of this move to our internal culture – we'd be firing ten drivers. Also, I would like to assess the potential for a strike should we decide to outsource this service.

Interviewer: Those are good points, but our drivers are not unionized and we estimate the culture will not change significantly. Can you think of anything else?

Student: Yes, actually. Looking at external factors, I can see some benefits in outsourcing. Especially if we sign longer-term contracts, by outsourcing we externalize the risk for the increase in the price of gas and the changes in government regulations. These are important risks to a company like ours and are significant benefits to our company. Additionally, outsourcing would maintain the flexibility of our distribution if our company expands.

Interviewer: Great answer. Now let's change hats and try to figure out how to make the in-house deliveries work. What would be some of your suggestions?

Student: Well, we have a few variables. For the in-house deliveries to work, we would need:

Investment < savings from in-house times payback period.

Therefore, we could do several things.

1. We could lower the needed investment. We could do this by leasing or renting the trucks instead of buying them.
2. We could increase the payback period beyond four years.
3. We could increase savings from in-house deliveries. Here, we have several options as well:
    a) We could increase the number of deliveries, either for our company or for smaller companies, in order to increase the utilization of our drivers.
    b) We could reduce maintenance costs by outsourcing that job alone.
    c) We could introduce new software to determine more efficient routing for our trucks, thus saving on gas and maintenance.

Interviewer: Excellent. Thank you.

Type of case: Reducing costs, in-sourcing versus out-sourcing

Comments: You're not always going to get the clients you want, and you need to think this through. Many consulting firms will try to reassign you if you have a legitimate reason for not wanting to be on the case, but they can't always control it because it has to do with scheduling. The student did well. He analyzed the simple chart and was able to fill in the blanks. He looked at both external and internal factors and came up with good recommendations on both sides of the issue.

+ CABANA FEET

Interviewer: Cabana Feet, LLC makes gel-flow flip-flops. These are like traditional flip-flops but have the comfort of a gel insole. They come in a variety of sizes and colors. Earlier this year, Brad Pitt wore them in his latest film, and they have become all the rage. Now, Cabana Feet is struggling to keep up with demand. Cabana Feet is the only flip-flop maker producing its footwear entirely in the U.S. This has been a selling point in their advertisements for the last 10 years. Thus, it can't outsource production to other flip-flop makers. Take a look at the chart below and lay out for me in broad strokes some short-term and long-term strategies that it might review.

Student: Our client is a company called Cabana Feet. They make gel-flow flip-flops. It looks like the company was producing about 6,000 pairs a month. Demand suddenly shot up when Brad Pitt wore their flip-flops in a movie. Cabana can't outsource because they are the only flip-flop maker in the U.S. and a big part of their advertising rides on the fact that their product is American made.

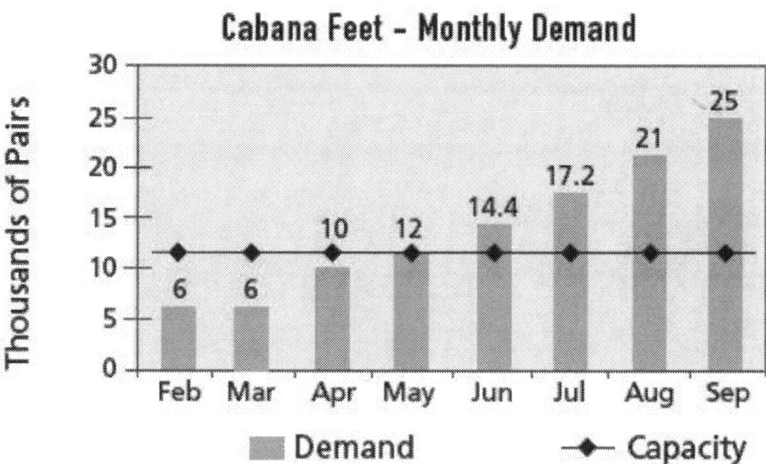

Interviewer: That's right.

Student: You want me to come up with some short-term and long-term strategies to help the company meet demand. Are there any other objectives I should be aware of?

Interviewer: No.

Student: Can I ask a few questions?

Interviewer: Absolutely.

Student: Judging by the chart, our capacity is 12,000 pairs of flip-flops a month.

Interviewer: Yes.

Student: I'm assuming that the movie came out in April.

Interviewer: Yes.

Student: This is September, so the 25,000 number is an estimate?

Interviewer: That's right.

Student: Have we been able to fill the orders up until now, or are there thousands of pairs back-ordered?

Interviewer: We've been able to fill the orders because of inventory; however, we'll run out of inventory at the end of the month.

Student: Do we expect the trend to continue? When does the DVD come out?

Interviewer: The DVD comes out in December. What are your thoughts on the trend?

Student: I would expect the trend to level off after the DVD's release. But our strategy must take into consideration two scenarios. First, what happens if Brad Pitt wears construction boots in his next movie and sales fall back to the 6,000 pairs a month number? And what can we do if it levels off at around 25,000 pairs?

Interviewer: Okay, good. What are you thinking? How can we meet demand?

Student: I have a couple of ideas. First, we put on more shifts if we haven't already. Ask employees if they want to work weekends and a third shift. If not, then hire new employees for those shifts. Second, I'd do a complete analysis of the current production line. See if there are any bottlenecks. See how we can squeeze more pairs out of each shift without compromising quality. Third, look for labor-saving devices or technologies that would boost production without committing to another production line. Fourth, build another production line or even another factory. Fifth, Econ 101 – raise our prices. And, sixth, outsource production.

Interviewer: There is no one inside the U.S. that can help us. So the only option is to go outside the U.S.

Student: Then go outside the U.S.

Interviewer: And throw away our marketing campaign of the last 10 years? We'd get crucified in the press.

Student: Not if we go to the business press and argue that this is a temporary measure, that for us to meet demand we need to go outside the U.S. Once we can meet demand with U.S. manufacturing, then we'll bring everything back home. Look, our sales jumped from 6,000 pairs a month to 25,000 pairs a month. Assume that 5,000 of the original 6,000 customers bought our shoes because they were made in the U.S. I think that number is high, but let's assume it to be true. That means that we have 20,000 new customers who are more interested in looking like Brad Pitt from the ankles down than whether the flip-flops are made in the U.S.

We can't miss this opportunity. If we don't get those flip-flops on the market, someone else will. We have to worry about knock-offs and new competition.

Interviewer: All right. By what percentage did the company's demand grow from March to April?

Student: It went from 6,000 pairs to 10,000 pairs. That's 10 – 6 = 4 4/6 = .66 or 66 percent.

Interviewer: I'm going to give you some additional information. At the plant, workers make $15 an hour. Supervisors make $20 an hour. Each shift uses 10 workers and one supervisor. Each shift is eight hours long. Assume 20 work days in a month. Got it?

Student: Got it.

Interviewer: What would be the labor costs of one shift if benefits equal 30 percent of wages and there is a miscellaneous cost of $232 per shift?

Student: Workers' wages, $15 an hour; times eight hours times 10 workers equals $1,200. The supervisor costs are $160. I got that by multiplying $20 by eight hours. Total wages are $1,360 times 30 percent equals 408. So $1,360 plus $408 equals $1,768, plus the miscellaneous cost of $232, equals $2,000 per shift.

Interviewer: Good. Now assume that the total costs per shift, fixed and variable, equal $2,000. Cabana makes $8 a pair, up to production capacity. What is the shift break-even point? How many pairs of flip-flops does the company have to make each shift to break even?

Student: That would be $2,000 divided by $8 equals ... 250 pairs of flip-flops.

Interviewer: Capacity is 12,000 pairs of flip-flops a month. Capacity equals two shifts a day, five days a week. Given a normal eight-hour shift, what is the maximum production per shift?

Student: For a single shift?

Interviewer: Yes, a single shift. I want you to think out loud when you do the math.

Student: Okay. I'll take 12,000 pairs and divide that by two shifts. So each shift makes 6,000 pairs per month. Next, I'll divide the 6,000 pairs by 20 work days in the month and I'll get 300 pairs of flip-flops per shift.

Interviewer: How much would a third shift increase our capacity?

Student: It would increase it by 6,000 pairs and push it from 12,000 to 18,000.

Interviewer: If we started a third shift using our current employees, what would be the cost of the third shift? How much would our profits per pair of flip-flops change? Keep in mind that wages would go to time-and-a-half. And you'll need to add in the miscellaneous cost as well.

Student: Workers' wages at time-and-a-half would jump to ... $1,800 ($22.50 x 10 x 8) and the supervisor's costs would be $240 (30 x 8). That totals to $2,040. Multiply 2,040 by 30 percent for benefits and that equals $612, so that's $2,652 plus the miscellaneous $232. So the total is $2,884. So $2,884 minus $2,000 equals $884 in additional costs. Divide the $892 by 300 pairs and it equals ... $2.97. Thus we have $8 minus $2.97 equals $5.03 per pair.

Interviewer: What are some of the pros and cons of adding a triple shift using our current workers?

Student: Can I take a minute to think this through?

Interviewer: Sure.

The student draws a line down the center of his page. He writes out the pros and cons and presents them in bulk – all the pros first, then all the cons.

Pros	Cons
Able to meet demand up to 18,000 pairs without major new investment	Possible worker burnout
More total profits	Lowers profit per pair
Helps keep competitors out	Higher wear and tear on the machinery
Saves on hiring and training costs of new employees	Might lower quality of product; may have to throw out some pairs
Easy to get back to normal production levels	Less time for maintenance
Better utilization of equipment	Suppliers might not be able to meet our demand

Interviewer: By adding a third shift we'll be able to produce only 18,000 pairs a month. You said earlier that you thought demand would level out at 25,000 pairs. If we add a new line that produces 800 pairs a day, this includes two shifts; is this enough?

Student: Well, 800 pairs a day equals 16,000 pairs a month, given 20 workdays in a month. Add to that the current capacity of 12,000 pairs and we total 28,000 pairs a month. If demand is greater than that, we can go as high as 42,000 pairs if we put on triple shifts on the new line and the old line.

Interviewer: Summarize the case for me.

Student: Our client, Cabana Feet, has seen demand for its flip-flops skyrocket from 6,000 pairs a month to 25,000 pairs within a six-month period. While we'll assume that demand might continue to grow for a few more months, we're thinking that it will settle down at around 25,000 pairs a month. Current capacity is only 12,000 pairs a month. We've been able to meet demand because of inventory on hand; however, the inventory is now down to nothing. We came up with six short-term and long-term strategies to fix the problem. The main options are putting on more shifts, streamlining our production process, and outsourcing production to another manufacturer outside the U.S.

We learned that our break-even point is 250 flip-flops per shift and that our capacity is 300 pairs per shift. We talked about the pros and cons of putting on a third shift, including watching our profit per pair drop from $8 to about $5 a pair. And finally, we are considering adding a new line, which could increase our overall production to 42,000 pairs a month. That's a 250 percent increase over our current double shift capacity.

Interviewer: Good. Thanks for coming by.

Type of case: Production and strategy case

Comments: The student did very well. He was quick to come up with some long-term and short-term strategies. He held his own when the interviewer pushed him about the outsourcing question. His math skills were solid and he tried to quantify his answer when he could.

+ WIRELESS WORRIES

Interviewer: In Q4, the number three U.S. wireless carrier slipped further behind its rivals in its number of customers, even as profits rose 35 percent. What do you think is going on?

Student: Profits are up, but the number of customers is down. We need to figure out why this is happening.

Interviewer: That's right.

Student: How many customers did we lose in Q4?

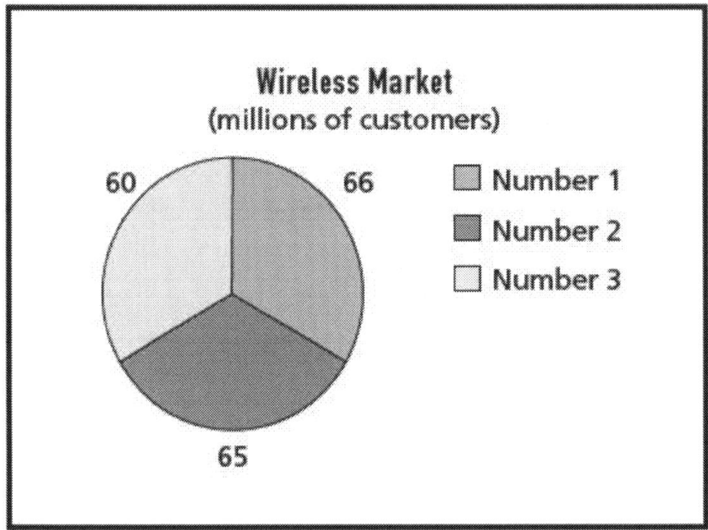

Interviewer: As you can see, we closed the year with 60 million customers. That takes into account a loss of 2.5 percent, or 1.5 million customers lost in Q4.

Student: Annually, that's 10 percent of our customer base for the year.

Interviewer: That's right.

Student: Besides figuring out why we're losing so many customers, are there any other objectives I need to be concerned about?

Interviewer: Not at the moment.

The student writes E(P = R –C)M.

Student: I'd like to start by looking at the industry. Are the other two major wireless companies losing customers as well?

Interviewer: Yes, but not in such large numbers. Traditionally, wireless companies lose about 1 percent of their customer base each quarter. However, they gain much more than they lose.

Student: Did we gain more than we lost?

Interviewer: Yes. We gained 2 million new customers that quarter.

Student: Next, I'd like to know why we are losing so many customers?

Interviewer: Why do you think?

Student: It could be any number of reasons: the other companies might have a better and more reliable network, more effective advertising, better pricing, cooler phones, or better customer service.

Interviewer: Assume all that is true, but it makes up only a small portion of our losses. Why else?

Student: Did we have a satellite problem, causing our network to go down for a while?

Interviewer: No.

The student struggles to come up with other reasons, so the interviewer tosses her a bone.

Interviewer: What if we wanted to lose those customers?

Student: I'm not sure I understand.

Interviewer: One of our major concerns is bad debt. We spend a lot of time, effort and money on bill collection. It's a runaway cost. We spend so much time trying to get new accounts that we don't do a proper job vetting our customers' credit. Here's a chart for you to study. What does it say to you?

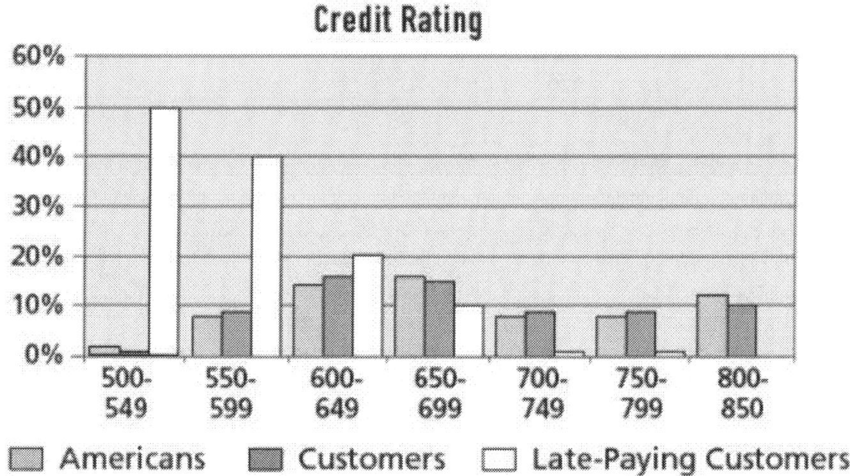

Student: It tells me that people with credit ratings between 500 and 600 are a problem. Is it worth keeping them as customers? Let's figure out how many customers we're talking about. According to the first pie chart, we have 60 million customers. It looks as if 1 percent of our customers fall into the 500 – 549 range. They pay late 50 percent of the time. Is it the same 50 percent who pay late every month?

Interviewer: Not necessarily. You can assume that everyone in that group has been late paying the bill at some point, some more than others.

Student: If we eliminate them as customers, that's 600,000 customers. The next group isn't much better. We can see that 40 percent of them pay late. This is a bigger pool. We're looking at 9 percent of the customer base, or around 5.4 million customers. If we dropped those two groups from our customer lists, that would set us back 6 million customers and put us at 54 million. In turn we would be 10 million customers behind the number-two wireless company.

Interviewer: So?

Student: How much does it cost us to collect late payments from each customer?

Interviewer: $50.

Student: How much is the average bill?

Interviewer: Overall, it's $75.

Student: So we're paying $50 to collect $75. Are our margins so great that we're still making money off those customers?

Interviewer: No. Profit margins are 25 percent.

Student: Do we charge a late fee?

Interviewer: No.

Student: What percentage of those customers abandon their accounts altogether, leaving us holding the bag?

Interviewer: Good question, but I don't have the figure for that. Run some numbers for me. How much will we be saving if we drop all 6 million customers?

Student: We have 6 million late-paying customers with average bills of $75. That's revenues of ... $450 million. Our margins are 25 percent, which brings the number down to a little less than $115 million. We need to add the cost of collection. Some customers pay late 50 percent of the time, others 40 percent of the time. Let's average it and call it 45 percent. So 45 percent of 6 million customers is 2.7. We have 2.7 million customers who pay late. We spend $50 trying to recover the money; that's $135 million. So we're losing $20 million a month going after those customers.

Interviewer: So what do you suggest?

Student: We can do a couple of things. Shed the high-risk late payers. Vet new customers better. Require them to have a 600 credit rating or better. Start charging a late fee and go after the customer collections every two months instead of every month. If we do that, we're spending $50 to go after $150.

Interviewer: That's right.

Type of case: Reducing costs

Comments: She just did all right. The student's math was solid. She figured out the annual loss of customers even though the numbers given to her were quarterly. She got stuck and the interviewer came to the rescue, but the student didn't pick up on the hint. She came up with a decent list of suggestions, which showed she listened. Also, she did a good job analyzing the second chart. It's a hard chart. It is not well designed and it has a lot of information on it. Oftentimes, the interviewers will give you badly designed charts to test your analytical skills.

+ THE DISCOUNT BROKERAGE RACE

Interviewer: Look at this chart. Your client is a discount brokerage. Most of its revenue comes from online trading. It achieved a 10 percent growth rate last year (Y1) and was ranked number six in the industry. In Y2 it fell to seventh. The company wants to get back its sixth-place ranking. How much will it have to grow to maintain that sixth-place ranking in Y3, given the rate of growth of its competitors?

Company	Industry Ranking	Current Size Y1 (Revenue)	Growth Rate	Y2	Industry Ranking
A	1	$1000m	1 %	1010	1
B	2	$900m	2 %	918	2
C	3	$800m	0 %	800	4
D	4	$800m	5 %	840	3
E	5	$700m	5 %	735	5
F	6	$600m	10 %	660	7
G	7	$600m	20 %	720	6
H	8	$500m	20 %	600	8
I	9	$500m	10 %	550	9
J	10	$400m	30 %	520	10
K	11	$300m	20 %	360	11
L	12	$300m	30 %	390	12

Student: Our client is Company F, a discount brokerage. In Y1 we were ranked sixth with a growth rate of 10 percent and sales of $600 million. In Y2 we dropped to seventh place with a growth rate of 10 percent and revenues of $660 million. You want me to figure out how much we will have to grow in order to get our sixth-place ranking back in Y3.

Interviewer: Yes, that's right.

Student: Is it fair to assume that the growth rates of all the other firms will remain the same?

Interviewer: Yes.

Student: Do you mind if I write on the chart you gave me?

Interviewer: No, go ahead.

Student: I'm going to do part of this through a process of elimination. Everyone below Company F growing at a smaller or equal rate, or whose revenues are significantly below ours, can be eliminated. So that's easily the bottom four – Companies I through L.

We know that A and B will remain the top two. So I'll concentrate on C through H, including us – F. So, first, I'm going to do the calculations for each of those and see where they stand.

Company	Industry Ranking	Current Size Y1 (Revenue)	Growth Rate	Y2	Industry Ranking	Y3	Industry Ranking
A	1	$1000m	1 %	1010	1		1
B	2	$900m	2 %	918	2		2
C	3	$800m	0 %	800	4	800	5
D	4	$800m	5 %	840	3	882	3
E	5	$700m	5 %	735	5	772	6
F	6	$600m	10 %	660	7	726	7
G	7	$600m	20 %	720	6	864	4
H	8	$500m	20 %	600	8	720	
I	9	$500m	10 %	550	9		
J	10	$400m	30 %	520	10		
K	11	$300m	20 %	360	11		
L	12	$300m	30 %	390	12		

If we stayed at a 10 percent growth rate, we'd have revenues of $726 million, which would put us in seventh place.

Interviewer: So, how fast do we need to grow?

Student: If we round Company E's sales off to $772 then that's our target number. We need to beat 772. So we need an increase of over $46 million (772 – 726). So 660X = 772. Divide each side by 660 and we get X equals ... about 1.17 or 17 percent. A minimum 17 percent growth in Y3 would put us in sixth place.

Company	Year 3	Industry Ranking
A		1
B		2
C	800	5
D	882	3
E	771.75	7
F	772	6
G	864	4
H	720	8

Interviewer: Okay, good. Which company would you invest in and why?

Student: I'd invest in Company G, provided it can continue its 20 percent growth rate.

Type of case: Numbers

Comments: This case was a pure numbers case. The student did well by eliminating what was obvious and using her time efficiently.

+ Government and Nonprofit Cases

Many firms have both commercial and public sector clients and the same core skills are needed for either client. While it is common to specialize in commercial or public sector consulting, it is not out of the ordinary for consultants to cross over and support both sectors. Fortunately, the four key competencies remain the same: structure of thought, confidence level, communication skills, and going beyond the expected answer. There are several primary distinctions between commercial and public sector cases.

In the public sector, one must have a stronger understanding of the stakeholders. Oftentimes, recommendations require consensus, building bridges across divisions, and navigating or showing commonalities between seemingly distinct agendas. In public sector cases, one must be critically aware of who the decision makers are (yes, this can be plural), who are the regulators, who are the influencers, along with possible detractors who need to be won over or neutralized. In these cases, you need to determine the chain-of-command and who should have a seat at the table.

Potential stakeholders could include employees, private citizens, donors, unions, watchdog and oversight committees, Congress, private and public sector partnerships, personnel receiving services, and vendors offering services.

Public sector cases have more of a mission motive rather than a profit motive. While cost savings and managing budgets are important, there should always be a tie back to how costs influence mission effectiveness and stakeholders. Public sector organizations provide a service, and managing scarce resources more effectively may enable the organization to provide services to better meet their mission. Budget should be viewed through a lens of the impact on the mission and stakeholders who use the organization's services.

There are certain levers that are more common in private sector cases than in public sector cases. In the private sector, you might be able to recommend re-structuring, outsourcing, mergers and acquisitions, and quick implementation of a technology solution. In the public sector, people are more likely to be re-purposed or re-trained rather than laid off, services may be "outsourced" through contracting or by forming strategic partnerships. Mergers or re-structuring of organizations may be a lengthy process that needs to consider impact on the mission, culture, and stakeholders.

In public sector cases, an organization or agency sets itself apart by showing impact. Oftentimes, public sector clients are competing for dollars – whether from donors, corporate sponsors, or Congress. Organizations make a business case for these dollars by showing mission relevance, addressing a public need, and showing impact. If another organization or agency with a similar mission set broadens its mission or shows greater impact, they may receive more money in a limited pool of dollars.

In federal cases, there is no competitive threat or response. The only threat is failure, which may harm the stakeholder's mission, chances of promotion, and your firm's chances of additional work.

Types of cases:

The types of cases will vary depending on your client. Is it a federal government agency, a nonprofit/NGO, a state or city tourism department, or the government of a developing nation? When preparing for a public-sector case, consider the operating environment, the mission of the organization, and the key stakeholders.

Common public sector cases may include, but are not limited to:

- Building a business case for receiving a larger budget from Congress
- Change management through the development of new systems, technology, and roles and responsibilities
- Consolidating services or building a shared services model between divisions or agencies
- Optimizing services to better meet public needs
- Updating outdated infrastructure or legacy technology systems

In other words, cases could be about innovation, building scale, operations strategy, optimization, cost reduction, investment, supply chain optimization, distribution of services, organizational behavior, collaboration with the private sector, enhancing mission delivery, and there could also be a market-sizing component.

What interviewers look for

For the most part, the competencies are similar in public sector and private sector cases. Interviewers look for structure, confidence, communication skills, analysis (qualitative and quantitative), critical thinking skills, and creativity. Coming up with solutions that others haven't thought about, that provide flexible, scalable and cost-efficient options, both for the short-term and long-term.

Interviewers will want to see that you are considering impact to the mission and stakeholders and you are considering common constraints that public sector clients might face.

7 common constraints

1. **Accountability** – Where does ultimate ownership for the output reside?
2. **Acquisitions** – What are the requirements for any outside solution? How much time will it take to receive sign-off for a contracting solution?
3. **Funding** – Is there money available in the budget to support this solution?
4. **Mission scope** – Is the solution aligned with the mission of the organization?
5. **Personnel** – Do personnel have the skills to complete their roles and responsibilities? What training is available to prepare personnel for their roles and responsibilities?
6. **Politics** – Is the political climate or the agendas of leaders and key stakeholders supportive of this recommendation?

7. **Time** – When does the solution need to be implemented? Are there steps that can be taken in the short, intermediate, and long term to move the organization toward an optimal solution?

Interviewers also want to make sure that you can speak the language (e.g. saying "agency" not "company" or "department," "taxpayers/donors" and not "shareholders," "mission effectiveness" not "bottom line," "repurposing" not "downsizing," "contracting" and not "outsourcing.")

Other differentiators include being able to use analogies by tying prior experience or understanding to the case – such as highlighting something experienced in the private sector and adapting/modifying it for the public sector. Context matters! When adapting something you read or from your previous experience, be sure to highlight how it would be adapted, how it would affect the mission and stakeholders, and how constraints could modify this solution.

Although politics could play a role and may put constraints on some of your options, leave out political editorializing. Show awareness of the political climate. Be nonpartisan and recognize that you are providing a service to a client who provides a service to the public.

Accessing risk and making a recommendation

Recommendations – lead with the answer and be definitive. Explain why (including the metrics if possible), how, the risks, and the next steps – both in the short term, intermediate term, and long term. In government cases, many recommendations can be built around the strategies of consolidation, automation, simplification, or elimination – reducing redundancies and streamlining.

A common lens for reviewing public sector cases is People, Process, Technology (PPT). **People**: What personnel do you currently have? What skills are needed? What incentives or training is in place? What is the chain of command? **Process**: Are there standard operating procedures (SOPs) in place? Are these SOPs documented and followed consistently? What are the measures of success? **Technology**: What systems are used? Are these systems aligned – do they "talk" to each other? How is data collected and is there any manual piece that leaves the data open to human error (input, interpretation, consolidation of data)?

Prioritize risks based on impact and likelihood of occurrence.

Here are some additional tips to prepare for such an interview.

Prepare like you would for a corporate interview. Spend time on Chapter 4. Scan the interviewer's website and elsewhere, looking for types of clients and projects it has had in the past. Search the interviewing firm for recent articles or news. Find the names of alums, faculty, and current graduate students who have either worked for the firm or have public sector experience. Talk to them once you have gained an understanding of the sector and conducted your due diligence.

For federal government interviews read Government Accountability Office (GAO) and Office of Inspector General (OIG) reports. These are "watchdog" reports on specific agencies and offices that ensure that the agencies are operating effectively. The reports provide an understanding of the issues, methodology, findings, and recommendations. It shows the interviewer that you have taken an extra step to prepare and it allows you to have an educated conversation about their agency or common issues impacting the public sector.

Read white papers on government and specific agencies written by the consulting firms.

Stay informed – there are a number of newsletters and websites geared toward the public sector. Follow the news – consider why issues may be occurring, who the stakeholders are, how they are affected, and what is the root cause of each issue. You should stay informed on views from both sides of the aisle, not just the current administration or your own political orientation.

Familiarize yourself with major government agencies, their missions and acronyms. However, if the interviewer throws out an acronym and you're not 100 percent certain what it stands for, ask. If you guess and get it wrong, you've lost the interviewer's trust. Because if you do that in something as important as an interview, what will you do in front of a client?

Sample questions:

State and Local Government:

1. Our client is the mayor's office of a major city on the eastern seaboard. It has hired us to help put together a bid for the Amazon HQ2 headquarters.

2. Puerto Rico was devastated by hurricanes. It lost much of its infrastructure, electrical power, and roads – and many of its best workers. The Governor's office has hired you to help revitalize the island's industry attractiveness.

3. The city of Santa Maria has hired you to help revitalize its downtown area, which is plagued with empty storefronts and a growing homeless population. What's the plan?

Federal:

1. The Department of Veterans Affairs (VA) budget was reduced by 10 percent. How do we best redeploy resources to lessen the impact on client services, while still maintaining a good public image?

2. Puerto Rico was devastated by hurricane Maria. It lost much of its infrastructure, electrical power, and roads – and many of its best workers. The Federal Emergency Management Agency (FEMA) has hired you to help determine who should be deployed to help Puerto Rico address the devastation and revitalize the island.

3. Health and Human Services (HHS) is looking to build a reputation for innovation. It has designated a program to access innovative ideas within the agency. HHS has hired you to help build the brand and extend the program across government. What steps would you take to help increase adoption of this program?

Nonprofit:

1. A nonprofit with the mission of honoring educators was recently commissioned by Congress to design a museum that tells the story of educators in America. This mandate has dramatically increased the nonprofit's scope and base. The nonprofit has hired you to help develop a strategy for this mandate. What steps should the nonprofit take to successfully launch the museum?

2. Our client is a nonprofit responsible for providing temporary housing to the homeless. The nonprofit and its donors have noted that while temporary housing addresses the immediate need, it may not address the root cause of homelessness. The client is considering merging with an organization that can provide support services that will reduce recidivism and enable the homeless population to become more self-sufficient. What organizations should it consider merging with?

3. A growing nonprofit has recognized a need for recruiting doctors for low-income neighborhoods, and intends to develop a corps of doctors committed to working in a low-income neighborhood for a designated time. They have hired you to develop a recruitment strategy. What factors would you consider in order to increase their prospects for success?

Read "The Best Shot" and "Mismatch – A Federal Case" on the following pages.

+ THE BEST SHOT

Interviewer: The Gates Foundation is the largest private foundation in the U.S., holding $38 billion in assets. The foundation has poured $218 million into polio and measles immunization and research worldwide. Foundation leaders have asked you to reduce the supply chain costs while expanding the vaccination program. How can this be achieved?

Student: The Gates Foundation has asked us to reduce its supply chain costs and expand its polio and measles vaccination program. Are there any other mission goals or objectives I should be concerned with?

Interviewer: No.

Student: Can you tell me a little about the current vaccination program?

Interviewer: Vaccines are among the most cost-effective health interventions ever developed. Immunization has led to the eradication of smallpox, a 74 percent reduction in childhood deaths from measles over the past decade, and the near-eradication of polio.

One in five children worldwide is not fully protected with even the most basic vaccines. As a result, an estimated 1.5 million children die each year – that's one every 20 seconds. These are preventable diseases. Vaccines are often too expensive for those in the world's poorest countries, and supply shortages and lack of trained health workers are the two main problems. Other problems include unreliable transportation systems and storage facilities – many of the vaccines require refrigeration.

Student: You said supply shortages. What companies manufacture these vaccines? And why are there shortages?

Interviewer: The two manufacturers are French drugmaker Sanofi Pasteur and Serum Institute of India. Production has been about 40 percent below what was requested, leaving about 50 countries without adequate supplies. So why do you think there are shortages?

Student: I would like to think that the companies are having a hard time getting the ingredients. But the skeptic in me thinks they are producing less so there will always be a need. Because if they produce enough and polio is eradicated, then they are out of business.

Interviewer: Interesting, but you are way off base. Both firms are very reputable.

Student: I'd like to take a minute to structure my thoughts. [*The student takes about two minutes.*] I'd like to break this down into several buckets – the key stakeholders, their roles and responsibilities, ways to reduce the supply chain costs, and ways to expand the vaccine program.

First, we have the key stakeholders, the Gates Foundation, maybe the World Health Organization, the 50 countries and their decision-makers, maybe other NGOs, the drug manufacturers, and the storage and transportation companies or organizations.

Second, the supply chain. We need to analyze the current process and then investigate whether there are options to consolidate, automate, simplify, or even eliminate parts of the process that are either slowing things down or just redundant.

Third, I'd like to look at ways to expand the program, provided we can determine how to eliminate the two major problems of supply and transportation.

What can you tell me about the stakeholders and decision-makers?

Interviewer: As you can imagine, with a program like this you have many stakeholders. You have national governments, other donors, international organizations like the WHO, UNICEF, and the GAVI Alliance, the private sector, academia, civil society organizations, faith-based organizations, and local communities – just to name a few. They all want to and need to participate.

Student: This seems overwhelming. And I'd assume there is a lot of redundancy. What exactly is the Gates Foundation's part? What are its priorities?

Interviewer: Gates supports the collection, analysis, and use of high-quality vaccine-related data, improving the measurement and evaluation of vaccination efforts. Gates also supports new diagnostic tools to help health workers access need. They support strengthening supply chain logistics. That includes storage, transportation, and distribution of vaccines.

Student: When you say support, you mean give money.

Interviewer: While that's a big part of it, they also contribute other things.

Student: Pardon me. I'd like to look at this problem from a 30,000-foot level. You have millions of children each year who need to be vaccinated. You have scores of organizations and agencies wanting to help out, clamoring for their share of the process. Helping out, yes, but also increasing the complexity of the situation. But you still have two major problems – a shortage of vaccine and the logistics of getting it to the end-user, the child. The Gates Foundation has thrown a lot of money and resources at this problem, and it has done a lot of good, but these two main problems remain.

Interviewer: Okay. What do you suggest?

Student: Tackle something you can control. The Gates Foundation should acquire the polio vaccine business from either Sanofi Pasteur or the Serum Institute. I would think that these firms would be interested in selling a division that is slowly becoming obsolete. By acquiring the division, the cost of the vaccine should go down. We could increase production, ensuring that there is enough vaccine to reach all those in need. They could also start to produce vaccines for measles and other early childhood diseases.

Interviewer: Both of those companies are huge. Serum is privately held and Sanofi Pasteur did around $40 billion in revenues last year. Even if polio and measles make up only 3 percent of its revenues, that's still around $1.2 billion. Gates would have to pay at least $3 billion for the division. Besides, Sanofi just opened a $430 million vaccine plant in Canada, so maybe production will increase.

Student: The other problem is logistics. What if Gates partnered with FedEx, or UPS or Amazon? Private-sector firms are more efficient and have greater experience in the area of logistics and transportation than the NGOs do.

Interviewer: Clearly you don't have the patience or tolerance to work with government and nonprofit clients. These are very complex problems with many partners and stakeholders. Yes, there is redundancy, even corruption to a certain degree, but ...

Student: That's not true. I have great respect for the work the NGOs of the world do. I apologize if it sounded like I underestimated their desire and abilities. But I have a hard time believing that Amazon or FedEx couldn't do a better job at transportation and distribution than the WHO. Yes, there would be organizations that would lose some funding if Gates allocated a big part of its budget to working with FedEx. But in the end, it is all about the children; they are the ultimate stakeholder.

Interviewer: Okay. Walk me through your plan to partner with ... pick one.

Student: FedEx has established distribution networks within most, if not all, of these countries. They already partner with reliable companies to ensure the delivery of packages for the last mile or miles. Gates can contribute by buying refrigeration units sited at these companies' warehouses. While these transportation companies already go to many of the towns, they might not go to all of the remote villages. This means two things. One, if they do start going to the remote villages, it would allow other vendors to get their goods to the village, and for village goods to be transported out to other markets. If they don't, then the NGO's distribution chain has an established central location where they can pick up the vaccines for transport to the villages. So instead of the NGOs taking them across country, they would be responsible for only that last leg.

In addition, FedEx won an award for its relief efforts in response to the 2015 Nepal earthquake. If I remember correctly, they partnered with Direct Relief and other nonprofits to transport critically needed medicines, medical supplies, food, shelter, and water purification equipment from the U.S. to Kathmandu. Their dedication to disaster relief programs makes them an excellent potential partner for the Gates Foundation.

Interviewer: You have a meeting with the director of the Gates Foundation vaccine program. What's your recommendation?

Student: Partner with FedEx to strengthen supply chain logistics, including storage of vaccines, transportation, and distribution. The Gates Foundation needs to consolidate, automate, simplify, and eliminate redundancies to speed up and enhance the distribution of vaccines. FedEx is good at scaling existing logistic solutions while investing in new ideas to improve mobility and guarantee consistency in drugs and delivery.

Why? FedEx already has experience in disaster relief in remote parts of the world. This experience can help consolidate and streamline the delivery of vaccines. It will also stimulate the economies of the villages as goods move in and out more efficiently. *But there are risks*: this action may irk certain NGOs and possibly some government officials who will want to control the process. In the short-term, though, next steps might include contacting the NGOs and government agencies to get their approval on these changes. Working closely with FedEx and the foundation could help control costs and fine-tune logistics. Long-term, we can work with the vaccine manufacturers to ship directly through FedEx to the closest airports and government agencies to ensure expedited handling through customs.

Interviewer: Great. Thanks for coming by.

(Case Takeaways)

- Talked of mission (the right language)
- Asked good clarifying questions to get to the two main problems
- Designed a good structure
- Defended himself when the interviewer attacked his patience with NGOs
- Developed a credible creative solution even after his first idea was shot down
- Laid out a strong recommendation touching on why, the risks, and the next steps

+ MISMATCH – A FEDERAL CASE by Evan Piekara

Interviewer: Your client is a federal agency that manages all national parks, many national monuments, and a number of historical and conservation sites. Under the current administration, Congress has been looking to consolidate efforts and eliminate real or perceived redundancies. They are conducting a review of the agency and are recommending a merger with an agency that protects the environment from air and water pollution and protects the public from health hazards and pollution. Your client has hired you to conduct an impact assessment of this recommendation. What steps do you take?

Student: Our client is a federal agency that manages national parks, monuments, and historical and conservation sites. The current political climate is focused on a wave of consolidation. As such, Congress is recommending that the agency merge with another agency with the mission to protect the environment and the public from pollution and health hazards. Our objective is to complete an impact assessment of this recommendation. Just to clarify, by impact assessment, you mean that we review options and determine the potential impact that this could have on the mission and stakeholders, correct?

Interviewer: That is correct.

Student: Great! At first glance, Congress may see many synergies between both of these missions. Our client manages parks, monuments, and historical sites, which is tied to the environment and conservation efforts. I want to gain a deeper understanding of both mission sets to better comprehend the goals of each agency. I remember visiting the Grand Canyon with my family, and I remember there was more than just a park to enjoy. By managing parks and monuments, is this agency also responsible for upkeep and maintenance, defining what qualifies as one of these designated areas, and providing services and education to visitors?

Interviewer: Yes and yes. Good start! Anything else that may be part of the agency mission?

Student: I remember there were park rangers, so the agency may also be responsible for protection. I also remember that there were opportunities to donate and that not all parks were free, so there might be some financial stewardship as well.

Interviewer: Great! I think you are capturing the mission. Where do you want to go from there?

Student: I'd like to get a sense for the political climate and the stakeholders involved. You mentioned that Congress is reviewing consolidation efforts. I am assuming this is in line with the current administration.

Interviewer: That is correct. Do you have a problem with the administration's approach?

Student: While I may not personally agree with the approach, my objective is to help the client assess the impact of this move and assist them with the analysis to best provide services to meet the agency mission.

Interviewer: Yes – let's keep politics aside. Please continue.

Student: I'd next like to clarify the mission of the agency that may merge with our client. This agency focuses on protecting the environment, and protecting the public from health hazards. I've got a sense that there may be some potential synergies between the missions. I am assuming that setting standards and criteria comes with conserving and protecting the environment. There may also be an education element to this so that the public is aware of contamination, pollution, and how to conserve. I'd also venture that the environment includes air quality, water quality, and land – and the last time I visited a national park all three of these elements were present.

Interviewer: Are you sure that you have not read Congress' study? You did miss a few crucial pieces. That agency also manages standards for fuel, oil, and pesticides, and helps communities develop sound environmental practices.

Student: Thanks for sharing these important elements and I'll be sure to work them into the impact assessment. Now that we have a basic understanding of the two missions, I'd like to get a sense for the stakeholders. We have to consider Congress as they seem to be the one reviewing and making a recommendation. We also have to consider the administration as they seem to be operating in a climate supporting consolidation and fiscal austerity. I'd like to make sure that these two critical stakeholders are aligned and that the end decision resides with Congress.

Interviewer: The administration and both houses of Congress skew Republican and seem to favor fiscal austerity. The recommendation will come from Congress.

Student: Good to know. I'll need to consider this in our assessment. I'd also like to consider other stakeholders. The public will be heavily impacted by this move. We'd need to consider whether this merger would disrupt environmental protection or public access to the parks and monuments. From what I know of private sector mergers, synergies are not always realized and there is usually a lot of time and effort put into ensuring that systems, processes, and skills align. I can imagine that this may be even more challenging in the federal space with constraints such as internal politics, different technology and legacy systems, different agency mandates determined by federal legislation, and distinct knowledge and skills.

Interviewer: I don't know. I've seen countless examples where mergers have led to synergies.

Student: One of my first jobs was working for a successful landscape company. They were purchased by a real estate company. Both thought there would be synergies – the realtors could hire the landscape company to make the homes look more beautiful at a fraction of the cost and then sell the properties at a profit. In theory, there are synergies. In practice, though, the cultures were fundamentally different. The landscape company's mission was more of an aesthetic one – to sustainably beautify the properties and the community. The real estate company's mission was to flip homes and make the largest profit. Profit dropped substantially, and ultimately the realtor fired many employees from the landscape company and began contracting out.

Interviewer: Interesting story. I do not see how that relates to two large federal agencies merging.

Student: Let me clarify my point. Synergies may exist, but it takes patience for those synergies to be realized. This is a cautionary tale of what happens if cultures and mission do not align. One company's mission was more on aesthetics, the other more on profit. This brought together two distinct groups with different motivations. I'd like to better understand another critical stakeholder – the employees. I'd like to know what the make-up is for each agency. Our client may be more service-based providing maintenance, protection, and education. The other "acquiring" agency may be made up more of scientists and engineers with a major standards, research, and development component.

Interviewer: Nice segue and clarification. You are spot on – about 80 percent of our client's staff are more service-based. They maintain the lands, protect the sites, offer tours and education, sell tickets. Some 20 percent of the employees are more specialized and develop the standards and criteria for designating these sites. The "acquiring" agency, as you termed it, comprises about 80 percent scientists and engineers and 20 percent services. Do you see a problem with this?

Student: We'd have to assess the impact on the missions and the stakeholders. Will we need to train the 80 percent of service-based people for our client to fill new roles at the acquiring agency or would they maintain their current roles? Would we need to hire more scientists and engineers to account for the additional oversight that the acquiring agency has? That agency has a major role in the development and enforcement of federal standards and regulations – a role our client does not have. Would we need to re-classify employees for our client to meet the standards of the acquiring agency? These are all questions that Congress should be considering.

Interviewer: They aren't considering these questions, but probably should. Go on.

Student: We'd also need to consider union involvement. If the employees are union, which they likely are, we'd need to understand their expectations for training and shifting roles and responsibilities.

Interviewer: Good insight. A lot of interviewees forget that consideration.

Student: Thank you. I'd like to also explore their current systems. My assumption is that both agencies use systems for tracking funds. Given the stewardship element for our client, they may need a system for tracking revenue. I'd also like to get a sense of what data each agency collects and how they track and store this data. I'd need to know whether these systems are compatible.

Interviewer: Our client and the acquiring agency have distinct systems for managing human capital, finances, and data. Moreover, our client operates on a fiscal year ending in late September and the acquiring company operates under the calendar year.

Student: This is good information. I could see this posing a challenge in managing data and funds, which could ultimately impact service to the public. These distinctions could also cause the merger to take longer, and could hinder perceived synergies from being realized.

Interviewer: How might this impact the mission?

Student: I'm glad you brought that up. Our client may receive funding, due in part, to ticket sales. This may help them cover some of their budget and expand or support the services they provide. They have an incentive to sell tickets and provide a great experience to visitors to these parks and other attractions. Like the example I gave before with the landscape company merger, aesthetics and the experience may be more important to this group. The acquiring agency, however, may have more of a focus on research and development – and regulation. We may have a mission mismatch, which could lead to a mismatch in priorities. One agency may suffer at the expense and priorities of another.

Interviewer: Congress has just informed us that they are tightening the timeline on the impact assessment and they want what you have to-date. How do you respond?

Student: On its face, it seems there are many potential synergies between these two agencies. However, a closer look reveals that this could negatively affect stakeholders, and there are risks that both agencies would need to mitigate for both missions to be efficiently and effectively realized. There will be some challenges with integrating personnel because of cultural, technological, and skills mismatches. This could result in unforeseen costs in training, migrating information, and designing processes and new systems. Ultimately, this could impact park-goers like me, along with the merged agency's ability to protect the public from pollution and other hazards. There may also be a critical mission mismatch. The acquiring agency may more heavily emphasize research and development – not to mention regulation. If this is where they use their funding, we may well see less services for publicly owned parks and other lands. Congress may want to assess other alternatives to get a full scope.

Interviewer: Good – so there may be some unforeseen costs. Congress would like to know other alternatives worth assessing.

Student: Congress should consider whether it makes sense for this agency to operate as a standalone (status quo), reduce its scope or raise the criteria for national parks and monuments to lower costs, increase admission prices to visit parks, or whether another agency may yield better synergies.

Interviewer: Very good. Thank you.

(Case Takeaways:)

- Strong opening focused on clarifying the mission of each organization and sharing assumptions that the mission may be more expansive than just what was shared.
- Solid stakeholder analysis – and considered the impact on the agency, employees, and customers.
- Excellent job including personal experience. Sharing experience going to national parks shows that the interviewee has an understanding and a vested interest.
- Artfully dodged getting into a political conversation. Expressed views, but kept eye on the prize.
- Despite the interviewer's response, shared a good personal example of a private sector merger gone wrong, and used this experience to highlight some of the constraints.
- Considered people, processes, and technology – and the constraints and impact on each. Summary took into account stakeholders, impact, and other alternatives.

+ Partner Cases

Partner cases are cases that you can do with your friends, regardless of whether they know how to give a case. There are five medium Level 2 cases, and five hard Level 3 cases. Your partner first needs to read the Roommate's Guide found below and then read the case all the way through, twice. The case gives your partner plenty of advice and information to make it easy and fun to grill you.

For some of the cases there are charts in the back of the book (see Partner Case Charts), some of which can be hand-drawn in a few minutes' time.

There is flexibility built into these answers and there is usually no one right answer. Have fun with these. After you have answered the case, turn around and give it to another friend. You learn just as much giving a case as you do answering one. The average student serious about a career in consulting will do at least 30 "live" cases. Nothing beats live case practice.

+ Partner Cases List

LEVEL 2 CASES:

LEVEL 3 CASES:

+ THE ROOMMATE'S GUIDE

If you have been begged, bribed, or blackmailed into helping your friend(s) prepare for case questions, here are some suggestions.

Your prep

- Read the question and the answer all the way through before giving the case.
- Be aware that there are multiple "right" answers.
- It's all right to give them help if they lose their way.
- Don't cop a know-it-all attitude.

Things to watch for at the beginning

- Are they writing down the case information?
- Is there a long silence between the end of the question and the beginning of the answer?
- Are they summarizing the question?
- Are they asking about the client's objective(s)?
- Are they asking clarifying questions about the company, the industry, the competition, and the product?
- Are they laying out a logical structure for their answer?

Things to watch and listen for during the course of the question

- Are they enthusiastic and do they project a positive attitude?
- Listen for the logic of their answer. Is it making good business sense?
- Is their answer well organized?
- Are they stating their assumptions clearly?
- Are they being creative?
- Are they engaging, bringing you into the question and turning the case into a conversation?
- Are they asking probing questions?
- Are they quantifying their answer?
- Are they asking for help or guidance?

Review list

- Was their answer well organized? Did they manage their time well?
- Did they get bogged down in details?
- Did they seem to go off on a tangent?

- Did they ask probing questions?
- Did they use business terms and buzzwords correctly?
- Did they have trouble with math, multiplication, or percentage calculation?
- Did they try to get you to answer the question for them?
- Were they coachable? Did they pick up on your hints?
- Did they speak without thinking?
- Did they have a positive attitude?
- Did they summarize their answer?

Final analysis

- Did they take your criticism well?
- Did they defend themselves without sounding defensive?

Aftermath

- Go out on the town!

+ STUCK

Problem Statement

Our client is the third largest peanut butter manufacturer in the U.S. Its brand, Mickey's, sells 120 million jars of peanut butter a year, but trails behind Skippy and Jif. Peter Pan is in fourth place, but only two market share percentage points behind us, so they are breathing down our necks. Mickey's sells to supermarkets and convenience stores nationwide, which makes up 60 percent of the company's sales volume. Sales to big box stores such as Costco and BJ's Wholesale make up 25 percent, but the biggest customer is Wal-Mart, and Wal-Mart alone makes up the remaining 15 percent.

Our client received some bad news. Wal-Mart is replacing Mickey's with Wal-Mart's private label peanut butter; however, the good news is that Wal-Mart wants Mickey's to produce the chain's private label. They want the same peanut butter, the same jar and cap, everything exactly the same except the label. I want to break this case down into two parts. First, I want you to list the key strategic issues and concerns that Mickey's should be thinking about when deciding whether or not to move ahead with this decision. Second, I want you to run the numbers to see if it makes financial sense.

Guidance for the Interviewer

Two questions the student might ask upfront: (1) What has been the sales trend in peanut butter? It's been flat the last two years and is forecast to be flat the next two years. (2) Why is Wal-Mart taking Mickey's off its shelf? It is part of a larger store trend, to replace the third player in various categories with Wal-Mart's private label.

An impressive MBA student should get six or seven of these issues, and undergrads four or five issues. Discuss with the student the ones she didn't get. Just have a general discussion about each; gauge her thoughts. I'm looking for the student to state the issue first, and then follow it up with a question.

- Profit: Will the new contract be profitable? Wal-Mart is known for squeezing margins.
- Brand image / brand equity: Will our brand take a hit if consumers find out that Mickey's and Wal-Mart's are the same product? How much will it hurt Mickey's when consumers don't see it on Wal-Mart's shelf?
- Capacity: What is the size of the contract and do we have the capacity?
- Cannibalization: Will we be stealing sales from ourselves?
- Market share: Regardless of whether we do this or not, Mickey's will fall to fourth place because they will be losing 15 percent of our volume. Mickey's doesn't get credit for Wal-Mart's label.

- Dependency on Wal-Mart: Currently Wal-Mart makes up 15 percent of our volume. If the volume increases, they could be responsible for up to 20 percent of our volume. And whenever one client has 20 percent of your volume, it's a concern, especially when it is Wal-Mart.
- Private labels for others: If we say yes, we can then make private label product for other stores. Will Mickey's get replaced in other stores with a private label?
- Project what happens if we don't accept the contract. Mickey's loses 15 percent of its volume, without much hope of making it up in any other market, and will have to shut down production lines and lay people off.

Data Bank

For the second part of the case, give the following information to the student.

- Skippy, Jif, and Peter Pan sell their peanut butter for $3.99 a jar in supermarkets; Mickey's sells for $3.69.
- Total yearly plant capacity is 150 million jars.
- Mickey's makes a per-jar profit in the supermarkets of $1.20, a per-jar profit in the big box stores of $1.00, and a per-jar profit in Wal-Mart of $.50 (selling as Mickey's).
- The new Wal-Mart contract is a one-year deal, calling for 50 million jars with a $0.25 per-jar profit.

Ask: Is this a good deal? Will our client be making more or less money with the new contract? Compare Wal-Mart to Wal-Mart.

Old deal: 120 million x .15 = 18 million x $0.50 = $9 million
New deal: 50 million x $0.25 = $12.5 million

The company makes $3.5 million more in profits; however, the new deal puts our plant into an over-capacity situation by 2 million jars. (120m –18m = 102m +50m = 152m jars) **What do we do? (How quickly did the student realize that there was a capacity issue?)**

These are some of the ideas the student will come up with (along with your response). As he offers these ideas, keep telling him "no." Even cut him off on one or two to see how he reacts. Does he remain calm? Or does he get upset or try to argue with you? How students react is more important than coming up with the right answer.

- **Mickey's can outsource the 2 million jars.** (No, because the Wal-Mart contract calls for Mickey's to produce the product, so we can't outsource – and we don't want to outsource Mickey's; it's our main product and we want quality control.)
- **Mickey's can build another production line.** (No, because a new production line is a long-term solution and we don't know whether Wal-Mart will extend the contract, plus it is expensive.)
- **Mickey's can add overtime or another shift.** (No, adding overtime would cost too much because we would have to pay the workers time and a half. Besides, they are working at full capacity, which means seven days a week, three shifts a day.)

- **Mickey's can acquire a smaller player and run the extra production through the acquisition.** (No, because an acquisition is a long-term solution and we don't know whether Wal-Mart will extend the contract, plus it is expensive.)
- **Mickey's can just ship 48 million jars to Wal-Mart.** (No, the contract calls for 50 million jars. If Mickey's can't do it, Wal-Mart will find someone else.)
- **Mickey's can pull 2 million jars from the big box stores.** (No, because that move will cost us $2 million in lost profits and we worked hard on the Wal-Mart contract just to make $3.5 million extra profit. It will reduce our Mickey's market share even more. In addition, we want to continue to supply the supermarkets and big box stores with all the peanut butter they need, plus fill the Wal-Mart contract.)

Solution

- Raise your price at supermarkets by $0.20.
- Mickey's price will still be a little less than the competition's while Mickey's will be making $1.40 per jar.
- Higher prices will reduce volume.
- Our analysts projected that volume will drop 10 percent – have the student run the numbers to see if this makes sense.
    - 60 percent of 120m jars is 72m jars. 72m x 1.20 = $86.4m
    - 72m – 10 percent or 7.2m jars = 64.8m or 65m jars. 65m x $1.40 = $91m. We produce about 7 million fewer jars but make about $5 million more.

Summary

The student needs to jump into this without any downtime to collect his thoughts. A good summary is about a minute, minute-and-a-half long. It is not a rehash of everything discussed; it is a short recap of the problem and two or three main points that he wants the interviewer to remember.

Mickey's received notice that they are being replaced in Wal-Mart by a private label; however, Wal-Mart has asked them to manufacture their private label. It is a one-year contract that would require Mickey's to produce 50 million jars at a profit of $0.25 a jar, leading to a $3.5 million increase in profits overall. After reviewing the larger strategic issues including brand equity and market share, Mickey's decided to move ahead. However, the new contract pushes demand 2 million jars over plant capacity. To correct this, Mickey's decided to raise the price of its peanut butter in supermarkets by $0.20, thus reducing demand by 10 percent (or 7 million jars), while making almost $5 million more.

A good interview consists of:

- repeating the question, verifying the objective, and asking if there are any other objectives.

- maintaining an even keel as the interviewer rejects the student's ideas.
- coming up with the price increase solution without any help from the interviewer.
- quickly recognizing that there is a capacity issue.
- developing a good short summary touching on the most critical points, but also bringing up points from both parts of the question.
- keeping well-organized and easy-to-read notes. Big points if the student made a chart like the one below.

Store	% of volume	# of jars	Profit/jar	$ profit
Super/conv	60 percent	72m	$1.20	$86m
Big Box	25 percent	30m	$1.00	$30m
Wal-Mart	15 percent	18m	$0.50	$9m
		120m		$125m

Mark of a good case discussion: While this is a first-round case, it is a difficult first-round case because there is only one right answer. I have given this case live more than 200 times and I can tell you that fewer than 10 percent of the students got the right answer of raising our price in the supermarkets. I look for two other things: (1) how quickly did they pick up on the capacity issue? And (2) how did they react when I cut them off and kept telling them, "No, what else do you have?" To me, this last issue is much more important than coming up with the right answer.

+ NERVES OF STEEL

Problem Statement

Our client is the second largest maker of steel filing cabinets and desks in the U.S. It is nearing the end of a four-year rolled-steel contract, which expires at the end of Year 7. Our client signed its steel contract in Year 4.

The CFO wants to know if it makes sense to stockpile two years' worth of steel at the end of the contract at the Year 4 price or sign a new contract at Year 8's price.

You can assume that the company uses 12,000 tons of steel a year and will continue to do so over the next five years.

Guidance for the Interviewer

Make sure that the student summarizes the question and verifies the objective. The student is looking at two options. Option one is to sign a new contract at Year 8 prices. Option two is to stockpile steel for two years, then sign a new contract in Year 10.

Ask the student what he needs to know. He should ask about:

- Cost of steel in Y4 contract: $600/ton
- Current Y7 cost of steel: $810/ton
- Steel to stockpile: 24,000 tons (12,000/year)
- Time value of money: $FV = PV (1+i)^n$
- Current interest rates: 5 percent
- Inventory storage cost: $50/ton annually paid at beginning of each year
- Steel price forecast: Economic conditions

While the student may not ask for all this information up front, give him some time to discover what he needs.

Steel Pricing Trends (in dollars per ton)

Y1	Y2	Y3	Y4	Y5	Y6	Y7	Y8
$263	$554	$615	$600	$610	$750	$810	?

Show the student this chart, or write it out for him. You are looking to see what conclusions the student can derive from this chart – which is not much. The numbers are all over the place and there is very little consistency. The most it can do is anchor the Year 8 price for him.

Ask him what he thinks the Year 8 price will be. He has a starting point of $810 (the Year 7 price). He should take into consideration the economic conditions around the world, particularly in the top three industries that use rolled steel: autos, aircraft, and appliances (which are tied to housing starts).

Remember that there is no right answer. Students are often reluctant to go out on a limb and give a number, but you need to force your student to come up with a price. (Let's assume he comes up with a Year 8 price of $850 per ton.) Once he has a price for Year 8, look to see what he does with it. Give him big points if he draws up the final slide.

The Final Slide

This is critical. If the student has the foresight to build the final slide, he will stand out from all the other candidates. Whenever you have a case that compares two or more strategies, options, or ideas and you are applying the same criteria, you should build "the final slide" almost immediately. As you calculate the numbers, fill them in on the final slide; it keeps all relevant information in one place and makes it easier for the interviewer to follow. When all the information is filled out, the student turns the final slide toward the interviewer and walks her through it. It is the best summary. It is similar to the final slide of a deck that a consultant would present to a client.

In this case it would look like this (assuming he came up with a Year 8 price of $850 per ton):

	Y8	Y9	Y10	Y11
Option 1 – new contract	$850	$850	$850	$850
Option 2 – stockpiling				

The student should also conclude that he needs to come up with a price for Year 10. If he stockpiles for two years, then the company will have to sign a new contract. Again, he should talk about where he thinks the economy – and those three industries in particular – are headed. Let's say he comes up with a Year 10 price of $900 per ton.

	Y8	Y9	Y10	Y11
Option 1 – new contract	$850	$850	$850	$850
Option 2 – stockpiling			$900	$900

The only two spaces left open in the final slide are the stockpiling numbers. They would stockpile 24,000 tons, enough for two years. Because they are stockpiling, they would need to pay for all of it upfront.

Inventory Costs

Inventory costs are paid on a yearly basis at the beginning of each year. When money is laid out at the beginning of the year, you need to figure the "cost of money." Remember: $50 per ton per year.

Year 1 / (24,000 x 50) = 1,200,000
$FV = PV (1+i)^n$ (n = 1)
FV = 1,200,000 x 1.05
FV = 1,260,000 or $1.26m

Year 2 / (12,000 x 50) = 600,000
$FV = PV (1 + i)^n$ (n = 1)
FV = 600,000 x 1.05
FV = 630,000 or $0.63m

Y1 = $1.26m
Y2 = $0.63m
Total Storage and Inventory Costs = $1.89m

Steel Costs

24,000 tons x $600 = $14,400,000
Interest rates are at 5 percent

$FV = PV (1 + i)^n$
$FV = 14{,}400{,}000 (1.05)^2$
FV = 14,400,000 x (1.10)
FV = 15,840,000 or $15.84m

Stockpiling = $15,840,000 + $1,890,000 (inventory costs)
Stockpiling = $17,730,000, or round off to $18,000,000

$18,000,000 / 24,000 tons = $750/ton (it always comes out to $750/ton)

	Y8	Y9	Y10	Y11
Option 1 – new contract	$850	$850	$850	$850
Option 2 – stockpiling	$750	$750	$900	$900

Summary

The interviewee needs to jump right into this without any downtime to collect his thoughts. A good summary is about a minute, minute-and-a-half long. It is not a rehash of everything you spoke about; it is a short recap of the problem and two or three main points that the student wants the interviewer to remember.

Did the interviewee ...

- repeat the question, verifying the objective and asking about other objectives?
- make math mistakes?
- design the final slide?
- draw the interviewer into a discussion?
- produce a good, short summary touching on the most critical points?
- have well-organized and easy-to-read notes?

Mark of Good Case Discussion: The key things to look for are the student's knowledge of the current economic conditions, the realization that the company will have to sign another contract two years later if they stockpile, and of course the use of the final slide. It is important not only that the slide be filled in, but also that the student turn it toward the interviewer and walk through his analysis and decision.

+ GPS APP

Problem Statement

Our client is a pair of college students who have built an app that will allow customers to download celebrity voices onto their smart phones' GPS systems. The client wants us to determine: the domestic market-size, the breakeven in terms of the number of downloads, the price, and estimated profits for the first year.

Guidance for the Interviewer

The student should repeat the question to make sure everyone is on the same page, and he should verify objectives (market-size, breakeven, price, and profits). The student should also ask whether there are any other objectives he needs to be concerned with – in this case the answer is no.

Most students will try to determine the market-size first. In this case, you are looking to see whether the student first determines the price of the app. He doesn't need to answer the questions in the order they were given. An exceptional student will determine the price first, as well as make a final slide almost immediately. See below for an example.

Data Bank

Our client will be first to market; no other app like this exists. There is a patent pending, but figure on one year before someone weasels their way around the patent.

Costs: In order to determine the price, the student first must ask about costs. Tell him the fixed costs are $500,000 and the variable costs are: one-third of the price goes to Apple or the other platforms, and a $0.50 per download royalty payment goes to the celebrity.

Price: There are three major ways to determine price: competitive analysis, cost-based pricing, and price-based costing.

Competitive analysis: Because we are first to market, there is no real competition. However, given the platform (iTunes, etc.) it is fair to try to compare this with other products being sold, such as songs, ringtones, and games. These items range in price from free to $9.99. It is a fair assumption that this product will fall somewhere in that range.

Cost-based pricing: The product's variable cost is one-third of the price plus $0.50 per download. Make sure that all costs are covered.

Price-based costing: What will customers be willing to pay? Will they equate this app to a ringtone? Or something a little more sophisticated?

It is good practice to use numbers that will make your calculations easier. Apple is taking a one-third fee. Songs and ringtones sell for $1.29 each. The student probably wants to use $3 as a sale price. One dollar goes to Apple, and $.50 goes to the celebrity, which leaves a profit of $1.50 for our client.

Domestic market size: To determine the market size, the student should calculate the number of cellphones in the U.S. and estimate the percentage that are smartphones. He should also determine who is old enough to drive and most likely to buy celebrity voices (probably ages 16 to 36). Have the student walk you through his thinking for each age group.

Assume a U.S. population of 320 million with an average life expectancy of 80 years, with even numbers of people in each age group. Below is an example. The student's assumptions might be different, which is fine, as long as he can justify them.

	Population	No. of cellphones	No. of smartphones	No. to buy app
0 – 20	80 mil	25m	10m	1m
21 – 40	80 mil	60m	40m	3m
41-60	80 mil	60m	40m	.5m
61-80	80 mil	55m	10m	.5m

He came up with 5 million apps. Also assume that the average person would purchase 2 apps, making the market 10 million apps the first year.

Breakeven:
BE = fixed costs / margin (price – 1/3 price – royalty)
BE = 500,000 / 3 – 1 – 0.5 = 1.5
BE = 500,000 / 1.5 = 333,333 downloads

Profits: If the client sells 10 million apps the first year, profits would be 10 million times $1.50 = $15 million minus start-up costs of $500,000 First-year profits are $14.5 million.

Final slide: This simple final slide can be drawn up immediately. Interviewers will watch the order in which the student writes the requests. Did he stick with the order given, or did he realize they were out of order? This final slide acts as a structure, a scorecard (making it easy for the interviewer to keep track of the numbers), and a summary. The student should turn the final slide toward you, the interviewer, and walk you through it.

Price	$3.00
Market size	10m apps
Breakeven	333,000
Est. profits	$14.5 million

Summary

The student needs to jump right into this without any downtime to collect his thoughts. If he made the final slide, then that is his summary. He should turn the slide toward you and walk you through it. If not, a good summary is about a minute, minute-and-a-half long. It is not a rehash of everything you spoke about; it is a short recap of the problem and two or three main points that he wants the interviewer to remember.

We were asked to determine four main factors concerning the GPS app: price, which was determined to be $3; market size, 10 million apps; breakeven in volume, 333,000; and profit the first year; $14.5 million. If these numbers hold up, this promises to be a very profitable venture.

A good interview consists of:

- repeating the question, verifying the objective, and asking about other objectives.
- drawing the final slide.
- making no math mistakes.
- using fair assumptions. keeping well-organized and easy-to-read notes.
- developing a good, short summary touching on the most critical points.

Mark of a good discussion: Did the interviewee figure out the price before the market size? Most students that I give this case to do not figure price first; they try to do market size. This is okay, but you're not going to stand out from the rest of the crowd. Whenever you get a case with a new product, especially when there isn't any direct competition, you should figure price first.

+ FINDING FULFILLMENT

Our client is an online toy store. They ship toys all over the U.S. Currently, they have one warehouse outside Boston where they receive and then distribute the toys. They ship to the end-user, the parents or the kids, through FedEx. The client wants to know if it makes sense to outsource product distribution through a third party such as Amazon.com or Danny's. I'd like to break this question into two parts. What are the pros and cons of outsourcing our distribution and in this case, does it make financial sense to outsource?

Guidance for the interviewer

The student should repeat the question, verify the objective, and then ask whether there are any other objectives. In this case there are no other objectives. Some students will try to lay out a structure, which is not necessary. The structure is basically a list of pros and cons and a running of the numbers. The candidate should ask for a minute to write down his thoughts and then give you all the pros first, then the cons. If he tries to do it off the top of his head, cut him off in mid-answer and say, "I get it. What else do you have?" How quickly does he move on to the next pro or con? Also, the candidate should realize that because this is a toy store, almost 80 percent of the business takes place in the last two months of the year. So the warehouse sits three-quarters empty for ten months.

Listen to his list, and then go through this list confirming what he said, but mentioning the ideas he may have missed.

Pros of Outsourcing	Cons of Outsourcing
Shutting down the warehouse will save warehouse expenses and labor costs. The warehouse sits three-fourths empty for 10 months out of the year.	An outside vendor might be more expensive.
Takes worry and stress out of fulfillment. Allows the client to focus on marketing and selling – what it does best.	Loss of control: can't individualize packages. If the client chooses Amazon, everything is shipped in an Amazon box. Loss of brand recognition.
Outside distributors have multiple warehouses around the country for faster delivery (can shave a day or two off delivery time), lower shipping costs, and use less capital if they expand.	What if this fails? The client already closed their warehouse and fired their employees so they'd need to find another vendor and have their entire inventory shipped to another distributor's warehouses. If this occurs during holiday season, they might not be able to find another distributor.
The client doesn't have to ramp up during the busy holiday season by hiring seasonal employees, then lay people off two months later. An accounting and HR nightmare.	Reduces profit (can't make money on shipping). We charge an extra one dollar per package shipped. This is a handling fee. Look at it as warehouse income.

Data Bank

Client information: Give this information to the student so he can figure out the second half of the question. Tell the student we are going with Danny's. Here are the numbers.

- Currently we ship 250 orders a day, 20 days a month, for 10 months.
- Holidays: They ship 2,000 orders a day, 20 days a month, for 2 months.
- Average toy sells for $20.
- Warehouse rental costs, utilities, and equipment cost $75,000 a year.
- Warehouse insurance costs $9,000.
- Yearly labor costs for four full-time employees and benefits totals $200,000.
- Thirty additional holiday employees at $10 per hour, 8 hours a day, for 20 days a month, for two months. No benefits.
- Danny's fulfillment center storage costs are $0.45 per cubic foot (10,000 cubic feet for 10 months, 100,000 cubic feet for two months).

- Restocking fee of $2 per item for any toys that are returned. They have a 3 percent return rate.
- The client pays the distributor a $1 handling fee per package.

Watch to see how well he organizes his notes. He should walk you through his calculations.

Number of packages; revenues and profits

250 orders a day, 20 days a month = 5,000 packages x 10 months equals 50,000 packages 2,000 orders a day times 20 days a month = 40,000 packages x 2 months equals 80,000 packages

Total number packages shipped last year: 130,000

Average revenue is $20 per package x 130,000 = $2.6 million

In-house Costs

Labor

Full-time = $200,000
Part-time = 30em x $10hr x 8hrs = $2,400
$2,400 x 20 days = $48,000 x 2 months = $96,000

Warehouse rent and equipment (yearly) = $75,000
Warehouse insurance (yearly) = $9,000

Warehouse Costs

$200,000 + 96,000 + 75,000 + 9,000 = $380,000

Warehouse income ($1 handling fee per package) = $130,000 (it is important that the student take this into consideration and subtract it from the warehouse costs).

Net Warehouse Costs: $380,000 – 130,000 = $250,000

Danny's Fulfillment Center
$0.45 x 10,000 = 4,500 x 10 months = $45,000
$0.45 x 100,000 = 45,000 x 2 months = $90,000
Extra shipping credit = 130,000
3 percent return rate = 130,000 x .03 = 3,900 x $2 = $7,800
$45,000 + $90,000 + $130,000 + 7,800 = $272,800

While the cost of shipping the toys in-house is $22,800 cheaper, the student needs to take other things into consideration and put it into perspective before making a decision.

FORCE THE STUDENT TO MAKE A DECISION.

After the student makes a decision, you can say, "Let me tell you why you're wrong!"

If he chooses to keep it in-house, your argument is:

- $22,000 is less than 1 percent of the revenues (22,000/2.6m = .008)

- They would need to sell only 1,900 more toys (about 1 percent) to make up the difference. This would free them to concentrate on marketing and selling more toys.
- The company could pass Danny's $1 handling fee on to the customer.
- Shipping costs would be less.
- The industry is headed toward free shipping during the holidays, so they would not receive $80,000 out of the $130,000 handling fee.
- If the company is worrying about a bad distributor, they could go with two distributors the first year and then choose one. They might lose some volume discounts, but this strategy would be far less expensive than shipping toys from ten of Danny's warehouses to ten warehouses owned by a new distributor.

If they choose to outsource distribution, your argument is:

- They would maintain control of their brand and delivery times.
- They have a warehouse sitting three-quarters empty 10 months out of the year. That is a real opportunity. The company could bring seasonal balance to their warehouse and maybe to their bottom line too, by generating additional revenues: Because the warehouse sits empty most of the year, the client could rent part of it out, or could begin to distribute products for other companies. They could expand their website to include items that ship in the spring, e.g. patio furniture, pool equipment, or toys.

After you tell the interviewee that he is wrong, and why, does he defend his answer without getting defensive or does he switch to your answer? Did he think through his original answer or just shoot from the hip?

A good interview consists of:

- Making no math mistakes.
- Stating fair assumptions.
- Keeping well-organized and easy-to-read notes.
- Turning notes toward you to make you more like a client and less like an interviewer.
- Developing a well-articulated recommendation.
- Defending his recommendation without getting defensive.

A great interview consists of all of the above, plus:

- Putting the $22,800 in perspective.
- Realizing that the handling fee could be passed on to the customer.
- Suggesting that the industry was headed toward free shipping during the holidays and what that would mean for the client.
- Exploring additional revenue opportunities for the warehouse.

Note: I've given this case at least 200 times. Only one person came up with the dual vendors; only one person suggested that the customers pay the handling fee; only four people came up with additional revenue streams for the warehouse. And *no one* spoke about free shipping.

+ KBO APPLIANCES

Problem Statement

KBO Appliances, a U.S. maker of kitchen appliances, saw its stock price drop from $34 to $30 a share on news that the experts had called the new line of products "pedestrian," meaning lacking imagination. While the CEO ordered the design team to redesign the major products, she also wants to enter the college market. She wants to know if it makes sense to develop and market a mini-fridge-and-microwave combo.

What is the size of this market? How would you price the product and how much profit could we expect?

Guidance for the Interviewer

The student should summarize the case to make sure everyone is on the same page. She should quantify the change in stock price by percentage (the stock dropped by about 12 percent), and should also inquire about whether there are any other objectives to be concerned with – in this case, no.

We are looking for several things. What does the student want to know in order to make a decision? Ideally, she would ask about everything listed on the chart below, but that is unlikely. You can give her the detailed information below if she asks for it. Whatever she doesn't bring up, question her about it – and then give her that information. You should have time to visit all eight issues. Keep in mind that there is no right answer. You are looking to see how the student thinks and communicates under pressure.

How the student lays out her notes is also very important. Did she set up a chart similar to the one below? This is known as the final slide. The final slide will make it easier for both her and the interviewer to follow the case. As she makes the calculations and thinks about the issues and variables that will come into play, she should fill in the chart. At the end of the case, she should turn the chart toward the interviewer. Her summary is just going through the chart touching on all eight issues and then making her decision. If she doesn't draw a similar chart, show her this one at the end of the interview.

Start off by asking her what she wants to know.

Market-sizing. This is a general population problem. Start with 320 million Americans. Assume that the average life expectancy of an American is 80 years and that there are even numbers of people in each age group. Thus, there are same number of 2-year-olds as 72-year-olds. That means each group has 4 million people. The average age of college students is 18 to 22 – covering five years (my daughter tells me it takes five years to graduate from college now), so that's 20 million Americans of college age. We care about only full-time students, those living in a dorm. Assume that 8 million go to college full-time; 2 million are freshmen, 2 million are sophomores, etc.

Assume that all freshmen live in dorms and that the number of students living in dorms falls off as they go through school. Also, most freshmen have a roommate, so cut the 2 million number in half. That's 1 million freshmen as the market. Assume that all of the others add up to another million, taking into account that students who buy the fridge will hold onto it year after year.

Also assume that the biggest purchasers of these microwave mini-fridges are the universities. They buy them, then rent them out to students. So we'll assume that the market size is 2 million units per year. The candidate's thought process is more important than the actual number. Regardless of what she comes up with, use 2 million as the market size.

Competition and product differentiation. Tell the student that all of the existing products look the same – white mini-fridge with a microwave screwed onto the top. Ask her how she would differentiate our product, then go with an energy-efficient fridge with a nice cow design.

	Mini-Fridge & Microwave
Market size	2 million units per year
Competition and product differentiation	3 current products priced between $300 and $350. Our product will be the fourth and will have a cow design on the outside of the product.
Cost (our manufacturing cost)	$150 per unit
Pricing	In determining the price, the student should take several things into consideration: (1) our costs, (2) competition, (3) what students are willing to pay and (4) the fact that the CEO wants to enter this market.[4] She should also take into consideration that there is a 20 percent retail markup. At what price do we sell to the retailer? Can we sell direct to schools and bypass the retailer? If we do that, then follow-up sales will be less because the schools will hang onto them year after year.
Estimated market share	Given the price, the student can now estimate the market share the company can expect. A reasonable number for the first year could be as high as 10 percent, but no higher.
Profits	Once the student figures out the price and our market share, she should figure out our estimated profits.
Competitive response	How will our competition react? Price war? A tiger design? Get the company's customers to sign a long-term contract?
Other factors	Will we cannibalize our other products? (no) What other markets (e.g., small business, senior housing, hospitals) can we expect to pull from?
Decision	Look for a "go" or "no go" decision.

[4] The CEO wants to enter the market so she can introduce the quality of her products and brand to students in hopes of having them make bigger purchases as they go through life (think long-term greed). This discovery should lead to pricing the unit on the lower end of the price range – probably the lowest.

Guidance for the Interviewer

The student should have touched on all the issues above in a similar order. Thus, we can't determine the company's estimated market share until we know the price. And we can't calculate profits until we know the estimated market share. Does the student see the big picture? Does she understand how everything is tied together?

Summary

The perfect summary is walking you through the final slide. Don't expect that – very few students ever make the final slide. If the student does it, she is exceptional! But she needs to jump right into the summary without any downtime to collect her thoughts. A good summary is about a minute, minute-and-a-half long. It is not a rehash of everything she spoke about; it is a short recap of the problem and two or three main points with a recommendation that she wants the interviewer to remember.

A good interview consists of:

- repeating the question, verifying the objective, and asking about other objectives.
- taking into account *why* the CEO wants to enter this market.
- making no math mistakes.
- keeping well-organized and easy-to-read notes (making of the chart).
- developing a good short summary using the chart and touching on the most critical points.

Mark of a Good Case Discussion: Besides drawing the final slide, did she have everything in the right order? Did she pick up on the fact that the universities are the biggest buyers and that having an energy-efficient model would be the most appealing to them? I also look to see if the student suggests a price war as a response. If she does, tell her to avoid that option in future cases if possible. Most firms view it as a knee-jerk reaction.

+ BULLETPROOF AUTO GLASS

Problem Statement

Our client is an applied materials manufacturer who wants to enter the bulletproof auto glass industry. They've developed a one-way bullet-resistant glass. Bullets won't come in, but you can fire out. This new glass is lighter and cheaper to manufacture. Word leaked out and their stock jumped from $15 to $18 a share. They want you to calculate the size of the worldwide bulletproof auto glass market, come up with a pricing strategy, determine the plant location, and make a decision on whether to enter this market.

Guidance for the interviewer

Make sure that the student summarizes the case and verifies the objective(s) (calculate market size, come up with a pricing strategy, determine plant location, and decide whether to enter the market). When summarizing, he should state that the stock jumped 20 percent, not $3. He should also ask whether there are any other objectives about which he should be concerned. In this case the answer is no. After he verifies the objectives he should take a moment and lay out his structure. Because this is an interviewer-driven case, no hypothesis is needed.

Ideally, his notes should look something like this.

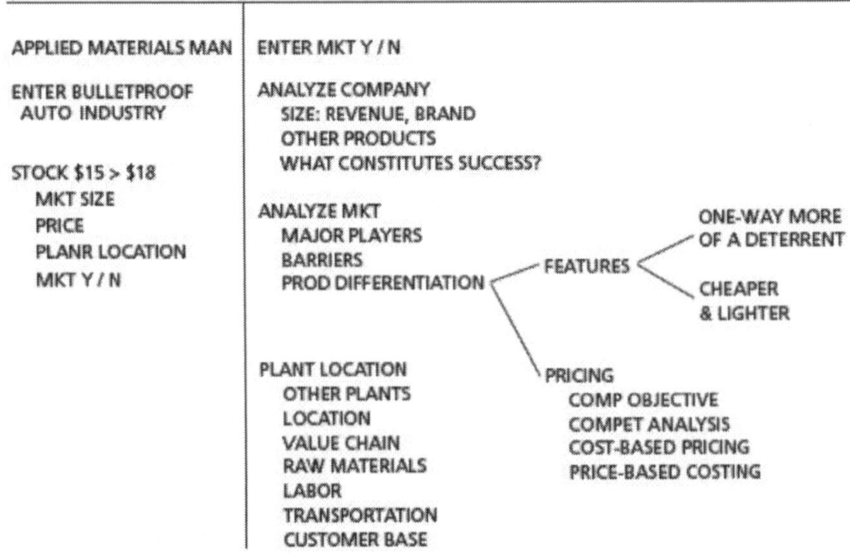

Because this is a new product, not only for the company but also for the industry, the student might want to solve the pricing issue first, before figuring out the market size.

Databank

The information below should help you answer any of the student's questions. If he asks you something you don't know, just say that it's not relevant. If he doesn't ask you about all these areas, turn the question back on him, i.e., "What do you think are some of the barriers to entry?" I look carefully at the structure. Ideally he should lay out his approach in this order: the company, the overall market, pricing, market sizing, plant location, and the best way to enter the market. Most students will jump right into the market sizing first, which is okay, but not optimal.

The company

- Size: revenues, brands: $15 billion in revenue, all b2b
- Other products? Any in auto industry? No. Flat-screen television panels, solar panels, semi-conductors, bulletproof walls, and windows for buildings
- Is the product patented? Yes
- What constitutes a success? 10 percent market share within 3 years

The market

- Major players and market share Four players, 25 percent each. Two are divisions of larger companies; two are smaller players. Growing by 10 percent a year last five years.
- Product differentiation Ours would be lighter, cheaper to manufacture, and one-way. No other one-way on the market. (Disadvantage: Once you fire out, the integrity of the glass is compromised.)
- Barriers to entry Contracts with original equipment manufacturers (OEM) usually take four years to get established OEMs make up 80 percent, aftermarket 20 percent

Note: If this company wants 10 percent market share and an OEM contract takes four years, then they need to take market share out of the aftermarket, which means that they need to get 50 percent of the aftermarket – very unlikely without an acquisition.

Pricing

- Company objective: 10 percent market share within 3 years.
- Competitive analysis: Four competitors between $400 and $450 /sq. ft.
- Best guess, that it costs them around $300/sq. ft. to manufacture – figure a standard industry 25 percent margin.
- Cost-based pricing. It costs us $250/sq. ft. The average vehicle uses 25 square feet of glass.
- Price-based costing. Do we think that customers would be willing to pay more for our product? Lighter means easier to work with, and saves on vehicle gas. But bulletproof glass isn't something that you would try to save money on – you'd want the best. Customers are not price sensitive.

Market-sizing

What is the size of the worldwide bulletproof auto glass market?

Clients that use bulletproof glass are militaries, corporations, and government agencies such as the FBI, local police, and their counterparts around the globe. Royalty, celebrities, mob bosses, drug lords, and armored trucks also use bulletproof glass. Plus, the market needs to broken down into the OEM market and the aftermarket.

The best way for the student to solve this is to make some assumptions about the U.S. and extrapolate it out to the world market. Start with assumptions:

1 percent of U.S. vehicles have bulletproof glass.
U.S. vehicles make up 10 percent of the world market.

Next, figure out the number of U.S. cars/vehicles on the road. This is a household problem.

Assume U.S. population is 320 million, 3.2 people per household, or 100 million U.S. households. Next, break this data down by income levels. He should draw this chart and walk you through his thought process for each level.

Income	Households	# Cars / HH	Total cars
High	10m	3	30m
Middle	60m	2	120m
Low	30m	.5	15m

He's calculated 165 million cars owned by households. To that, he should add military vehicles, taxis, rental cars, limos, government cars, university cars, RVs, and armored cars. He can bundle all those together in a single number. It makes his calculations easier: in this example say 35 million. Now the total is 200 million cars on the road. Assume a car has a life expectancy of 10 years, which means 20 million new cars sold every year.

20 million new cars x .01 = 200,000 new cars with bulletproof glass in the U.S.
180 million used cars x .01 = 1.8 million used cars with bulletproof glass
Total 2 million cars in U.S. have bulletproof glass
The U.S. has 10 percent of market – total market is 20 million cars with bulletproof glass worldwide

Remember, his numbers might be very different, which is okay provided that there were solid assumptions and logic behind his thoughts.

Plant location

He should be asking several questions. Where are the company's other plants? What are the bulletproof glass sales by region? Where are his customers?

Current plants are in Ireland, Germany, Israel, the U.S., and Brazil. The company manufactures bulletproof glass for buildings in their Ireland plant. Other issues to take into consideration are the value chain, raw materials, labor, transportation, and customer base. The OEMs are located in Detroit, Tokyo, Berlin, and South Carolina.

Another consideration is whether acquiring a smaller player is discussed. If the company acquires a competitor, they may use that company's plant to produce, if they have the capacity.

BPG (auto) market by region and by user

Middle East 35 percent
South America 25 percent
Asia 20 percent
U.S. 10 percent
Other 10 percent

Entry into the market

What the question is really asking is not only should the company enter this market, but how? What you should be looking for here is for the student to suggest acquiring one of the smaller players, particularly if it has an OEM contract. Remember, it takes four years to get one. This will speed up the process and help the company reach the 10 percent market share in three years because each player represents 25 percent of the market.

Here are five ways to enter the market. The student should review these, stating the advantages and disadvantages of each.

- Start producing on their own and try to grow it organically.
- Make an acquisition.
- Sell their technology to another company.
- Produce the glass for all the other companies (private label).
- Do a joint venture.

Final slide: When a student gets a question that asks for "these four things" he can usually make a final slide on a separate sheet of paper at the start of the case.

This acts as a scorecard as well as his summary. He should fill it out as he goes along and then turn it toward the interviewer and walk him through it.

Below are some answers; the student may have come up with different ones, which is fine as long as he used logic and his arguments made sense.

Market Size	20m
Price	$500 / sq. ft.
Plant location	Ireland
Enter market	Yes

Summary

He needs to jump right into this without any downtime to collect his thoughts. A good summary is about 30 seconds to a minute, possibly a minute-and-a-half long at the most. It is not a rehash of everything he spoke about; it is a very short recap of the problem and two or three main takeaways that he wants the interviewer to remember. If he made the final slide, that will serve as his summary. He should turn it toward you and walk you through it.

While most students will suggest that the company enter the market, one thing I look for is whether they suggest an acquisition and how they incorporate that into their overall market entry strategy and plant location discussion.

A good interview consists of:

- Repeating the question, verifying the objective, and asking about other objectives.
- Laying out a clear structure, starting with the company.
- Asking solid and poignant questions.
- Making no math mistakes.
- Keeping well-organized and easy-to-read notes.
- Drawing a final slide.
- Developing a good, short summary touching on the most critical points.

Mark of a good discussion: Did the student ask probing questions to get all the information from you that you had to offer? Did he have a full understanding of the problem? Did he realize that it is not only about entering the market, but how to enter the market? Was he able to determine market size quickly or did he get gummed up on the enormity of the question? And, finally, did he draw a final slide?

+ STATIN BLUE

Problem Statement

Our client is a large pharma company similar to Johnson & Johnson. It has developed a new cholesterol drug called Statin Blue. Because Statin Blue is on the lower end of the statin chain (meaning that it is weaker than traditional prescription cholesterol drugs), the company has the option of releasing this drug either as an over-the-counter product or as a prescription drug.

You need to:

- determine which market the company should enter, as a prescription drug or as an over-the-counter product.
- figure the breakeven in terms of the number of customers for both markets.
- calculate the estimated profits for both markets.
- list the pros and cons of entering the prescription market.

Guidance for the Interviewer

Make sure that the student summarizes the question and verifies the objectives (determining which market to enter, figuring the breakeven in terms of customers for both markets, calculating the estimated profits for both markets, and listing the pros and cons of entering the prescription market). She should also ask whether there are any other objectives she should be concerned with. In this case the answer is no. After the student summarizes the question and verifies the objectives, have her start with the pros and cons.

When she lists the pros and cons, check to see whether she asks for a moment to write down her thoughts. By asking for a moment (up to 30 seconds), she can list the pros and cons any way they pop into her head; however, when it comes time to tell them to you, she should list all the pros first, then all the cons. Make sure she doesn't ping-pong back and forth between pros and cons.

Prescription:

+Price – can charge more
+Insurance coverage
+Perceived higher value
+Good established sales force
–Highly competitive market
–One dominant player (Lipitor with 49 percent of the market)

Over-the-Counter:

+Easy access – don't need to see a doctor
+High volume
+Easier to market

+Company brand name recognition
+Potentially huge, untapped market
–Patients in the high-risk category already on prescription drug
–Viewed as less effective (which it is – 10 percent)

Entering the Market

After listing the pros and cons, the student should ask about the market. Force her to ask about the prescription market first. What does the student need to know about entering a new market?

Who are the major players?
What market share does the company have?
How do their products differ from those of Statin Blue?
Are there any barriers to entry? (Has the company received FDA approval for both markets?)

Special note – Our company does not produce any of the other Statin products

Data Bank

Our Client

- Large pharma with a large drug portfolio. Fifty percent of its products are over-the-counter and 50 percent are prescription drugs. This should tell the student that our distribution and marketing channels are well established in either market.

Prescription Market (Rx)

- Current market size: 14 million Americans and $14 billion in sales. Show the student the chart at the back of the book.
- If covered by insurance, the patient pays $15 a month co-pay.

Over-the-Counter Market (OTC)

- No such market exists.
- The OTC version of Statin Blue would cost the consumer $15 for a month's supply.
- No insurance coverage.

Statin Blue

- Think of it as Lipitor Light – it's less effective.
- Similar side effects as with regular Statin drugs, just less intense. Side effects include muscle pain, diarrhea, sexual dysfunction, cognitive impairment, and possible liver damage.

Costs

- Costs are $40 million a year. This is the only cost number the student needs to know.

Pricing

- The cost to the end user will be the same regardless of which market we use. By prescription, the patient will pay a $15 a month co-pay. For OTC the patient will pay $15 for a month's supply.

Profits

- The company makes a $20 profit per bottle sold in the prescription market. The patient would use one bottle a month, 12 bottles a year. Yearly profit is $240 per patient per year.
- The company makes a $5 profit per bottle sold in the OTC market. The patient would use one bottle a month, 12 bottles a year. Yearly profit is $60 per patient per year.

Rx Markets: *Walk the student through the chart below*. Explain that if your cholesterol is less than 180, you are very healthy. If it falls between 180 and 200, the doctor will tell you to exercise more and eat some Honey Nut Cheerios. Patients with cholesterol levels between 200 and 220 are the prime target for Statin Blue. This group makes up 10 percent of the overall prescription market. However, we think we will be able to get only 4 percent of the overall 14-million-person prescription cholesterol market (which is 560,000 patients). If your cholesterol levels are over 220, then the doctor will prescribe one of the seven drugs in the first chart.

Before there was Statin Blue, if your level was 210 or above, the doctor would most likely prescribe one of the seven current drugs; however, you would be over-medicating and at risk for the side effects.

250	Big Trouble (represents 10% of the overall prescription cholesterol market)	
220	Other Prescription Cholesterol Drugs (represents 80% of the overall prescription cholesterol market)	
200	Statin Blue (We believe that the patients whose cholesterol levels fall between 200 and 220 make up 10% of the overall cholesterol market.)	10%
180	Honey Nut Cheerios & Exercise	
<180	Healthy	

OTC Market: The market-sizing of the OTC market is the hardest part of the case.

Assumptions:

- There are 300 million Americans.

- There is an 80/20 split between Americans with health insurance (the ones who would have access to the prescription market) and those without health insurance (the ones who wouldn't have access to discounted prescriptions).
- Of the 240 million Americans with health insurance (300 million times 80 percent = 240 million), we know that 14 million or 5 percent have a cholesterol problem (14/240 = 5.8 percent or round-off to 5 percent).
- That leaves an uninsured population of 60 million (300 million x .2 = 60 million). Thus we can assume that at least 5 percent of the uninsured, or 3 million people, have a cholesterol problem (60 million times 20 percent = 3 million). I would add in an extra 1 million because the uninsured don't receive constant health care and have a higher rate of obesity, heart attacks, and strokes.
- Out of the 4 million uninsured who likely have a cholesterol problem, we'll assume that 25 percent or 1 million people would buy this drug. Many have higher priorities (like feeding their families or paying rent) than spending $15 a month on a drug for a problem that they can't see or feel.
- To that 1 million I'd add a group of people ages 20 to 40. These are people who don't have a cholesterol problem, but their parents or relatives do. Because cholesterol levels are tied into genetics, they know that they are on the same path as their parents and may want to take something now to prevent problems later.
- Three hundred million Americans divided into four even generations of 75 million each: Thus there are 75 million Americans ages 20 to 40.
- Assume that 5 percent of their parents have a cholesterol problem. Five percent of 75 million is 3.75 million, or 4 million. Out of that 4 million I'll assume 25 percent will take this preventive measure and buy Statin Blue. That equals 1 million preventers.
- Total of 2 million customers for the OTC drug (this number is not set in stone.) It is not critical that the student use the same assumption numbers, just the same logic – and even then, as long as there is logic to the thoughts, that is fine.

Breakeven Calculations

- Prescription Breakeven:

$40 million in costs divided by a $20 per-bottle profit equals 2 million bottles divided by 12 months equals 166,667 customers.

- OTC Breakeven:

$40 million in costs divided by a $5 per-bottle profit equals 8 million bottles, which divided by 12 months equals 667,000 customers.

Profit Calculations

- Prescription: 560,000 customers x $240 = $134.4 million
- OTC: 2 million customers x $60 = $120 million

What would you do?

The Final Slide

This is critical. If the student has the foresight to build the final slide, she will stand out from all the other candidates. Whenever you have a case that compares two or more strategies, options, or ideas, and you are applying the same criteria to both, you should build the final slide almost immediately. As you calculate the numbers, fill them in on the final slide; it keeps all relevant information in one place and makes it easier for the interviewer to follow. Once all the information is filled out, the student turns the final slide toward the interviewer and walks him through it. It is the best summary. It is also similar to the final slide of a deck that a consultant would present to a client. (Show the student the chart at the end of the case when you are walking through her analysis.)

	Prescription	OTC
Market Size		
Breakeven		
Profit		
Market Choice		
Other Concerns		

Summary

The interviewee needs to jump right into this without any downtime to collect her thoughts. A good summary is about a minute, minute-and-a-half long. It is not a rehash of everything you spoke about; it is a short recap of the problem and two or three main points that the student wants the interviewer to remember.

Did the interviewee ...

- repeat the question, verifying the objective and asking about other objectives?
- make math mistakes?
- design the final slide?
- develop a logical and well-thought-out market-sizing process?
- draw the interviewer into a discussion?
- produce a good short summary touching on the most critical points?
- have well-organized and easy-to-read notes?

Mark of a Good Case Discussion: Besides the final slide, students should bring up ...

- Competitive response to our entry in either market.
- Entering both markets.
- Which market would the company enter first? (prescription)
- What are some of the pros and cons?

Synergies include a common manufacturing plant. We can also take advantage of established distribution channels and marketing strategies.

Notes: Make sure the student's notes are neat, well-organized, and easy-to-read. At the very least she should have divided her notes into prescription and OTC. Did she draw a line down the middle of her paper? Did she do her prescription and OTC calculations on separate sheets of paper?

+ BOTTLED WATER

Problem Statement

Last year Americans bought more than 4 billion gallons of bottled drinking water. Our client sold 1 billion bottles of spring water in the .5 liter size. In the past, our client has purchased the empty bottles from a guy named Ed for 5 cents each. These bottles are made from polyethylene terephthalate (PET), which is a combination of natural gas and petroleum.

Ed wants to raise his price by one penny, which would increase the client's costs by $10 million. The client is considering in-house bottle production but currently does not have the resources to do it. The CFO wants you to determine whether this makes sense. The CFO requires a two-year payback (breakeven) on investments and wants to know if the company should in-source the bottle production.

Besides determining whether to in-source bottle production, can you tell me what market share our client has of the U.S. bottled water industry?

Guidance for the Interviewer

Make sure that the student summarizes the question and verifies the objective (determining whether to in-source bottle production) before determining market share. He should also ask whether there are any other objectives he should be concerned with. The answer is that there are no other objectives to be concerned about in this case.

How to figure out market share:

It needs to be done by volume of water. Tell the student to assume that one pint equals .5 liters.

If he asks (and most students do) ...

2 pints = 1 quart
4 quarts to the gallon; thus, 8 pints = 1 gallon

Easiest way is to turn everything into pints:

4 billion gallons = 32 billion pints
1 billion .5 liters = 1 billion pints
1 billion pints / 32 billion pints = about 3 percent of the market

Ask the student: Before we get into the numbers, just off the top of your head, can you lay out the pros and cons of in-house production?

Pros	Cons
Possible lower price	Added risk
More control over costs in the future	No experience
Produce and sell to competitors	Big investment setup costs
	Economic variables out of our control

If the student misses any from the list above, don't tell him what he missed. He'll figure it out later. Show the student this chart.

Y1	Ed	Client
COGS	60m	?
Building	N/A	\$6m
Equipment	N/A	\$4m
Labor	N/A	?
Utilities & Maintenance	N/A	\$.04m
Transportation	N/A	?
Admin	N/A	\$1m
Cost per bottle	\$0.06	?

Explain that the left-hand column represents the costs associated with bottle production. The middle column represents what the client would pay Ed (1 billion bottles times 6 cents each equals \$60 million). The right-hand column represents the client. Some of the numbers have been filled in; others are still a mystery and need to be figured out.

Data Bank

COGS – The cost per gallon of PET pellets is \$5. It takes 10 gallons to make 1,000 bottles. We want to make a billion bottles.

Answer: \$50 / 1,000 = \$0.05 per bottle
\$0.05 x 1 billion bottles = \$50 million

Labor – Twenty people x \$4,000 a month each equals \$80,000 a month.

Answer: \$80,000 x 12 months = \$960,000 per year (don't round up).

Transportation – It costs $0.005 to transport one bottle.

Answer: $0.005 x 1 billion = $5 million.

The completed chart should look like this:

Y1	Ed	Client
COGS	$60m	$50m
Building	N/A	$6m
Equipment	N/A	$4m
Labor	N/A	$.96m
Utilities & Maintenance	N/A	$.04m
Transportation	N/A	$5m
Admin	N/A	$1m
Cost per bottle	$0.06	$0.067

$67 million / 1 billion bottles = $0.067 per bottle

Client $0.067
Outsource -$0.060
$0.007 x 1 billion bottles = $7 million

The first year, we pay $7 million more than if we had purchased the bottles from Ed.

Tell the student: For Y2 assume that production is up 5 percent to 1.05 billion bottles. COGS should increase by 5 percent; the building and equipment are one-time expenses and can be zeroed out. Labor, utilities and maintenance, and administration remain the same, but transportation is up by 5 percent. The new chart should look like this:

Y2	Ed	Client
COGS	$63m	$52.5m
Building	N/A	N/A
Equipment	N/A	N/A
Labor	N/A	$.96m
Utilities & Maintenance	N/A	$.04m
Transportation	N/A	$5.25m
Admin	N/A	$1m
Cost per bottle	$0.06	$0.056

Have the student come up with the new dollar total, which is $59.75 million.

(52.5 + .96 + .04 + 5.25 +1 = $59.75)

I never make the student divide 59,750,000 by 1,050,000,000; just tell him it equals around $0.056 per bottle.

Thus $0.06 - $0.056 = $0.004 less than what we would pay Ed.

However, make the student figure out that $0.004 x 1.05 billion = $4.2 million.

To summarize so far:
Year 1: down $7 million
Year 2: up $4.2 million (so we are still down by $2.8 million).

Remember: The CFO wanted a two-year payback.

Tell the student that in Y3 the company will end up with a $3.31 million profit, so we are $510,000 in the black.

What do you tell the CFO?

The student will most likely say that we won't break even in two years; however, if we stay the course, we will become profitable in Year 3.

Tell the student that the CFO wants a two-year payback and that he needs to figure out (1) a way to break even through increasing revenues; and (2) a way to break even by lowering expenses.

Revenues side: Produce more bottles to sell to competitors.
Expense side: Lease the building and equipment.

Summary

The interviewee needs to jump right into this without any downtime to collect his thoughts. A good summary is about a minute, minute-and-a-half long. It is not a rehash of everything you spoke about; it is a short recap of the problem and two or three main points that the student wants the interviewer to remember.

Did the interviewee ...

- repeat the question, verifying the objective and asking about other objectives?
- make math mistakes?
- know how to value a company?
- produce a good short summary touching on the most critical points?
- have well-organized and easy-to-read notes?

Mark of a Good Case Discussion: One thing I look for that students almost never do is to stop before they go in to the meeting with the CFO and say, "If I go in to the meeting now, I will have to tell the CFO that we can't do it in two years. Before I go in, I want to figure out a way to do it in two years. That way I can tell the CFO, yes we can!"

This shows great forethought and a can-do attitude that any consultant would love.

+ SMACKDOWN RIVALS[5]

Problem Statement

Our client, Smackdown Rivals, is a publicly traded sports entertainment company. Smackdown has successfully conceived and developed a very popular genre of wrestling that has cultivated an impassioned international fan base; it is marketed and distributed globally across live and televised events, digital media platforms, and a wide variety of consumer products.

Smackdown had revenues of $526.5 million last year, with an operating profit of $70.3 million and a net profit of $45.4 million. Smackdown has 72.85 million shares outstanding, and it has been paying dividends of $1.44 per share. The company has enjoyed a good growth trajectory and has been expanding internationally. In fact, in the past few years international revenue has been growing at twice the rate of domestic revenue. Smackdown currently employs almost 600 people, not including the approximately 150 wrestlers who are contractors under exclusive agreements with the company.

The COO has asked for your advice. Analysts have praised Smackdown's ability to generate cash, its lack of debt, its healthy revenue trajectory, and its generous quarterly dividends. But, a few analysts have voiced concerns that costs have been rising out of proportion to growth. In addition to pleasing analysts, the COO knows, the company needs to be as efficient as possible in its operations so it can fuel strategic investments that allow international expansion and other growth possibilities.

The COO wants to keep growing the company aggressively, but he needs to make really solid choices on where and how to grow. If a future creative idea doesn't work out, it could be an expensive loss for the company. On the other hand, if Smackdown is too conservative in its growth investments, its fan base could begin spending its entertainment dollars elsewhere.

I need you to take the following five steps:

1. Determine whether costs are indeed rising out of proportion to growth.
2. Explain whether the analysts have a valid concern about costs.
3. Based on your observations, tell me what you would advise the COO to do, if anything, regarding costs.
4. Give your opinion about how the COO should determine the appropriate cost structure for this business.
5. Give your opinion on Smackdown's recent dividend payments.

[5] (Written by Lynda Knoll Cotter)

Guidance for the Interviewer

Make sure that the student summarizes the question and verifies the objectives before starting to answer your questions.

Questions 1 and 2: Calculate whether costs are rising out of proportion to growth. Explain whether the analysts have a valid concern about costs.

- Show the student Chart 1 below and give her time to review the statement.
- Using Chart 1, the student should be able to calculate the YOY (year over year) growth and cost percentages to answer Question 1.
- The student might ask for more details. Give the student Charts 2 and 3 (profitability ratios and a headcount) and Chart 4 (a breakdown of the revenues by business unit).
- The student should calculate the YOY percentage growth for revenue and costs as in the table below:

YOY Percentage Growth

Area	2006–7	2007–8
Revenue	17.0%	8.4%
Total Costs	19.6%	8.6%
Cost of Revenue	22.0%	4.4%
Selling/Gen./Admin	13.5%	20.3%

From the data provided, the student should be able to make the following observations:

- We have revenue data by line of business but not cost data, so it is difficult to make observations by line of business.
- At a high level, total costs and revenue are staying roughly in sync. At a more detailed level, SG&A costs just took a big jump, 50+ percent, in proportion to other costs and revenue. The concern of the analysts appears to be valid. The student may speculate that some analysts could be worried that SG&A costs will continue to rise more quickly than revenue, and the company needs to have plans to ensure that the rising SG&A will not become a trend.
- The student might point out that the number of employees did not rise in 2008, yet SG&A costs as a percentage of revenue increased by almost 10 percent.
- The "All Other" bucket of expenses is a high number for a catch-all category, and the student should ask what is included in the "All Other" expenses. You can tell the student that it's good she asked, but the details are not available.
- The student should note that there was a dramatic increase in advertising and promotion (over 100 percent) in the last year.
- Revenue from studios appears to be a new revenue stream, and it is growing the most rapidly, at over 50 percent from 2007–08. The student might hypothesize that the growth in advertising and promotion could be coming from this new venture.

- The student should comment on the increase in bad debt, and the student may wonder whether credit policies should be tightened. The student may realize that the increase in bad debt might not be from ignoring credit policies, but instead from paying closer attention and being more aggressive in writing off uncollectible debt.

Question 3: Based on your observations, tell me what you would advise the COO to do, if anything, regarding costs.

- It would be difficult for the student to make detailed recommendations on cost-cutting without more detailed information on what the costs represent and how they are allocated to each line of business.
- The student should understand that costs are an investment made to grow the company. The Smackdown leadership team, analysts, and investors want to ensure that the company is using its investments in the parts of the business that have the most potential.
- The student should suggest that the COO pursue further investigation in the areas in which costs have increased the most (e.g., advertising and promotion, bad debt, all others).
- On Chart 2, the student should be able to explain the difference between the two profitability ratios. The definitions are:
- **Gross Margin**: The percentage of revenue remaining after subtracting the cost of goods sold.
- **Operating Margin**: The proportion of revenues remaining after taking out costs of goods sold and SG&A expenses.
- The student should be able to explain that the operating margin is going down, presumably because of the increase in SG&A costs.
- It would also be good if the student asked to see the costs of other companies in the industry, to get benchmark information. Although benchmark data is usually fairly easily available, with this particular company you would need to benchmark the different areas of the business separately – so you can tell the student that this information isn't available right now, but that benchmarking in general is a good practice to follow.

Question 4: State your opinion about how the COO should determine the appropriate cost structure for this business.

- The student might suggest that Smackdown should control costs differently for a growing part of the business than it does for a non-growing part of the business.
- The student should consider that a new business could require substantial startup costs and may lose money in the first year or two.
- These are good points, but regardless of whether or not a business unit is experiencing growth, the key is to control costs. A business unit leader shouldn't ever have a "no-holds-barred" approach to hiring and other expenditures, regardless of how fast that area is growing.
- The student should suggest that the cost structure for the business be based on the results of ROI analyses for new areas of growth, and that leadership should reduce costs for those lines of business that are not in a growth mode.

Question 5: State your opinion on Smackdown's dividend payments.

- The student should say that Smackdown is currently using all its profits for dividends, which is not a sustainable policy in the long run.
- The student should also mention that growth companies tend to not pay dividends, more often using that money to instead fuel growth.
- The student should understand that dividends can be a very important part of shareholder value, and should speculate about why this company has such a high dividend. The student may surmise that because the company is in a non-traditional business, the dividend could be used as the backbone of its stock valuation.

Smackdown Rivals
Trending Schedules
Statement of Operations
($ in millions, unaudited)

	2006	2007	2008
Revenues	$ 415.3	$ 485.7	$ 526.5
Cost of Revenues	244.9	298.8	311.8
SG&A	96.1	109.1	131.3
Dep. & Amortization	8.7	9.4	13.1
Operating Income	$ 65.6	$ 68.4	$ 70.3
Interest and Other, net	9.8	8.0	(1.0)
Income before Taxes	$ 75.4	$ 76.4	$ 69.3
Interest and Other, net	26.6	24.3	23.9
Effective Tax Rate	35%	32%	34%
Income from Continuing Operations	$ 48.8	$ 52.1	$ 45.4
Discontinued Ops			0.0
Net Income	$ 48.8	$ 52.1	$ 45.4
EPS - Continuing Operations	$0.68	$0.72	$0.62
EPS - Net Income	$0.68	$0.72	$0.62
Memo:			
EBIDTA	$ 74.3	77.8	83.4
EBIDTA margin %	18%	16%	16%

Smackdown Chart 2

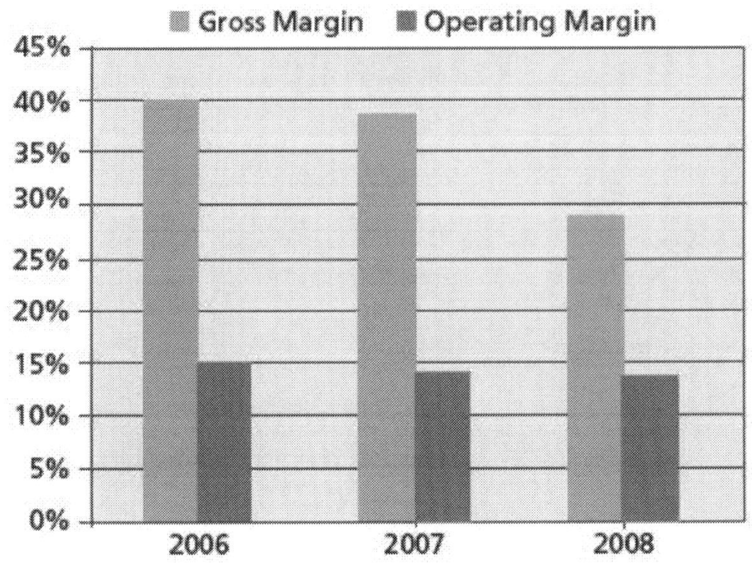

Smackdown Chart 3

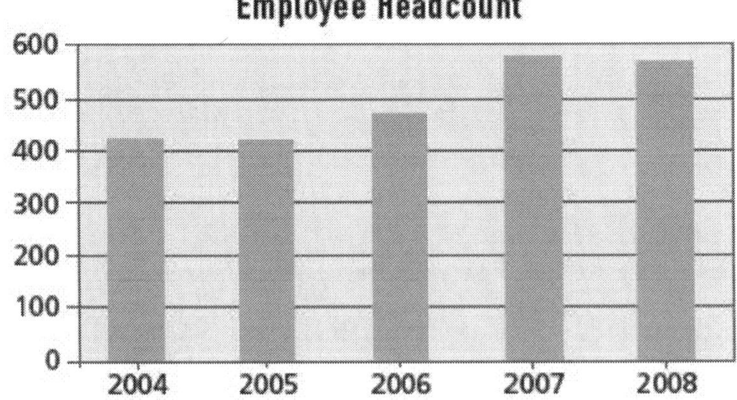

Smackdown Chart 4

Revenues	2006	2007	2008
Live & TV entertainment	$292.2	$316.8	$331.5
Consumer products	95.0	118.1	135.7
Digital media	28.1	34.8	34.8
Smackdown Studios	0.0	16.0	224.5
Total revenues	$415.3	$485.7	$526.5

Smackdown Chart 5

	2006	2007	2008
Staff related	$44.7	$50.3	$55.2
Legal accounting and other professional	10.9	14.0	16.6
Stock compensation	4.7	7.8	8.0
Advertising and promotion	5.2	5.4	11.6
Bad debt	0.5	0.1	2.5
All other	30.1	31.5	37.4
Total SG&A	**$96.1**	**$109.1**	**$131.3**
SG&A as a percentage of revenue	23%	23%	25%

Summary

The interviewee needs to jump right into this without any downtime to collect her thoughts. A good summary is about a minute, minute-and-a-half long. It is not a rehash of everything you spoke about; it is a short recap of the problem and two or three main points that the student wants the interviewer to remember.

Did the interviewee ...

- repeat the question, verifying the objective and asking about other objectives?
- quantify her findings?
- make math mistakes?
- produce a good short summary touching on the most critical points?
- have well-organized and easy-to-read notes?

Mark of a Good Case Discussion: This is a tough case. Did the student get rattled by what was asked of her, or did she jump right in? Did she know to ask for more data and what information to pull out? With this case, it is easy to get overwhelmed, so award extra points for staying calm and working through it.

+ TEDEX

Problem Statement

Your client is TedEx (very similar to FedEx). It has annual revenues of $40 billion. It ships 2.5 billion packages a year. The average customer ships five packages per year.

In a survey, its customer service ranked high in all areas except lost package compensation. The complaints included:

- TedEx never tells me when my package is lost.
- Time-consuming, multi-step process that puts the responsibility on the customer.
- Four-week payout timetable (takes four weeks to get a check).

What are the lost packages and poor service costing TedEx, and how can it improve its customer service?

Guidance for the Interviewer

The student should repeat the question to make sure everyone is on the same page, and she should verify the objective – how can we improve customer service and increase profits? She should also ask whether there are any other objectives she needs to be concerned with – in this case the answer is no other objectives.

The case should be broken down into two parts, costs and service. On the cost side, we are looking for three numbers: (1) insurance payouts (assume that TedEx pays insurance claims out of its own pocket), (2) business lost because of poor service and (3) the amount incurred by TedEx when a package is lost. On the service side, we are looking for ways to streamline the reimbursement process.

Data Bank

The student should ask, how many packages does TedEx lose each year and what does this cost them?

Tell her: TedEx loses 3 percent of its packages, and 80 percent of those lost packages were insured for the minimum $100. This is the group we care about – this 80 percent. We are assuming that every package automatically is insured for $100 regardless of the contents of the package.

Of the 80 percent of the lost packages with an automatic value of $100, 20 percent of those customers give up on their claim because the process is too cumbersome. Of that 20 percent, 25 percent abandon TedEx and switch to another carrier.

Here are the numbers: TedEx loses 3 percent of its packages (75 million: 2.5B x .03 = 75 million) and 80 percent of those (60 million: 75 million x .8 = 60 million) packages were insured for the minimum $100. We are assuming that every package automatically is insured for $100 regardless of the contents of the package.

Of those 60 million lost packages with an automatic value of $100 (remember, this is the group we care about), 20 percent (12 million: 60 million x .20 = 12 million) of the customers give up on their claim because the process is too cumbersome. **Assume that customers lose only one package, so think of packages and customers as the same**.

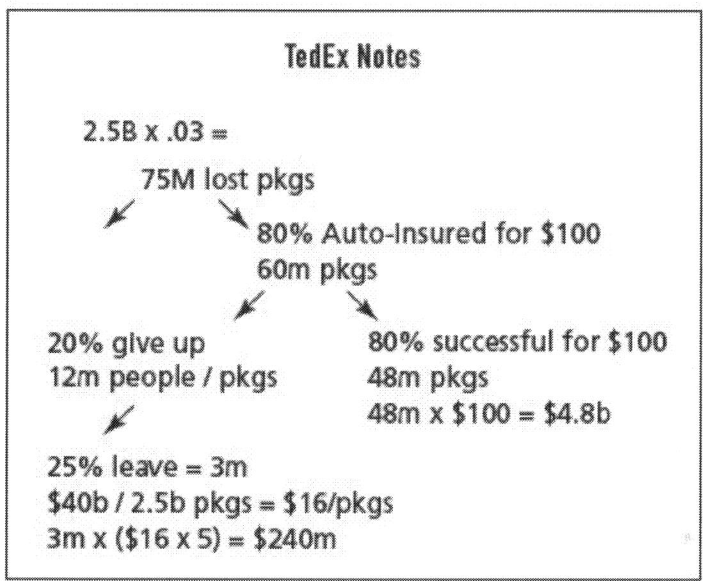

Note: How the student lays out her notes becomes very important. The biggest mistakes I see in this case result simply because the student's notes are a mess. If she uses a tree design, then her notes will be clean and easy to follow, and she'll be able to find the information she needs quickly. Ideally, her notes should look something like the above. If they don't, then at the end of the case, show her this.

How much does TedEx lose in future sales?

Twenty-five percent of the 12 million, or 3 million (3 million: 12 million x .25 = 3 million) switch to another carrier. If the average revenue per package is $16 ($16: $40 billion/2.5 billion = $16) and if the average customer ships 5 packages a year, that is equal to 15 million (15 million: 3 million x 5 number of average packages sent = $15 million packages a year times the $16 average revenue per package). Thus, TedEx loses $240 million a year in future sales – with customers switching after a frustrating experience ($16 x 15 million = $240 million).

How much does it cost TedEx to process the lost package claim?

Assume that it costs TedEx $4 per claim considering labor, processing time, and overhead; 60 million packages times $4 equals $240 million.

How much does TedEx pay out in insurance?

Assume that TedEx pays its own insurance; 80 percent of the 60 million claims are successful, which means TedEx pays $100 each for 48 million packages, or $4.8 billion in claims.

The three numbers we are looking for:

1. $240 million in lost business next year
2. $4.8 billion in insurance payouts (48 million x $100 = $4.8 billion)
3. $240 million in lost package processing costs (60 million x $4 = $240 million)

That totals $5.28 billion. **Ask the student what percentage of the total revenues that represents**. Answer: about 13 percent (5.28/40 = 13 percent).

Guidance for the Interviewer

Tell the student that a team down the hall came up with options to streamline the process. The outcome was:

1. The $4 lost package processing fee was reduced to $1 per lost package.
2. The customers who were going to leave TedEx actually stay.
3. TedEx received very high marks on its customer service.
4. The number of successful claims rose from 80 percent to 100 percent.

Ask: What does this mean for TedEx?

1. The processing fee was reduced to $60 million from $240 million.
2. We don't lose $240 million in defecting customers.
3. TedEx's customer service received high marks (which was one of the objectives).
4. Insurance payouts grew from $4.8 billion to $6 billion; TedEx is now paying out $1.2 billion more in insurance claims.

Ask: How can we reduce the amount of money TedEx pays out in claims?

1. Reduce the number of lost packages.
2. Reduce the dollar payout per claim from $100 to $50, which would save $3 billion. Not all packages are worth $100.
3. Instead of paying out cash, TedEx could credit the customer's account; in this way:
    a) They keep the customer.
    b) There's no dollar payout.
    c) It might take customers three to six months to use up the credit, or they may never use it.
    d) If the customer does use it and TedEx's margins are 50 percent, then it is paying out only $25 in actual services.

Summary

The candidate needs to jump right into to this without any downtime to collect her thoughts. A good summary is about a minute, minute-and-a-half long. It is not a rehash of everything you spoke about; it is a short recap of the problem and two or three main points that she wants the interviewer to remember.

TedEx has received poor marks on customer service relating to lost packages. It is also paying out an extraordinarily high 13 percent of its revenues in lost package expenses. We've worked to streamline the claims process, which resulted in better customer service marks, but this also greatly increased the amount of money TedEx pays out in claims. We've come up with three ways to reduce those payouts: reduce the number of lost packages, reduce the dollar amount of an automatic payout from $100 to $50 and credit the claim money to the customer's TedEx account. These three steps should greatly reduce the amount of money TedEx pays out in lost package claims.

A good interview consists of:

- repeating the question, verifying the objective, and asking about other objectives.
- making no math mistakes.
- keeping well-organized and easy-to-read notes.
- recognizing quickly that streamlining the process will cost TedEx more in claim payouts.
- realizing that TedEx might have made the process cumbersome on purpose so that fewer people would claim the money.
- developing a good short summary touching on the most critical points.

Mark of good discussion: Did the student realize that increasing successful claims from 80 percent to 100 percent was going to be expensive? Did she recognize that maybe TedEx had made the process cumbersome on purpose so that fewer people would claim their money (think mail-in rebate)? In addition, the last idea (crediting the customer's TedEx account) is the one idea that very few students ever get. So if they get it, they deserve big points.

6 : Final Analysis

Most of this is psychological. The biggest assets a candidate can bring are a measure of confidence, a perspective of self-worth, and a good night's sleep. The interview structure is daunting, the people generally intimidating, and the atmosphere tense, but you can slay all these dragons immediately when you choose to arm yourself with a positive self-image. In the end, it's not whether you are right or wrong, it is how you present yourself, your information, and your thinking. This is the measure of marketability for the firm – and it is what they seek to determine through an imperfect process.

Practice before your interview. No athlete you ever admired stepped up to the plate or went out on the playing field without warming up. You need to do the same thing. You need to get into the right mindset. Log on to CQI and run through some math problems, market-sizing cases, or maybe even a full case. Do a few case starts with the video vault. It's difficult to walk in off the street and do a case cold. When you did two or three practice cases with your friends, you probably did better on the second or third case than the first, even if the first case was easier. Get into the zone. You don't want the interview to be your first case of the day.

Finally, it's only you against the beast (the case question, not the interviewer). We can't be there with you, but we've given you the tools to feel confident and to have a good time. If you're excited about the challenge and the interview, then you're headed into the right profession. If you dread what's coming, you may want to re-evaluate your career choice. When discussing career choices, Winston Churchill advised his children, "Do what you like, but like what you do." It's all about having fun.

It's easy to forget that the firms know you can do the work – they wouldn't be interviewing you if they didn't think you were smart enough to succeed. Now it's just time to prove them right.

Case closed!

More Resources: Just in case you need more practice, check out CQ Interactive at casequestions.com

7 : Partner Case Charts

+ NERVES OF STEEL

Steel Pricing Trends (in dollars per ton)

Y1	Y2	Y3	Y4	Y5	Y6	Y7	Y8
$263	$554	$615	$600	$610	$750	$810	?

+ BOTTLED WATER

Y1	Ed	Client
COGS	60m	?
Building	N/A	$6m
Equipment	N/A	$4m
Labor	N/A	?
Utilities & Maintenance	N/A	$.04m
Transportation	N/A	?
Admin	N/A	$1m
Cost per bottle	$0.06	?

+ SMACKDOWN RIVALS

Smackdown Rivals
Trending Schedules
Statement of Operations
($ in millions, unaudited)

	2006	2007	2008
Revenues	$ 415.3	$ 485.7	$ 526.5
Cost of Revenues	244.9	298.8	311.8
SG&A	96.1	109.1	131.3
Dep. & Amortization	8.7	9.4	13.1
Operating Income	$ 65.6	$ 68.4	$ 70.3
Interest and Other, net	9.8	8.0	(1.0)
Income before Taxes	$ 75.4	$ 76.4	$ 69.3
Interest and Other, net	26.6	24.3	23.9
Effective Tax Rate	35%	32%	34%
Income from Continuing Operations	$ 48.8	$ 52.1	$ 45.4
Discontinued Ops			0.0
Net Income	$ 48.8	$ 52.1	$ 45.4
EPS - Continuing Operations	$0.68	$0.72	$0.62
EPS - Net Income	$0.68	$0.72	$0.62
Memo:			
EBIDTA	$ 74.3	77.8	83.4
EBIDTA margin %	18%	16%	16%

Smackdown Chart 2

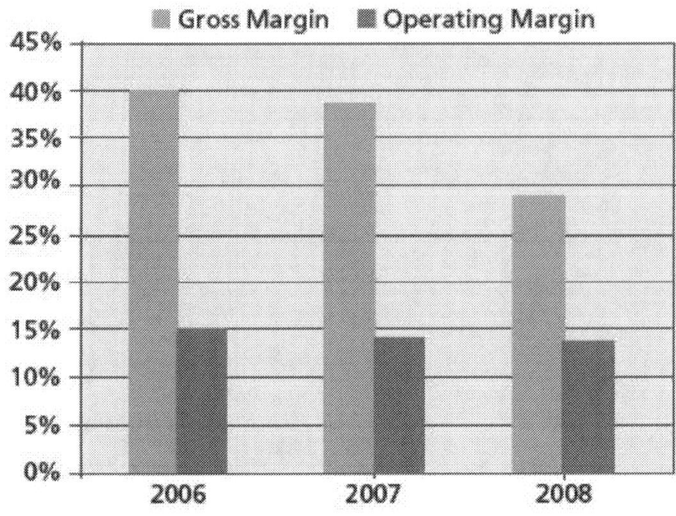

Smackdown Chart 3

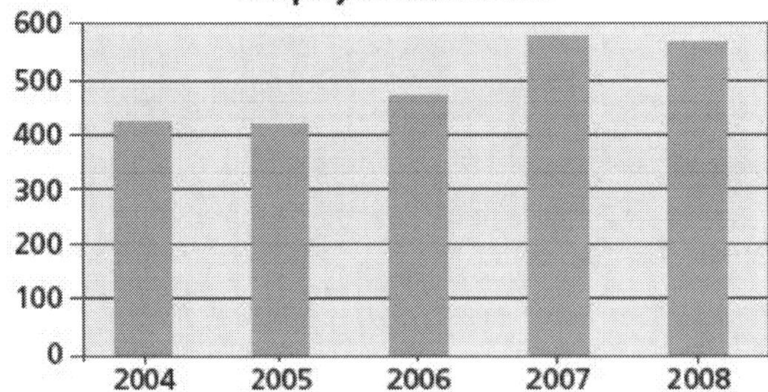

Smackdown Chart 4

Revenues	2006	2007	2008
Live & TV entertainment	$292.2	$316.8	$331.5
Consumer products	95.0	118.1	135.7
Digital media	28.1	34.8	34.8
Smackdown Studios	0.0	16.0	224.5
Total revenues	$415.3	$485.7	$526.5

Smackdown Chart 5

	2006	2007	2008
Staff related	$44.7	$50.3	$55.2
Legal accounting and other professional	10.9	14.0	16.6
Stock compensation	4.7	7.8	8.0
Advertising and promotion	5.2	5.4	11.6
Bad debt	0.5	0.1	2.5
All other	30.1	31.5	37.4
Total SG&A	**$96.1**	**$109.1**	**$131.3**
SG&A as a percentage of revenue	23%	23%	25%

About the Author

Marc Cosentino is the CEO of CaseQuestions.com.

For almost three decades Cosentino's work has towered over the field of case interviews. He has advised and coached over 100,000 students. Marc has written five books involving cases and consulting.

Case in Point is now published in four languages and was called the "MBA Bible" by *The Wall Street Journal*. It has been the best-selling case prep book on the planet for the last twelve years and the number one consulting book and number two selling interview book worldwide for the last decade.

Cosentino travels internationally giving case workshops at 45 schools annually, training students on how to answer case questions, training career services professionals on how to give case interviews, and teaching PhDs in private sector firms how to think like a businessperson. He consults with and designs cases for private sector firms, government agencies, and non-profits. Cosentino is a graduate of Harvard's Kennedy School and the University of Denver.

PHOTO: MARTHA STEWART

Additional Products by CaseQuestions.com

CaseQuestions Interactive
Online Training: Math Drills, Market Sizing, Case Starts, Videos and 12 full cases to work through

15 Videos: 10 case starts and 5 full cases with commentary

Manufactured by Amazon.ca
Bolton, ON